D1528041

MY FATHER THE SPY

DECEPTIONS OF AN MI6 OFFICER

BILL BRISTOW

WITH EXTRACTS FROM MAJOR DESMOND BRISTOW MI6

Paperback First Edition
First published in Great Britain in 2012 by
WBML ePublishing & Media Company Ltd.
6 Old Gloucester Road, Ross-on-Wye, HR9 5PB
www.wbmlpublishing.com

ISBN 978-0-9572855-3-8

Copyright © Bill Bristow 2012

Catalogue No.   201200004

Acknowledgements

I would like to dedicate this book to Desmond Bristow (my father), Tomas Harris, Kim Philby, Anthony Blunt, Guy Burgess, and all those other double agents who gave me a very confusing mixed up childhood. On the other hand this has made life exciting and beyond the normality of most. It still amazes me when I say 'my father was friends with Kim Philby' to see the look on people's faces!

My father died 7 years after we completed A Game of Moles. Not many Secrets about the work of a secret service man were included. Enough time has passed since his and my mother's death to reveal all the contents of his story. I leave most of the original manuscript from A Game of Moles Deceptions of An MI6 Officer.

THANKS to all my friends and family who have supported my efforts to write my version of the book. This includes secrets my father felt he could not reveal about his work, also his personal affairs.

My Father always went on about the Spanish and Portuguese collaborators who quietly, secretly and invariably dangerously, helped the Allied cause and received no thanks or commendations. They were, and are, amongst all those hundreds of unsung heroes from the never ending stories from World War 2. We should remember we are here to day due to the sacrifice of millions who died.

My thanks also go to Mark Lodge, (my business partner at WBML Publishing), for his suggestions to both improve and ensure completeness of the book and for his efforts in proofreading and formatting.

The Times Correspondent Michael Evans wrote on 8th October 1983:

'A FORMER MI6 officer published his autobiography yesterday despite an official warning that he could go to jail for two years for breaching his pledge of secrecy. Desmond Bristow, 76, was given the warning by the Treasury Solicitor. During discussions with the defence ministry over his manuscript for A Game of Moles, Deceptions of an MI6 Officer, he and his publishers were ordered to leave out names of former Intelligence officers and "to drop the word agent." He said yesterday: "I could not believe it. Are we really supposed to hide the fact the British secret intelligence service employs agents?"'

This threat of jail for two years really upset my mother at the time. I never believed they would carry this out. It is such a school boy act. It is that attitude of 'I told you so,' which really infuriated my father and me. Whilst on that subject, the real names of most of the agents are now in the book.

The amount of tax payer's money the Treasury Solicitor must have made out of this stream of correspondence beggars belief.

Journalist Nigel Nelson wrote on 14th November 1993:

'Although John Major keeps banging on about open Government, Britain remains the most secretive society in the Western World. This is what happened. Desmond and his film maker son Bill get together to pen dad's memoirs. A Game of Moles tells the story of Desmond's wartime work with MI6, of his friendship with Kim Philby and a few post war escapades.

All fascinating stuff for a spy freak like me, but about as harmful to the nation's security as a Whitehall canteen menu.'

This leaves me wondering how much of the Secrets Act is to protect the ministers and the civil servants and their dealings with corruption. When this was the threat leveled at my father at that time what would they have done with the likes of Burgess, Philby and Maclean? And why was Blunt allowed to slip through the punishment net?

Acknowledgements for 'A Game of Moles'
by Desmond Bristow

My thanks go to those who discouraged me to write due to the official secrets act and possible political embarrassment and to those who encouraged me to write, hoping there would be political embarrassment! A few ex-MI6 colleagues even.

Gratitude I offer my son Bill, for the long hours he spent compelling me to elaborate upon details which I had forgotten, or thought not to be relevant to my own manuscript. In this he was helped by my wife Betty.

Finally I thank all those friends and colleagues, no longer with us, whose friendship contributed to "the best days of my life". Those still living know who they are.

NOTE. Sadly today not one of those friends is still living.

1   Churchill's Funeral

On Friday morning January 29th 1965 my school headmaster came into my dormitory to tell me to pack my toothbrush and to put my school blazer and smart trousers on. My parents would arrive shortly to pick me up. I was going to a funeral. He may have explained to me at the time but I was more excited about missing a whole day and half of school. Matron came in with a clean white shirt which I put on. She helped me with my tie, and put clean socks and underpants in my bag. She made a terrible fuss. My shoes polished, I went downstairs and was told to wait in the headmaster's drawing room for my parents. This became rather nerve racking. Whose funeral? Was it Uncle Horace, or auntie Blodwyn. I hoped not as I really liked Auntie Blodwyn.

This was serious, we were never allowed into the headmaster's drawing room unless it was for a beating, or a serious talk. This was an English Boarding school. The doorbell rang; I hoped it was my mother and father. Yes. The headmaster came out with me and was extremely friendly. (Not normal at all.) We drove up to London. My mother and father explained we were going to the funeral of Sir Winston Churchill, a great man. He had been the Prime Minister during the war and father had been invited to attend. We arrived in London, and as we were getting out of the car, a soldier took our luggage and another parked the car. We entered a rather smart building and the doorman took our luggage from the soldier and escorted us up to a flat which had a balcony overlooking an area where the Horse Guards were obviously preparing for the big day.

Today I realise we went to Westminster Hall where my father met some people whom he knew. My mother kept a very firm hold of my hand. She was beautifully dressed and my father had a set of medals I had never seen before. It was then I started to realise my father must have been quite important.

The following day the crowds seemed to go on forever. I clearly remember watching the Gun Carriage draped with the Union flag passing by; soldiers looking very stern and somber. People were sobbing. My mother had tears running down her face, my father stared at the coffin, with a distant look on his face with his chest out, full of pride, and obviously upset. Although I did not understand, I felt the weight in the air of thousands of heavy hearts. Never really thinking of it before, but there was an air of humility amongst all of the adults. It was the passing of a very great man. The privilege of being there was perhaps wasted on me at the time; but now, older, I realise how privileged I was. Two silver crown coins with Winston's head on, were given to me some time later.

After this my curiosity as to who my father had been during the war needed to be satisfied. During a school holiday and one of my father's absences from the house, I found a uniform. Major, British Army Intelligence Corp, with some ribbons. I found a German luger pistol with holster and magazine, German sunglasses, a German cap, a German medal and some French Medals. I was just 10 years old. Earlier in the year some of my father's friends talked to my mother of traitors, and his work in the secret service. Who and what was MY FATHER? Had he been A TRAITOR?

From 1962 – 1969 I attended Holmwood House Preparatory School for boys; (potential young English Gentlemen). My friends at school had stories of their father's or grandfather's flying Spitfires, or Bombers; or officers at the Battle of Tobruk, or in some Naval Battle. What was my story about my heroic father? Had he really been a traitor? I wondered and hoped, with the fanciful imagination of a 10 year old who read the comic Victory, he had a good tale to tell. I often asked him what he had done during the war. With his light hearted laugh he would always manage to change the subject and not answer with any detail. He had been in the army in North Africa, and no more.

I can remember conversations between my father and his friends when they asked if they thought a friend of his was a traitor. Traitor was a word I was learning in History. I also remember my mother having to go to Switzerland. When she came back she had bought me a Swiss watch. In fact she had been to see Tommy Harris's widow in Mallorca via Switzerland. Tommy Harris, my godfather, had died in a strange car accident in 1964 the year after his and my father's friend Kim Philby had defected to Russia. I was too young to fully understand; I just knew it was not good.

This really bothered me. It actually had an effect on me at school and in general. Finally, December 1967 when I was 12 years old, I took the German Luger from his wardrobe top shelf. I held it and looked it and admired it with school boyish interest, wondering how many people it had killed. With a combination of fear and determination I strode down the stairs into the study, put the Luger on the table. As my fingers press the keys on my MacBook Pro I can feel my trepidation all over again. I can hear myself.

'Why do you have this and all those other German bits of uniform and French medals? Are you a Traitor?'

I can still hear his laugh; that all-encompassing laugh. He had no idea how serious this was for me. For the first time in my life, I yelled at my father. 'Shut Up'. I ran out and went to my room.

I could hear the argument between my father and mother. It's all my fault I thought. Tears ran down my face. Finally, there was a knock on my door. My father walked in. His shoulders were down. He looked smaller. He sat on the bed and took my hand.

'No I am not and never was a traitor.'

He was nervous and unable to tell me very much.

'During the war I worked for the Secret Service and the Army.'

He explained enough to put my mind at rest about his being a traitor. My mind just started to compile thousands of stories and questions. This book answers all the questions I had.

My father's modesty and self-effacing attitude about his work made the 'A Game of Moles' book difficult for me, as the most serious episodes were a form of amusement for him. For me they were a serious exploration into his life as a Spy and Spy Master which he did not fully reveal in the book.

My father died in November 2000 from a massive stroke. His six week long and painful death was horrifying and an emotional agony to witness. This strong man, full of life, humour and bouts of wisdom was slowly and agonizingly leaving me. I would sit with him, holding his hand and talking to him. Sometimes I would get angry with him; angry because this was not the way he should be leaving us. His death should have been in the swimming pool, or walking Fido his mastiff dog, or even writing his notes. Better still on one of his canvass picnic chairs with a glass of red wine, under the 200 year olive tree in the Patio.

I would talk to him about life, and why? And Mum. My Angry talks would be about not allowing us to put all his stories in the book. During this time I made a promise to myself to rewrite the book and include all the details of his work as a Spy, which he had insisted remained a Secret. More than ten years have passed. And here it is. It is still partly his book including additional information about his activities, with the addition of how being the son of a spy may sound glamorous and interesting. Perhaps in some ways it is; but in so many other ways it is quite damaging.

For a long time after the war my family was not aware of what I, Desmond Bristow, had been doing between 1940 and 1954.

Perhaps I had been so cagey that they were not even interested. Then, at the age of ten, our youngest son William began asking odd questions. This was in 1965. He had seen some French decorations and questioned my wife Betty about them. Betty invariably told Bill to ask me. I cannot recall how I replied to his enquiry. Later when he became more enlightened he pressed me to write my memoirs, such as they were. Reluctantly I began to do jottings.

By then, 1967, my erstwhile friend and sometime department boss, Kim Philby, had become a notorious figure as a prime traitor. Since his take-off to Moscow from Beirut in 1963, I had sometimes argued that he must be an MI6 double agent run by a most secret section, not to be found in either 54, Broadway (the MI6 headquarters) or at Leconfield House where MI5 was much more comfortably accommodated.

My father wanted to think at the time the powers-that-were had taken Malcolm Muggeridge's advice, closed both outfits and started up in an unknown place with new staff. A secret service within the secret service.

Alas, for my father this was not so; his friend deserved his traitorous notoriety. Even though my father had left MI6 in 1954 he fell under suspicion; maybe because he left. I have found notes in which he expresses his own feelings towards Philby's treachery to him personally and the country. There is a side of my father which understands Philby's reasons for this idealism, which I will reveal later on in the book.

In first place it was clear that the "moles" (traitors) had blackened the reputation not only of MI5 but MI6 also. No one then, nor any official body, had seen fit to issue a counterblast. It was not fair, I felt, to allow these traitorous characters and to cast their miserable shadows over everyone who had been involved in MI5 and MI6. It was nerve racking and very demoralizing and certainly not amusing to be asked what my KGB connections were and had been.

My first jottings came when I briefly recorded my association with Kim. By 1983, I began to appreciate not only Philby, but Tommy Harris, Garbo and others also deserved some attention.

Bill, who had been in Los Angeles for ten years and involved with making films, documentaries and general television work, suggested he would come to Spain for a father-and-son co-operative effort. The book 'A Game of Moles' is the result of that collaboration and is mostly of a straightforward nature but sometimes beset by acrimonious moments.

2   Childhood to College

1st July 1917. Birmingham Hospital Births: Desmond Arthur Bristow.

Ada Bristow had left her home in Spain to give birth to her second son to avoid him being born in Spain and therefore being a Spanish subject.

One week after his birth Ada, her new born son Desmond, and the maid stepped aboard the ship and returned home to Spain.

Richard Bristow was the mining Engineer and Director of Santa Rosa and Sotiel Coronada copper mines next to the vast Rio Tinto mines.

A colonial and privileged life with maids, a chauffeur and 750 Spanish miners with their families all lived under the rule of Richard Bristow, Desmond's father my Grandfather.

Mountains, olive trees, steam engines whistling and puffing around mining pits, dust, goats, donkeys and freedom; this was the life my father had as a child. Along with his horse and donkey, he would travel along mountainous foot paths, the rocky Rio Tinto and Odiel river beds; often venturing out for more than a day at a time. The life his son, (me), can only ever dream of and fantasize about. To me his life had been one which today I envy.

From the wild countryside on Huelva Andalucia, and the mining towns of Sotiel Coronada and Santa Maria where my father, Desmond roamed free; he made his first trip in the autumn of 1925 by steam ship to England as a Dulwich Preparatory schoolboy.

I had heard a lot about school and England from my brother. England was very green compared to Spain and the magnificent buildings around the school and in London were quite a change. Prep school was very much the same for me as for anyone else who went to one. Not speaking very good English created some extra problems for me, but being athletic helped. The staff were wonderfully understanding and helped me and many other foreign-speaking children to adapt to English boarding-school life. Rugby, cricket, swimming and of course languages were interests. I would sit with friends, mostly either colony children or foreign children, on the fire escape at night and watch the numerous firework displays at Crystal Palace. The restriction on my freedom took a little getting used to after the very free life on the mine, but having so many children around of my age alleviated the problem to a certain extent.

My father after his first year at school did not return home for over two years due to some civil unrest in Spain.

He told me stories of two Russian boys who had lost many members of their family during the wars in Russia. Although he never said anything to indicate how this absence from his home at the age of 8-9 upset him, it clearly did. It explained his distance from his parents throughout his life.

In 1931 Dulwich College accepted me after my few successes at Dulwich Prep school. Life was fairly similar to prep school, just freer in some ways and stricter in others, because one was older. I managed to do well in sports and relatively well academically, winning a place at Magdalene College Cambridge.

Rowing, (I became captain), reading French and Spanish, drinking certain amounts of port and the other college activities made up three of the most enjoyable years of my life. The college buildings were beautiful, and lush green lawns gently sloped down to the river, where chaps wearing boaters and highly colored blazers could be found punting up and down trying to find picnic spots for their girlfriends. Cambridge inspired good-spirited bad behavior. One year, in an effort to raise money for Poppy Day, a friend poured petrol over me, struck a match, and all ablaze I dived off a bridge into the river Cam where the flames sizzled out before doing any damage.

Cambridge was interspersed with train and boat trips to the Iberian Peninsula for holidays on the mines, or on the beach at Punta Umbria where my parents had a beach house. These trips, made between 1936 and 1939, were always tense and nervous due to the Spanish Civil War.

Six months at The Sorbonne in Paris should be mentioned. He met people such as Hemingway and would often eat at

La Coupole, a trendy restaurant where the likes of Picasso and Hemingway and others would hang out. This is where my father improved his French to the point where he spoke both French and Spanish fluently and would often be mistaken as a native. This ability with languages was an important factor which influenced his destiny of working for MI6.

3   Spain: To St. Albans with Philby

The Spanish Civil War ground to a bloody halt in March 1939. I left Cambridge in May and spent the early part of the summer rowing at Henley. After participating in the Regatta I sailed to Spanish shores for the summer holidays while waiting for a job in Chile or Canada as a trainee timber company manager. When the inevitable World War was declared, I realised it was not going to be a job in Chile or Canada. I wanted to join up, but the bureaucratic blockade characteristics of a dictatorial state after a civil war delayed my being permitted to leave the country, so I lost my place for an immediate commission.

Permission to leave was eventually granted and I was invited to escort three middle aged English ladies from Madrid on the train journey through Spain and France on to England; reluctantly I agreed.

I left the house in Sotiel Coronada on October 3rd, never to see it again as my beloved home. Francisco drove us to Seville, the bustling beautiful station echoing with childhood memories of school trips. Again, the painful goodbye to my parents on the platform with the beautiful iron and glass roof. The fateful steps onto the night train to Madrid; this time I was going to war. Steam and whistles filled the air and my train slowly pulled out. The ten-hour journey brought us under the glass dome of Madrid`s Atocha station, which had been shattered in the Civil War. Madrid was a shell of its former glory; there were food shortages, no cars or horse carriages and very few people in the streets; hotels were glad for any business.

A regal reception followed at the sumptuous Hotel Nacional. I spent a night thinking of what I was leaving behind, mixed with feelings of fear and excitement of where I was going. Fear due to the scenes of devastation I had witnessed during the Civil War; and excitement as it seemed the right thing to do.

After this rather restless night I met the three ladies for breakfast and escorted them onto the train taking us to the border town of Irun. I have to admit, in their own English way they kept me amused and somewhat alleviated my depression; like their, what seemed, petit concerns of how they would wash their stockings if there was no water in the hotel and had they brought enough clothes for the dinner parties they might attend. On a grander scale; one of them was worried whether she was going to be good enough to drive a tractor on a farm where she was going to work in the Land Army.

The countryside north of Madrid added to the trepidation I was feeling. It was pockmarked by shell holes and empty trenches that wound their snakelike courses amongst barbed wire and twisted tanks and trucks. If this is the aftermath of war, what am I doing? I asked myself. As we slowly rattled northwards, the dangling power lines, broken telegraph poles, bomb-shattered dwellings and gunshot scars of war stressed this question every kilometer we travelled. The arrival at the French frontier thankfully gave me something to do, bringing me out of my gloom.

Shepherding the ladies from one country to another was no problem, but the luggage was a different story; there were no porters or trolleys. The scene presented a sort of climax. There we were with piles of luggage, leaving Spain a country ravaged by the effects of civil war, setting foot into France about to become the centre stage of the European element of the Second World War.

Hendaye on the French side was bustling, organised and almost felt normal, except for the hordes of young men in uniform carrying guns. I enjoyed the buffet goodies of French pastries and coffee during our short wait.

The train, twice its normal length, smelt of sweat, and though full to the brim was very quiet. One could sense the anxiety and fear and the hundreds of different stories occupying the minds behind all these strangers' eyes. Being brought together under such circumstances played havoc with our lives and imaginations.

We drew away from Hendaye at 2am. The crisp morning air of that 5th October helped ease the cramped conditions; the frequent stops to pick up conscripted *poilus*, in uniform and armed, heading north to the front, made me feel more and more like a Spanish sardine and confident the war would be over by Christmas.

Food was a problem. At Angouleme I clambered out of the train, walked around the station where I managed to acquire six croissants, a kilo of bananas and a bottle of water from the packed station buffet. As I wandered onto the opposite platform my train started to pull out. Panic struck; holding onto the supplies I ran for it, only to have my path cut by a goods train. Without thinking, I jumped onto the buffers between two of the moving wagons, hopped across the coupling and down on the other side; as I made a grab for the handrail of the last carriage on my train it stopped; almost making me fall over. The bag with the bananas dropped to the floor. I picked them up in a hurry and made my way through the crowded passages. Breathless I reached the three old ladies, who smiled and effervesced with thanks. The train remained in the station for another hour.

In Paris, where the 'can-can' was still kicking, restaurants still cooking, the café au lait flowing and the people full of joie de vivre, we transferred to the boat train and finally arrived at Victoria Station, London. It was surprising to me being across the Channel. London, where I stayed for one night, was not full of joie de vivre. Sandbags were in many doorways, people were very serious. The following morning I caught the train to Cambridge and went to the university recruiting office. It really seemed that I had lost my place, having been delayed from leaving Spain; there were no vacancies for me in the war, and I was instructed to come back every two or three days. Strange, thinking of it now, that I had to wait to join in the war. To fill in time and save money I coached rowing and lived at Magdalene College for three weeks. At the end of the third week, having been rejected again and again, I decided to go on and see my girlfriend Betty who lived near Worcester, where I secured lodgings and drove tractors through the winter of 1939-1940.

On 27th February 1940 I trudged through the snow to Worcester station and caught the train to London, took the underground train to Westminster, walked to the War Office, wended my way through security checks and piled-up sandbags and approached the Colour-Sergeant in charge of volunteers. I explained about missing my commission due to the hold- ups in Spain, and then my waiting in Cambridge.

He looked me straight in the face and asked,

"What do you want me to do about it, young man?'

"Well, I'm bored, I'm broke and I want to join up, and I was wondering if you might have any vacancies in this war?' I replied.

Two weeks later I was marching in the ranks of the Oxfordshire and Buckinghamshire lads, many of who did not know their left foot from their right. There were four of us with university education in my barracks and we quickly became caretakers. Writing letters to parents and girlfriends was often an enjoyable benefit of being educated. One individual would compose letters of incredible passion to his girlfriend in Banbury. Darning socks and sewing buttons on tunics was one of the drawbacks. Promotion to corporal was soon followed by my transfer to Bloody Bulford officer's training camp.

Sergeant Davis was not the bullying sergeant I had expected; on the contrary he was a fairly soft-spoken man whose main duty was to get us fit, which he did. At Bloody Bulford I became the friend and chess opponent of

Leo Long, who nearly always beat me. Leo Long became famous for being the Russian agent who was a G2 officer to General Montgomery after D-Day.

Again I was subjected to drill trainings, part of the price of being in the infantry. After a week of intensive drill and field exercises I took some leave to see Betty. During my wait for the connecting train at Oxford I was standing on the platform when a hospital train with wounded from Dunkirk pulled in. The horror of war struck me as hundreds of young men like me limped, and hobbled, many on crutches, or carried on stretchers, with arms or legs missing and bloody bandages around their faces and eyes. Many who could walk but not see would help those who could see but not walk easily. Slowly they moved down the platform; nurses helped and guided them to the waiting ambulances. Suddenly the idea of being an infantryman lost its appeal.

Thankfully, on my return I was asked to attend an interview. Several interviews later I became a lieutenant in the British Intelligence Corps. My training at Oxford was only interrupted by trips on my Matchless 500 motorcycle to see Betty.

During this time, the Germans had overrun France and The Blitz had started, which demonstrated the might of the German army and air force. For many days London was ablaze. Major cities were hit, causing a feeling of resilience and stiff upper lip; and a deep down feeling of 'we might not win this war'. Along with the other officers in my section of the Intelligence Corp, we all agreed

Chamberlain had been an old fuddy-duddy and too weak a person to lead Britain. We also discussed the Old Guard in the Army and their need to wake up out of their superior sleep. We hoped, with Winston Churchill now Prime Minister and with his connections with America through his Mother, he might persuade the U.S. to join in.

Training consisted of learning all about enemy uniforms, hand weapons, tanks, airplanes, ships, habits and the German way of life. We also learnt the true art of discretion. I translated many military slogans and technical terms from the Spanish army into English, and English military terms into Spanish. In April 1941 my appointment as an instructor on the Spanish and Portuguese armies bewildered me since I thought I was only slightly less ignorant on the subject than the rest of our defence establishment. Actually my constant travelling back and forth to Spain had given me a knowledge which I only came to realise when I tapped into it. The concern at the time was the Spanish might decide to help Hitler since he had helped Franco during the Civil War. This I was sure would never happen. My father, through his contacts in the mining industries, had insightful information about the interior of Spain and how devastated and exhausted it was.

I was stationed in Cambridge where I felt quite at home. The work was rather boring and office bound, but the security of the job encouraged me to propose. On 18th May 1941 Betty and I were married.

Despite all the intrigue and complications of their life caused by my father's work and the family suspicions of his being a Russian agent, my parents remained married until their deaths.

After a few more months of lecturing, and promotion to Captain I started to feel as though my potential and my language talents were being wasted. There was only so much one could say about the Spanish and Portuguese armies; they were under-equipped and not very fit. The Spanish suffered very badly during the Civil War and the Portuguese, well ...they were Portuguese. I gave my arguments as to why I felt Spain would stay neutral suggesting the Portuguese were far more likely to help the German's than the Spanish. The only impediment to the popular German feeling amongst the people was The Anglo-Portuguese Treaty of 1373; which still stands today and is the oldest treaty between two nations.

One day I was told that a gentleman from the War Office had come to see me; this was Richard Broomham-White, who explained briefly about the need for Spanish-speaking officers, asked a couple of irrelevant questions, and generally chatted. It was arranged for me to go to London, to the War Office, to meet Lieutenant Colonel Cowgill who wanted to interview me.

Lieutenant Colonel Felix Cowgill, sitting behind his large oak desk, fired questions about my fluency in Spanish and my knowledge of the country. Sitting behind the Colonel was a pleasant-looking civilian taking notes and obviously studying me very carefully.

'How would you like to work on a rather secret project?' the Colonel asked.

'Anything to get my backside out of the seat in the office at Oxford,' I replied.

On 3rd September I found myself the passenger in a car going to St. Albans, the driver being the pleasant-looking civilian. He immediately put me at my ease and offered me a cigarette. After some preliminary chit-chat about the traffic and times at Cambridge, he started to explain where we were going and what we would be doing. He had a slight stammer.

'The old mansion, Glenalmond, h-h-headquarters of S-s-Section V is where you are going to be working with me in the Iberian sector of the Counter-Intelligence Department, MI6. There'll be about h-h-half a dozen of us collecting all the information we can about German movements in Spanish-speaking countries, including S-s-south America'.

As I watched the green countryside dashing by the car window, I thought to myself, 'I'm in the Secret Service.' He continued talking while guiding the car through the curving country lanes. The sun shining through the hedgerows reminded me of the sunbeams in the old flour mill at home in Spain.

'By the way, I know you know my name but any way, how do you do? I am Desmond Bristow', I informally introduced myself as we arrived at St. Albans.

The driver, throwing his cigarette out of the window, looked at me and with his slight stutter replied,

'H-h-how do you do, Desmond. I'm Kim Philby'.

My father would talk about Kim as being a very good friend and obviously had a great deal of respect for him at that time. I am glad to say he did not allow his traitorous exposure to cloud my father on how he felt at the time.

4   Snake Pit for the Abwehr

After driving through the old Roman town of St. Albans, we arrived at the private gravel driveway leading to Glenalmond, an Edwardian brick mansion tucked away behind large English Hedgerows with a rather run-down garden. The reception officer greeted us and while waiting for our security clearance I couldn't help noticing the atmosphere of excited and nervous efficiency. New telephone lines were being installed, filling cabinets put in place and runners were carrying important-looking dossiers from room to room. Clearance granted, Philby and I made our way up the stairs and knocked at Colonel Cowgill`s office.

Having said our formal salutation to Colonel Cowgill, we were ushered by his secretary downstairs to the Iberian sector office. Large French windows opened onto a small back lawn, and a path which wound in between some chestnut trees around an old lily pond, full of green water, and on down to a very overgrown rose garden. My desk, situated along the inner wall of the room, was thankfully near an old cast-iron stove. The few pictures on the walls were of naval officers who had once been connected with the Secret Service, and now appeared to be spying on us. The rest of the wall space was taken up by notice boards with constantly changing messages.

That evening Kim gave me a lift to my digs and waited outside while I dropped my luggage off. Mr. and Mrs. French provided bed and breakfast, and sandwiches or hot supper depending on what time I arrived back from work. They were the typical middle-aged English couple doing their bit for God and country, which was getting rent for housing chaps working on those 'Ssshhh, very secret things up at the old manor'. Kim honked the horn.

'Come on D-D-Desmond, the pub will be out of b-b-beer if we don't go now'.

The King Harry on Harry Lane was to become our main relief centre, publicly speaking. The smoke-stained beams, log fire and the smell of beer stored in barrels creeping up from the cellar, created an atmosphere conducive to conversation; it was the typical English pub. The evening was very pleasant; we told each other about our backgrounds, our families and various interests. I liked Kim Philby, my boss, and he seemed to like me; we got along very well, which made the prospect of my new work all the more exciting.

The first week was taken up establishing a routine and dividing the tasks between us. Our merry band of Iberian specialists was Kim Philby and Tim Milne from Oxford University. Tim was a bit older than me, humorless and rather reserved. His job was sorting through the pouch and choosing which of the intercepted Abwehr messages would come to us or go upstairs to the German, Dutch and French sections. (The Abwehr was the German intelligence service).

He and Kim were friends from before the War, having walked around Europe together. With hind sight, knowing now that Philby was working for the Russians even then, I can see it was bloody smart of him to maneuver Milne into that position, because Milne would have alerted Kim whenever anything important was snared by ISOS, (Intelligence Service Oliver Strachey), and Philby would have been able to pass it on to the Russians.

Trevor Wilson, in his mid-thirties older than the rest of us, had landed in the Iberian section for no obvious reason other than his knowledge of Morocco, and perhaps his comedic abilities; he could always make us laugh, except Milne of course. Trevor had been a purchaser of skunk excrement in Abyssinia for the French perfume company Molyneux, and spoke excellent French befitting a purveyor of skunk dropping, which proved useful in our North Africa spy operations.

Frank Hyde, a jovial character who enjoyed wearing his uniform, had been a liaison officer with the British navy in Barcelona at the outbreak of the Spanish Civil War. One day, while polishing his buttons, he told his sad tale about a Spanish Communist committee in his neighborhood.

'They knocked on my door and as I opened it they put a gun to my face.'

'You have a fascist parrot', they said.

At that very moment my parrot squawked,

'I am a royal parrot and I'm for Spain and Portugal'

Frank started to crack a smile,

'My maid had taught the poor creature these dangerous words'.

He then started to laugh,

'You'll never guess? These four anarchistic Commie chaps took my feathered friend outside, gave him a trial, found him guilty, then shot him'.

As you can imagine, we all burst out laughing.

Last but not least, was Jack Ivens who had been importing fruit from Portugal and Spain before the War, and with whom I worked closely in the beginning. I can't say much about Jack, other than he was a soft-spoken family man who adored his Greek wife.

"Anything to get my backside out of a chair", I'd said at the interview, only to find myself boxed up in an old brick manor house hidden by tall hedgerows. Chasing German and Italian spies had seemed like an exciting challenge. The challenge was to stick at it hour after hour in the most menial way possible. In those early days my job was looking for any likely suspects, by cross-checking the hotel lists and airline passenger rosters being sent to us by our chaps in Madrid and Lisbon. There were plenty. Thousands; and thanks to the geniuses at ISOS, a section of Ultra, we also received intercepted, decoded and deciphered messages being sent by agents of the Abwehr from Spain to Germany. We were building a data base of enemy agents, and analyzing their plans.

When my father and I discussed his work at Glenalmond Manor he would always become agitated; very resistant in giving details. At the time of working together I was ignorant of the meaning of ISOS and Ultra. Even after a day or two of me trying to get him to explain exactly what these were; he would not. I always felt distanced from him due to his reticence to share this with me. It was these moments where his secret world created a barrier between father and son.

For those interested, from my own research and to be fair my father eventually cracking, I discovered ISOS was named after Oliver Strachey a decipher expert who had been working in the secret communications world since World War 1. His system enabled our listening services to pick up German coded radio and telegram messages and for ISOS at Bletchley Park to decipher the codes and reveal enemy plans, worries, weaknesses, and every day movements.

I find all this fascinating; yet my father was almost smug and at times dismissive of its mystique and cleverness. This has upset me as I felt as though I was a total stranger. I could never understand why he would not enjoy educating, sharing this with me.

One Nazi wireless operator based in La Coruna was often a target of our humour. His intercepted messages often contained an accident of one nature or the other. One day Trevor gleefully reported,

'Hans Bugge has finally done it, poor bugger. His latest report to the Abwehr reads, and I quote, "I ran into an oxcart while riding my motorcycle, went over the cliff and broke my arm. Nothing else to report, signed Hans".'

Trevor's next antidote to the monotonous but tense days of roster-scanning was when he discovered a regular passenger from Istanbul to Madrid named Mustapha Kunt.

All this may seem ridiculous, reading it now, but there was a lot of tension. The importance of roster-checking was high and often understated; it was incredibly dull; silly humor kept us going.

One foggy morning in late October, the motorcycle courier brought over a batch of German messages from our men in ISOS. Tim Milne, scanning the intercepts, remarked,

'This sounds very odd.'

The room was icy cold as I had only just lit the fire. Kim was sitting by the bay window wearing the scarred leather jacket he had picked up in Spain during the Civil War. He glanced over and asked,

'What does it say?'

'Madrid's telling Berlin their V-Man, Arabel, has reported the information of a convoy in the bay of Caernarvon', replied Milne.

Arabel? The name had never cropped up on the wires before.

Philby not wasting a second, picked up his green phone, the scrambled line to MI5, and dialed the number for Herbert Hart who ran MI5's Abwehr research department.

'H-h-have you seen this message from M-Madrid on the Caernarvon convoy, Hart?' asked Kim.

This was the first time I noticed Kim clicking his fingers, which I soon realised was to help him fight his stammer. The rest of us in the room stopped what we were doing and listened intently. For me this Arabel was a welcome distraction. I was going through a battered Lisbon directory page by page, trying to match up a telephone number with a name and street address. It was obvious from Philby's conversation that MI5 had also received a copy of the messages from ISOS and was extremely worried.

'Get Scotland Yard onto it', Philby told Hart, clicking his fingers again, which obviously did help him stop his stammer.

'Ask them to see if any l-l-likely character in that area of North Wales fits the bill. We'll go on watching and see what comes of it. Bye for now.'

'So!' exclaimed Jack Ivens, 'It seems as though we have a Spaniard at large. Surely he must be a sailor off one of those merchant ships tied up in Liverpool'.

'Why should he or she to be a Spaniard?' I asked. 'Arabel could be a Dutchman or woman, Swedish national or whatever.'

I sat playing with a cigarette, Trevor fiddled with his glasses. We were all looking at each other. I glanced over to Kim and asked, as though he would know the answer,

'I wonder what means of communication our mysterious Arabel used.'

Kim shook his head and, raising his eyebrows, said quietly to all of us'

'Listen, we must not get c-c-carried away on a guessing game, it wastes time, and if this character is important there will be another reference from ISOS soon enough'.

Without saying it, Philby had told us to get back to our routine work; but of course one could not help wondering about our Arabel.

At the beginning of the following day we received a written report from Commander Ewen Montaque, MI5`s liaison officer with the Admiralty.

"CONVOY. CAERNARVON. DOES NOT EXIST."

The excitement of the previous day gave way to disappointing normality. The next report arrived a few days later from Commander Burt, MI5`s controller of Scotland Yard`s Special Branch.

"AFTER EXTENSIVE SEARCH. NORTH WALES AND LIVERPOOL. A NEGATIVE ON OUR SPANISH FRIEND ARABEL."

But despite all negative reports from our departments investigating Arabel, a second message from him to his German masters was picked up by ISOS a week later and immediately sent to our office. However, what he or she said only added to our perplexity. The cable bore the same code as the previous one used by the Germans working in Madrid.

"60 ABWEHRSTELLE 1, BERLIN. ARABEL STATES
CONVOY SAILED FOUR DAYS AGO IN
SOUTHERLY DIRECTION."

'What`s going on?' Kim asked with exasperation. 'We know there is no bloody convoy. Why and who is this Arabel and why is he so obviously lying?'

'Shouldn't we alert stations in Madrid and Lisbon?' asked Trevor.

'No; em-emphatically no,' replied Philby. 'That might blow ISOS. We can`t let the Germans know we have cracked the c-c-codes. Either Arabel`s a complete phoney, and a r-r-ruse to catch us out', Kim stopped and then slowly added, 'H-he is still around for some reason. Five thinks he might be a member of the S-S-Spanish mission in London.'

This made sense, as many Franco`s Falangist officers were rabidly pro-Nazi, and did not agree with his wish for Spain to remain neutral, therefore one of them might have infiltrated the London Embassy at the German`s bidding. We figured this would also explain why Arabel was filling through Madrid. Then, with the strong Nazi support across the Irish sea, others in the section thought Arabel might have been in Ireland not England at all.

The hordes of refugees then arriving in Britain were run past very tough interrogators who were set up at Wormwood Scrubs and at the Royal Victorian Patriotic School in Battersea. MI5, who ran these interrogators, checked and double-checked and none of the newcomers matched up with Arabel.

Having the distinct feeling this Spanish mystery was going to become larger, and our office very much busier in the near future, now seemed a good time as any to visit my pregnant wife in Worcester. Having cleared it with Kim Philby and Felix Cowgill, I set off on the train, still wondering who Arabel could be, and if the Germans were trying to catch us out. It was interesting sitting on the train with the other passengers; their uniforms very clearly explained who they were. Their conversations open, and more often about all of horror and heroics; but at least they could talk about their activities. I had some cover story explaining my circumstances and why I was in St Albans; none of it true, of course. Mind you, just having a cover story made it all the more tempting to talk about work. Thank goodness Betty was pregnant and I could occupy my mind with that.

Not having seen Betty for over two months, my excitement as the train approached Worcester was hard to contain. Seeing her again and pregnant, I forgot all about being a Secret Service man. The village postman, who had given Betty a lift to Worcester, drove us back to Kerswell

Green. The six-mile journey down the narrow winding lanes was over far too quickly, as was the whole weekend. Getting up very early the next morning to help feed and clean out the pigs, and generally lending my wife a hand with her Land Army duties, put me back in touch with a reality hard to maintain when working in the heady world of espionage and secrets. The cottage she shared with her mother was warm and comfortable.

After cleaning out the second pigsty I washed my boots off, walked to the end of the garden and took the Matchless 500cc out of the shed. I pushed it up the garden path towards the road, and asked Betty if she wanted to go for a spin up to the bluebell wood and back. In response to her hesitation, I told her I had decided to take the bike to St Albans with me and consequently managed to acquire a couple of extra petrol coupons.

Oh what joy to feel her arms around my waist as we leaned in and out of the corners, the wind pushing me against my precious passenger and pulling at our hair. We stopped on a grass verge and went for a walk in the woods, making the most of the little time we had together. After our walk I kick-started the motorbike into life and Betty climbed on to the pillion seat. In my haste to get home before it started to rain, I managed to accelerate too fast, leaving Betty sitting on the verge which caused some concern for the expected baby; (I hasten to add that our daughter Rosanne was born healthy in January 1942).

I left the next day, Sunday, in the pouring rain, and arrived at Mr. and Mrs. French`s tired, wet and sad; yet somehow looking forward to the Monday morning in-tray, my mind again wondering about our Spanish German spy.

The office was not the hive of activity I had expected; Arabel had been quiet, it was still raining, and the most excitement was created by my motorbike. While running my eyes and finger over names and addresses in the Lisbon directory Kim turned to me.

'Desmond, we have three arrivals from Spain; H-H-Huelva to be more precise. They need to be interrogated. Since this is your domain, you'd better get going'.

I took the train to London and was met by Detective Inspector Reginald Spooner of Special Branch who gave me the background. During what seemed a rather arduous task at first, these three Spanish longshoremen in Huelva informed me of how the Germans had given them money to load explosives on to English ships. From the report I read about the shipping in that area, very little had been sunk and none by explosives on board.

Each one, individually, told me how they consistently took the money and dumped the explosives into the sea, thus saving British lives, ships and tons of supplies. This was a very risky game these three had played, and when the Germans became suspicious, the Three Charlies, as we called them, managed to stow themselves away on a British ship and arrived in England.

I was rather tense for the first day, not being used to cross-questioning people. With the help of Reginald Spooner, by the end of the third day I had become quite apt at cross-examining. Their stories checked out. The irony for me was they told their stories filling in every detail of who their families were and where they were from. Unbeknown to them they knew my father and the mines I had lived on as a child. With this, and all the other evidence we had at hand, it was clear they were telling the truth. For their efforts the Three Charlies were given jobs in a group called the Pioneers Corps.

I arrived back at HQ at 6:30 on Thursday evening, in time for a session in the glass conservatory at the back of Glenalmond, commonly called the Snake pit. The dust and dead palm trees, the sound of glass clinking as the pink gins were stirred, set up the atmosphere for relaxed chatter about work. I quickly recounted my last few days as an interrogator and relayed my astonishment that the Three Charlies had successfully got away with their counter-sabotage activities.

Trevor peered over the top of his glass.

'Arabel has been at it again; even Kim the expert is at a loss.'

The Abwehr's trust in this creative liar grew with every creative message he sent to them. From the German radio messages sent from Madrid to Berlin we found out that Arabel's Abwehr contact Frederico was swallowing his agents every tale. We could only suppose the Germans were either extremely gullible or they were setting a trap, as Philby had suggested. We threw ideas around the room for a while, but we were at a loss as to who and why this Arabel was and where.

My father would often remember moments as clear as day, which were, to my mind, irrelevant yet important to him.

As the session drew to an end I stepped out of the back doorway into the dark autumn evening. A damp mist was hanging in the air as I emerged from the Snake pit onto the lawn. I walked around the side of the mansion to the front driveway. I listened to the crunch of the gravel under my feet, zipped up my jacket, put on my tan pigskin gloves and started up my Matchless. The throb of the single-cylinder engine echoed as I wiped the evening dew off the seat. I felt a tap on my shoulder which made me jump a little. Philby was standing behind me, his collar pulled up around his neck.

'Desmond, give me a lift and I`ll stand you a Jameson`s at King Harry`s.'

I took it slowly down the drive to the road as the bike needed warming up. Once at the gate I accelerated quite hard, skidding a little on the gravel as we entered the road. The headlight beam cut through the darkness and shone on the damp fallen leaves; the elm trees on either side created large dark shadows and intensified the loud throaty noise of the engine. My nose was running by the time we arrived. In the pub, the chill was soon relieved by the fire and the spirit of Mr. Jameson`s best Irish whisky. Kim seemed a little anxious that night; I assumed it was due to the ever-growing pressure our sector was experiencing.

'Everything OK?' I asked.

'Yes, fine. Our section is becoming more important by the minute, and we're all doing very well, I'm glad to say'. He continued almost in the same breath without his usual stutter, 'I was wondering what you think and feel about Franco?'

I was somewhat taken aback by the question, as it seemed rather out of place. Also; I will admit that I was not anti-Franco as so many people were.

'Well he has both us British and the Germans interested in what was once a totally divided country. I think he is good for Spain and providing the Commies and anarchists don't regain strength hopefully he will rebuild the country. Spain has vast tracks of land for farming and has great mineral resources such as coal up North and copper and tin down South. In my opinion it needs a strong hand; why do you ask?'

Sipping on his whisky he looked at me and pondered.

'Yes, I think you could be right, I got that f-f-feeling when I was covering his nationalist side as The Times Correspondent. Just wondering if you had any feelings about his leaning towards the Germans or to our side?' He finished his whisky and ordered two more.

'Kim we all know he is a Military Dictator, and there are a few of those around; but he does not get on with Mussolini at all, and he is too religious to get too entrenched with the German regime. Dictators scare us and rightly so, for us and our war effort his remaining neutral is very useful and strategically very important. I do not see him joining either side. Why would he? In my father's letters, he does not say much about the politics of Spain but he is concerned as are the other mining companies. None of them have the feeling Franco will actually come out and openly support either side; Spain is far too weak and unstable to fight.'

He leant back in his chair and unfastened his coat and took a long look into his glass.

'Yes I suppose you are right. H-how's Betty?' he suddenly asked, changing the subject. His stutter had returned.

When I read this piece written by my father I think, as any one might, "Did my father really say all that at the time? Was the conversation longer and more revealing; had my father analysed it more closely?" At this moment in his life my father might have started to work for the top KGB double agent. He might well have become a double agent.

Perhaps somewhere in my mind I wished he had. On the other hand this would have meant he had deceived all of us. Having a feeling of doubt about ones father's beliefs and actions is very disheartening. Does one ever know the truth about anyone?

After prodding from my son and thinking back on it now he was obviously testing me as a potential partner in his work for the Russians.

We drank and talked family and work. I dropped him off at his house late that night and picked him up early in the following morning to take him to the garage where his car had been serviced. He was leaving for London after lunch as he was on night duty at Secret Service HQ, 54 Broadway, a chore we all unfortunately had to do at some point.

The Iberian section was by now a hive of nervous activity. We had an ever increasing number of reports arriving from Lisbon, Madrid, Tangier and Gibraltar. In Madrid, Lisbon and Tangier we (Section V) had our own stations from mid-1941; prior to this we accepted what the general MI6 chaps reported. These stations would receive reports form consular representatives (agents). In Spain the towns covered were Bilbao, San Sebastian, Vigo, Zaragoza and Seville. Lisbon drew information from Oporto. As a result of our newly formed organization abroad more and more information of a purely counter-espionage nature was reported by these consular posts, often naming Germans and Italians suspected of being secret agents. In early 1941 these reports had been a trickle, now (late 1941) they were a torrent. We had a big field of neutrality to operate in, enabling our agents to operate without too much danger despite the number of Germanophiles in both Spain and Portugal.

From late 1941 to spring 1942 our card index became a very detailed data base register of thousands of names, addresses, and telephone numbers, and we spent many evenings checking the relevant files and creating a cross reference system.

I remember the feeling of gloom while I was reading ISOS messages and found one containing a solitary telephone number. My Sunday visit to the pub with Kim or Jack, and my Sunday motorcycle ride had to be ditched in favour of the arduous task of matching a name and address with Madrid 27533. This tedious challenge was very satisfying when yet another enemy agent was identified. This work gave us an incredible insight into the operations of the German network in Spain.

The urgent replies required to the ever-increasing number of telegrams and letters from stations kept the seven of us and three secretaries busy for long periods without a break. By January 1942 we were working as a very close unit; our socializing in the pubs had to become less and less and the clinking of glasses and rattling of tongues and brain cells in the Snake pit happened more and more. Pubs were a dangerous place to talk and our secrets were becoming bigger. We had to condition ourselves not to talk shop anywhere and since I found the work exciting and fascinating it was hard at first, especially with my wife. Somehow I found a way of switching off the work side of my life, perhaps helped by the fact I'm a Gemini. Jack Evans and I often helped each other with our problems and our workloads.

Office procedure was as follows: at 8.30 am we would peruse papers left over from the night before and clear any backlog. At 10.30 the bag would arrive from Broadway, containing the correspondence from Section V stations, which had first been delivered to MI6 HQ from the foreign office. Since all mail came to England by diplomatic bag from Madrid, Tangiers, Lisbon and Gibraltar independently, it was anybody's guess which bag would arrive on any one day of the week. Once having bet Trevor that the Madrid bag would arrive on Wednesday two weeks in a row, I received free pink gins for a week in the Snake pit. Unfortunately betting did not go down at all well, so the opportunity to make the most of my lucky streak ended abruptly. Often mail would be preceded by a telegram demanding an urgent response to a letter about to arrive. Some of this correspondence had to be sent to another station.

Our picture of the Abwehr grew day by day; more names, activities and possible targets constantly being revealed.

Interludes seemed infrequent. One Friday morning just before Christmas, Kim walked into the office came over to me and asked without stuttering,

'Hey Desmond! I was wondering if you wanted to come up to London for the weekend? I am staying with some good friends of mine, Tommy and Hilda Harris who are very involved in Spain and have been for many years. Tommy is a very good artist and Hilda is great fun and a very good cook.'

Tommy Harris was my God Father; it was when working on The Game of Moles with my father I started to realise how much the spy world had been a part of our family's world. It has affected my outlook on the world. Politics, economics and the press have a very dark and subversive underbelly for me. Yet it is the world we live in and that is that. The way of espionage and its back story has never left my way of looking at world events whether political, idea-logical or industrial. For me there is always something behind what we see and believe.

I accepted willingly and we left just after lunch. It was raining and very cold. I remember having to fix the lights on Kim's Vauxhall just before we arrived in London. When it started to get dark he turned them on and they fused.

Chesterfield Gardens was in a very beautiful part of London. Hilda Harris greeted us at the front door of the large house. Kim made the introductions, and Hilda took me up to my bedroom on the third floor. The wardrobe was a seventeenth-century cupboard with brass-studded lattice work on its doors; very Spanish and very rare in England. I washed and changed. Walking downstairs I could not help noticing the virtual museum pieces of furniture and art decorating the landings. There were a few Christmas decorations and a rather strange sculpture made up as a Christmas tree.

After the inevitable drink, Kim excused himself and drove off, supposedly to see his mother. Hilda, Tommy and I walked around the corner to a little hole-in-the-wall restaurant and started an early supper. The three of us hit it off. We talked about Spain and Tommy's father who was Jewish and had introduced Spanish furniture and art to the streets of London when he opened his antique and art shop on St James's Street. Tommy did not talk a lot about his Spanish Mother. Hilda was very funny and quite bawdy. She had been a dancer with one of the famous troops.

Shortly before we were turned out of the restaurant Kim arrived and ordered a drink.

'Desmond I am going to persuade Felix to employ my sister. She speaks a little French and is good with a typewriter.'

'Good idea, Kim,' I replied a little surprised at his openness in front of the Tommy and Hilda Harris.

We returned to their house and sat up drinking, and talking about the Civil War. Kim explained that Tommy was working for MI5 and was closely associated with many members of the intelligence and the Secret Services.

The following day at breakfast we talked about the Spanish Embassy staff, and who amongst them was busy in the intelligence field. Tommy was then in the second week of interrogating a suspect Spanish journalist who ended up not being an agent for the Abwehr, although some of his articles had been sent to Berlin. We knew that Senor Alcaza de Velasco was running a small group of agents for the Spanish foreign minister, Senor Serrano Suner. ISOS was showing some, but not many, reports of very little significance were reaching the Abwehr in Madrid. Tommy was becoming MI5's Spanish expert.

We ate and drank very well. As Sunday afternoon rolled on, it started to snow. Kim and I drove back to St Albans, talking a little about the War, and a lot about the Tommy and Hilda Harris. Tommy was an enchantingly enigmatic character who from this first meeting it was apparent he had a multitude of talents and boundless energy.

I thanked Kim for what had been a marvelous break.

'OK, Desmond. Just thought you would enjoy meeting Tommy and Hilda. By the way do not talk too much about this in front of the others. See you in the Morning; I'll pick you up at 7 am.'

I remember reading a letter from Madrid dated 23rd December 1941:

'Herr Mueller arrived in Madrid on an official visit yesterday. Attended very discreet meeting with Sr Serano Suner (Spanish foreign minister). After lunch Mueller met with Johan Bernhardt for two hours. This morning left by Swiss Air flying to Berne.'

We alerted our head of station in Berne, who promptly had Herr Mueller watched. We found out he was one of Germany's top metallurgists, visiting Spain to secure the purchase of wolfram, a rare mineral used to harden steel. Our card index read, "Herr Mueller no known connection with Abwehr. Metallurgist, German arms company." A letter sent, and telephone call made, to the Ministry of Economic Warfare promising to inform them of further developments was of no direct advantage to us. It helped our cause in proving the usefulness and co-operative attitude of the newly-formed band of merry men in the Iberian sector. The information we passed on enabled our purchasers in Spain to outbid the Germans; thus we gained and our enemy lost a supply of much needed wolfram. Besides the foreign correspondence, messages were constantly passing to and from other departments including the army, navy and air force.

Christmas passed by with a rapid clinking of glasses huddled around the fireplace in the Snake pit. Snow decorated the hedgerows and a few paper cutouts decorated the halls and offices thanks to the secretaries.

Despite the snow and ice the bag always arrived at 10.30 clutched in the arms of the often near-freezing motorcycle dispatch rider, who would stop by the hall stove to remove the icicles from his moustache. Personal mail was also very efficient despite the blizzards and I received a telegram on 14th January 1942 from my wife's mother: "Betty gave birth to your daughter, January 13th. Congratulations."

Five days later I arrived on leave at Yew Tree Cottage. The baby was crying, Betty was smiling with pride. Betty's mother had kept the Christmas tree up and lighted the fire. Kim, before I left, had taken me to the pub for celebratory drink and given me a bottle of Champagne so we toasted parenthood and a late Christmas in a very cosy fashion.

Two days later back in St Albans my colleagues gave me a very warm reception and all the usual congratulations. Kim and his wife invited me to dinner that night, where we discussed the war, babies, and my renting a little house down the street.

'You should be living with your family while you can,' Kim advised. 'The chances are you may be posted abroad at some point.'

Having thanked Aileen for the rather overcooked meal, and Kim for the friendly advice, I walked home. As I listened to the crunch of the snow beneath my feet, I decided to move Betty, her mother and our daughter to St Albans.

5th February, 10.30 am: the dispatch rider arrived skidded a little in the snow walked in removed the icicles from his moustache delivered the Bag and left. Tim distributed the content and I looked through my batch for the telegrams. Finding one from Lisbon I quickly opened it.

"Lieutenant Demarest US naval attaché has informed me he has been approached by a Spanish national named Juan Pujol wanting to work for us in Britain. He has a story about sending messages to Germans from Lisbon." It was signed Benson, our shipping attaché in Lisbon.

When remembering this section of his story, my father became enraged by the rather narrow mindedness, a weakness, of Cowgill. With the beauty of hindsight, he realised this weakness played straight into Philby's hands. Cowgill had been recruited as head of this section due to his expertise of supposedly recognizing Communist spies and infiltrators. My father would not allow his true thoughts to be entered in the original book. Cowgill was at times worse than useless and if it had not been for Philby, Section V would not have worked.

Yet at the time of the book he seemed to be supportive of Cowgill. Why?

Philby was in Curzon Street in London, conferring with MI5. Lisbon wanted a quick response. I read the message out to the others rushed upstairs and knocked on Colonel Felix Cowgill's door.

The colonel was sitting behind his large wooden desk, the photograph of his wife and dark green labeled phone (scrambler) on one side, the red labeled phone, (his direct link to Menzies, the chief of MI6), and the black phone on the other. He was talking on the black phone. He put his hand over the mouthpiece and indicated for me to sit down. I noticed the maps recently pinned around his office, which showed the extent our stations where spreading in Europe. A shy and secretive man, the colonel always wore his uniform. The khaki green set off against the indelible tan gained from his exploits in northern India before the War, when he was a police officer tracking down Communist agitators. He hung up and asked what I wanted.

'Felix, sorry to bother you. Since Philby is away I thought you should take a look at this telegram from Lisbon.'

When he had read the message he looked across his desk, and said in his quiet voice,

'Could be a double agent, we must be very careful. If we are too hasty we might give ISOS away and the Nazis will know we have broken their codes.'

His other reason for caution was to protect our secret from MI5; the rivalry between the two camps perpetuated by Cowgill was really quite amazing and in my mind juvenile and possibly very disruptive. After all, many people's lives might depend on our information and by not being more open with our internal section; some very important details could be missed.

Pushing him as far as I felt I could,

'Shouldn't we do something about it now?' I asked.

This was potentially very important and should be acted on at least to make sure this man in Lisbon did not disappear.

'We wait for Philby to return.'

He handed the message back indicating it was time for me to leave.

Dismissed by this idiot, who seemed too scared to take responsibility of his position, I couldn't help feeling irritated by his apparent lack of interest and his willingness to fob off the responsibility of a decision on Kim. It also occurred to me, Kim Philby had obviously not fully informed the Colonel about our suspect agent. In my mind there was no doubt this was the man sending the phoney messages to the Germans in Madrid; the man we had Special Branch search Liverpool and northern Wales for. The man we had MI5 comb the Spanish Embassy and refugee arrivals for. This had to be Arabel.

5   Arabel becomes Garbo

Kim arrived back from London at about 3.45 pm, walked into the office and stamped the snow off his shoes. As he hung up his old leather jacket by the stove I handed over the message from Lisbon, and said,

'I think we have something rather big here. I think it might be Arabel.'

He read the message, patted me on the shoulder and turned towards the door. He stopped, looked over at me with a smile of excitement and exclaimed,

'By God Desmond, I think you are right.'

On that, he rushed up to the Colonel. Ten minutes later I heard him running down the stairs. He walked quickly across the office, picked up the green phone and, out of breath, rang Lieutenant Colonel Robertson of MI5, familiarly called Tar.

'T-T-Tar, a Spaniard called Pujol has approached the Yanks in L-Lisbon offering to work for us. He claims to have Abwehr connections in M-M-Madrid and wants to come to England, where h-he feels he could be of use to us.'

Tar agreed with Kim that we must have Pujol interrogated in Portugal with the idea of bringing him over to England. When Kim raised the question of security once on English turf, Tar's voice boomed down the phone with a sarcastic tone.

'Oh, come on, Kim. I think we can handle this little Spanish sardine; once in England, where is he going to swim to?'

The following morning a telegram was sent to Ralph Jarvis, our head of station in Lisbon, instructing him to set up a discreet interview. Jarvis contacted his best local agent, Gene Risso Grill, and told him about Pujol. Between them they decided it was best for Gene to conduct the interviews as he was far less likely to be watched by the local Portuguese police, who were very pro-German at that time. Besides, he spoke the best Spanish.

Jarvis contacted Captain Benson and told him to arrange for Juan Pujol to go to a café in Estoril, just north of Lisbon. Gene, who recounted this story to me when I met him in 1944, told me,

'Never before, or since, have I been as nervous as I was at that first interview with Juan Pujol. Believe me, I thought every German agent was watching me and everybody around the area and in the café was a German agent.'

Gene arrived at the café. It was an unusually warm day for February and more people were out than usual; many of them sitting at the little cast-iron tables on the terrace. The café smelt of fresh coffee. The terrace was built like a horseshoe so that every seat was sheltered from the cold wind and benefited from the wonderful view of the

Atlantic waves crashing on the white beaches below. While the sardine fisherman, wearing personally designed sweaters and colorful hats, pulled in their catch, their women sat on the sand repairing torn nets. Many day travellers up from Lisbon, and small groups of refugees, were wondering along the promenade to kill time before an evening's gambling at the famous Estoril Casino. His task seemed totally incongruous with the setting, which apparently helped them relax. A man answering Pujol's description walked up to the bar and asked in Portuguese with a Spanish accent,

'Tea with lemon, no sugar please.'

Gene sat down beside him.

'The view is much better at the table by the steps leading down to the beach.'

Pujol gave the right response and got up they moved across to the far table. After the initial five minutes of tension, with Gene constantly watching over his shoulder, they relaxed and started to talk. Gene was able to cross-question Pujol very easily as the latter was eager to prove his case. He handed over the invisible ink with copies of the messages he had sent to the Germans and gave Gene information to work on. They arranged to have more meetings in the same place, but at different times of day. After these subsequent meetings the friendly little Catalonian seemed genuine enough to Gene.

Several messages came and went through our office in St Albans. Kim had taken to conferring with me during our evening visits to the pub, where he felt he had privacy from the others. When he and I became convinced this was almost certainly the German agent Arabel he sent a message off to Jarvis, "Make arrangements for transport of our friend to Gibraltar as soon as possible."

The tricky part was to make sure the Germans did not find out that Juan Pujol, their Arabel, who was supposed to be in England at this time, was in fact in contact with the British in Lisbon. Captain Benson made the arrangements and told Gene Risso Grill to escort Pujol through the harbor, up the gangway, past the Portuguese police, onto the British merchant ship due to leave for Gibraltar.

We received the message. "Our Spaniard is safely on board and sailing to the Rock."

Donald Darling of MI9, in charge of escaped prisoners of war and anybody else wanting to return to England, met Pujol, gave him money, showed him around Gibraltar and generally looked after him for two weeks. Donald quickly came to the same conclusion as Gene about Pujol, and with his sharp sense of humor named him Mr. Bovril; this was to prevent that sinking feeling coming over any of us. The final message sent from us at St Albans put Mr. Bovril in a seat on a Sunderland seaplane headed for Plymouth.

On the evening of 25th April the Sunderland landed in Plymouth harbor. Mr. Bovril was met by Cyril Mills and Tomas (Tommy) Harris of MI5. The following morning Harris and Mills escorted Bovril on the train to the Royal

Patriotic School for initial interrogation and filing of his arrival in England.

On 28th April I caught the morning train to London, the underground to Hendon and walked to 35 Crespigny Road, the house assigned to Bovril by MI5. Cyril Mills greeted me and introduced Pujol. My undercover name on this occasion was Captain Richards. Juan, a short man with slicked back dark hair revealing a high forehead and warm brown eyes with a slight mischievous glint, smiled as I shook his hand. The room was sparsely furnished, with just a table and four chairs set against a window overlooking the small back garden of the semi-detached house. I spent the next four hours translating the messages he had sent to the Abwehr into English. In the afternoon I started the preliminary debriefing. As the representative of MI6, it was my task for the next eight days to interrogate this enigmatic Catalan.

After our initial meeting, on the train back to St Albans, I reflected on how relaxed Pujol seemed, considering the ordeal he was going through. My train pulled into St Albans at 6.30 pm; I jumped onto my motorcycle and sped to Glenalmond, wanting to tell the others about Juan Pujol.

When I stuck my head around the office door to find only Tim Milne and a new arrival to the Iberian section, Francis Watts, I knew where the others would be. Kim, Trevor, Frank and Jack were having their evening natter and pick-me-up in the Snake pit. I asked Jack to pour me one of his specials.

Kim smiled at me through the smoke of his cigarette and asked,

'Well Desmond. H-h-how is our friend?'

'Very well,' I replied. 'Surprisingly relaxed, seems to enjoy answering any questions I put to him. He is delighted with the treatment he has received from everybody. He especially enjoys bacon and eggs for breakfast; apparently he hasn't seen bacon since 1936.'

'Being spoilt by our chaps in MI5 already, is he?' interjected Jack.

Trevor, never one to miss a dig, asked,

'Besides his culinary preferences, what else did you find out?'

'Well, without any doubt it is he who sent the messages to our opponents in Berlin. He is Arabel without any doubt.'

'No doubt in your mind at all, Desmond?' asked Kim.

'None at all. He knows the dates and the contents of every message, and I don't think he is a German agent; it seems as though he has invented himself out of some romantic notion about spying, or else just for the money. Apparently the Germans were paying him quite well.'

'Well, its early days yet.' replied Kim as he offered me a cigarette. 'It sounds as though he is going to be useful. Have another drink, Desmond. Two more, when you are ready Jack.'

Frank, asked whether Pujol's Catalan was any good.

'How would I know, I speak Spanish!'

'Of course,' said Frank. 'How the hell did he understand anything you had to say?'

This ribbing was all in good fun but I found it rather irritating at time.

Jack, handing me my other drink and lighting my cigarette, laughed.

'Besides do you like him, Desmond?'

'Well yes; he makes for better company than you chaps these days.'

Trevor asked in his gentle voice,

'Does his breath smell of garlic?'

'No! Skunk shit, just like your perfume, you ass.'

With the joking aside, I confirmed he seemed to be genuine in his desire to work for us and from what I could tell at that time, possessed a phenomenal imagination, with a good deal of naivety, a good sense of humor and plenty of guts. I was sure 5 could make good use of him.

Trevor offered me another drink; I graciously refused, wanting to get home to my wife and daughter now living just down the road from Kim and Aileen. Kim and I left together; he had become a regular passenger on my motorcycle.

For the next few days I did not return to Glenalmond. After my daily sessions with Pujol I went straight home from the station to Sandy Lane.

The interrogation fell into a routine, and became more like conversations. Pujol's life, the Civil War, his likes and dislikes. He was concerned about his wife and young son whom he had left behind in Portugal. It had been with his wife's help and encouragement he had started the stories of being an agent in England and sending, the made up messages to the Germans. His information had been gained by reading naval books, a travel guide and air travel brochures. His agent in Lisbon was a fictitious KLM pilot. His child like imagination and ability to make it real was quite staggering.

He was blissfully unaware we had deciphered all of his messages and full scale searches had been carried out looking for him. A question I seemed to go over and over again with him was why had he created this very dangerous illusion and contacted the Germans? I'm still not sure of his reasons even today.

On the fourth day, 1st May, Tommy Harris greeted me at 35 Crespigny Road. This was a great relief, especially when he told me he had just been appointed Pujol's case officer. Up to that morning it had been Cyril Mills, who did not speak a word of Spanish and was far too pompous and unimaginative to make anything out of Pujol and his small web of agents. Mr. C Mills had been working on the assumption he was going to be the case officer. Instead Tommy and Pujol were going to be working together, to build up a phoney spy network which would feed false information to Pujol's German contacts and onto Berlin and Hitler.

We spent the morning going over Pujol's reports to the Abwehr. Analysing his style: how he used punctuation; what letters of the alphabet he emphasized more than others; the way he crossed his t's and dotted his i's. Pujol had already developed a loose pattern of content, and it was essential the written dialogue remain in a similar vein to his previous letters to Frederico in Madrid. Coffee was brought in every so often by the watchman. Tommy seemed to have the size of Pujol very quickly and in between rolling and smoking his Spanish black tobacco cigarettes, manipulated his new agent in any direction he cared to. This was going to be some duo, I thought.

In the afternoon, listening to Pujol's life story and his motives for wanting to be a spy all over again, I observed how he responded to Tommy. His motives for working against the Germans seemed obvious as he told the story, yet again, about his brother witnessing atrocities committed by the Gestapo in France. His feeling of the Germans wanting to rule Europe, how they had just walked in to France. The bombings he had heard about. He had all the right answers. (Interestingly, my wife became great friends with his wife after the war and apparently his brother had never set foot in France. This is why today I'm still not sure of Pujol's motives).

By the end of the day I was saturated with Pujol's life story and in need of conversation other than spy talk. I offered Tomas a beer at the local. As I closed the front door, he rolled yet another cigarette, raised his eyebrows, shook his head and smiled in a very knowing way. Tommy was quite tall and slim, with a very angular and rather Spanish aristocratic face. His smile at that moment was quite haunting.

'Desmond, he is obviously Arabel. It is hard to believe such an outwardly simple man has the Germans fooled and had us worried for so long. He is such a dreamer and so willing. While the Germans continue to swallow his communications he is going to be a marvelous double agent to operate with. Something we must make sure of.' He turned to me, 'I'm not too keen on beer, how about a glass of vino at the Euston hotel?'

The hotel interior was sumptuous compared to my normal drinking and chatting houses. Tommy's half Spanish, half English mix, his work as an art dealer, his artistic and linguistic abilities were all part of this very cultured, intense and humorous man. It was the beginning of a friendship that lasted until his tragic death in a strange car accident in Majorca 1964.

By the end of the week Tommy and I had managed to convince our superiors; Pujol was genuine. I could see in the hands of Tommy Harris, Juan Pujol could be a marvelous line of false information, which would lead the Germans up all sorts of garden paths. Juan Pujol and Tommy Harris became 'Garbo'.

Tomas and Juan started to create a large phoney spy network, using the fictitious KLM pilot Juan had invented in Lisbon as the spearhead.. The combination of Pujol's rather naïve and creative imagination and Tommy's creative and deeply intelligent mind fueled by the XX committee strategies was to prove devastatingly successful.

Within a few days the XX committee was supplying Garbo with information to send to the Abwehr.

My time with Tommy and Garbo sadly came to an end. I learnt a great deal during those ten days, giving me a background to the operations of double agents. I became especially aware of the huge ramifications required to maintain one side oblivious of the real intensions of the other.

I was invited to the XX committee which took place on Wednesdays in MI5's headquarters. The full-time committee members chose the casual attenders, such as me, very carefully. Our security and loyalty had to be one hundred per cent. It was indeed the most secret club of the Secret Service in Britain.

I remember very clearly waking up on the first Wednesday. I had spent the previous evening polishing my uniform buttons, belt buckles and shoes. The first time I had worn my uniform in months.

My father was 25 years old at this time making him one of the youngest members of MI6, and very young for being a Captain in The Intelligence Corps. He recounted this event to me almost as though he still had a feeling of embarrassment as to how important his role had become.

For me as he slowly relaxed into revealing his Spy life to his son, I started to have feelings of pride. I just hoped all my fellow class mates might read the book at the time 'A Game of Moles' was published back in 1993.

This first meeting with all those important people gave me the butterflies. All I could eat for breakfast was half a piece of toast; the train journey to London was over far too quickly. I suppose I started to realise the heady responsibility and the fact, I was becoming a rather important cog in the Secret Service wheels; it had all been fun and rather easy up to this point. Now like Garbo, I was seriously IN.

As I turned into St James's street I took a deep breath; 'Chin in, shoulders back, chest out,' I mumbled to myself. 'Come on, Derry, this is exciting, you are becoming important.' Another little voice told me it might have been easier had I been in the infantry. I was able to dismiss that thought very quickly by recalling the wounded soldiers I had seen at Oxford station. Sand bags were still in evidence along the street barricading windows and doors. When I walked through the doorway of MI5's office the security watchman stood to attention and saluted me. This simple gesture boosted my self-confidence and I saluted back. After he checked my papers he indicated the old steel cage lift which took me down to the Basement level.

The room was square, bare and cold. So was the table in the middle with chairs around. Tar Robertson, a big haughty fellow with his friendly eyes and an assertive way about him, came up and shook my hand.

'Hello, Desmond, glad you could make it old boy.'

Noticing my shyness Tar put me at my ease straight away. While looking at my polished buttons and pressed uniform, he continued,

'Don't worry. We're an informal lot here really. Let me introduce you.' Which he did.

The names my father revealed to me were like watching a series of war movies and documentaries. Some featured in 'The Man Who Never Was,' the story of deception messages found on the dead body of a man dressed as an airman. He was discovered by some Spanish fishermen off the coast of Huelva, Southern Spain, near were my father had lived as a child.

John Masterman, the Head of the Committee, MI5, Oxford University; John Marriot the Secretary MI5, a London solicitor; T. A. Robertson, Lieutenant Colonel, MI5; Ewen Montague, Lieutenant Commander, Naval Intelligence; John Drew, Home Defence Executive; Colonel Bevan, Army Flight Lieutenant; Hugh Cholmondeley, Air Force Cambridge, and myself for this meeting and the following four Wednesday meetings.

We discussed the false information that Garbo should pass on to the Germans. My contribution was to advise on what information a Spaniard such as Pujol might initially put over to them and in what way he might text it. I liaised the information back to Tommy Harris. I suggested Tommy Harris attend these meetings, and he was present at the last two I attended and from them on dealt directly with the committee.

My workload at St Albans was growing since the Germans and Italians had started a spate of sabotage on our shipping in Gibraltar and around the southern coast of Spain.

6   Gibraltar

Early in May Felix invited me up to his office to discuss the growth of Section V and how well we were all doing. Several times during the conversation he brought up the subject of Gibraltar and sabotage and his feeling for the need for someone to go to the rock from our section. I began to wonder where all this was leading. He stopped talking, rubbed his chin stubbed out his cigarette, looked across his desk and said in his quiet voice,

'Desmond you do realise that you are the man for Gibraltar. You like the Spaniards and obviously know that area better than most natives.'

'I willingly accept.'

My car and boat trips to and from Gibraltar as a child and adolescent had given me a familiarity with the terrain, culture, and language (Andaluz) which would now be very useful. Besides it was becoming increasingly frustrating for me dealing with messages about blown-up ships and German intelligence activities without being in control of events and the flow of information to England.

I would need a secretary and after many interviews a choice was made; Dom O'Shagar. He had started his career as an Irish Priest and at the age of twenty seven he had given up the celibate life to open a shop in Vincent Square near Westminster Cathedral where he sold wooden and wax effigies, so popular in Catholic circles. How the department found him I have no idea but his Spanish was good and having an ex-priest around made me feel spiritually safe if nothing else. He came up to St Albans several times to be briefed.

I made several trips to Medmenham the headquarters of aerial photography to study aerial photographs of southern Spain, Gibraltar and the bay of Algeciras. It was astounding to see the number of merchant ships only a few hundred yards from the Spanish shoreline of La Linea. I realised why sabotage was so easy for the Italians and Germans.

A farewell party organised by Kim and Trevor in the Snake pit, gave all of us an evening off from the war. It was warm; many people from other departments who I had only seen in hallways or on the stairs, joined in. Somebody had brought an old record player and the music of Gershwin and the new sounds of Duke Ellington floated across the back lawn of Glenalmond Manor. Luckily I had one day's leave in order to do my final packing and be at home with Betty and Rosanne which enabled me to recover from the hangover.

The morning of the 4th June, Betty accompanied me to Paddington. I boarded the train for Plymouth. We hugged and kissed. Our held back tears and smiles came and went as we said goodbye. The pressure pushed the large piston, the wheels turned slowly and the steam from the boiler came hissing out and filled the platform immersing Betty in a cloud. I sat back in my first class seat reflecting all that had happened over the last year. The beautiful English countryside so green and sumptuous flashed by the window. The clickety-clack of the wheels taking me closer to my new assignment brought the tune of "Chatanooga Choo-Choo" to mind. For a brief moment I wondered if I would see any of my St Albans pals again. This thought quickly disappeared as the idea of heading almost home to Gibraltar and flying in a Sunderland, which I had only ever heard about.

It makes me wonder how my father remembered these sorts of details. If I had been in his place would I have thought of Chatanooga Choo-Choo? No! I would certainly have been excited by being sent on the mission to set up the MI6 Section V office in Gibraltar. His romantic memories often seem out of place, but I suppose he thought he might have been killed; the threat of death was going to be more prevalent now than back in St Albans. I know he considered he was getting into the war in a more intense way. One thing I will tell you; my father hated flying.

At Plymouth, an RAF driver took me to a small RAF establishment near the harbor where they gave me tea and biscuits; to calm my nerves I assumed. O'Shagar was already drinking his tea when I arrived. At dusk we were taken to the harbor and put on a small boat which chugged through the mist, honking its foghorn. Then in front of us looming up out of the mist was a huge sleeping whale with wings on, or a Sunderland flying boat, my transport to Gibraltar. Safely on board we started moving out of the harbor. It was exhilarating to feel the machine skid across the water and slowly rise out of the mist.

At midnight a member of the three-man crew brought more tea and biscuits. The noise of the engines and the small bucket seats made sleep difficult. Early next morning we seemed to be miles from anywhere no land visible; just the odd ship riding through the rough seas of the Bay of Biscay below. By 09.00 hours southern Portugal was visible and the plane closed in towards land. By 10.00 hours, flying along the Straits, we could just make out the Rock of Gibraltar peering at us through the low cloud. I put out my cigarette, fastened my safety belt, my sweaty hands clamped tightly around the small armrests.

It is here where I imagine him with white knuckles and as nervous as hell; wondering what dying would be like in a plane as it crashed into the water.

The sea got closer and closer and the waves bigger and bigger. The flying whale landed in a big envelope of spray crashing through the rough waters of the bay on the Atlantic side of the rock. Section V now had a man in Gibraltar.

A small boat manned by field security crew drew alongside. A big man covered with oilskins and water came aboard to greet us.

'Captain David Thompson, at your service.'

He handed a waterproof jacket to O'Shagar and me, then turning around quickly to step back on the boat added,

'Better move it, this weather is getting worse and the plane must get back.'

Thomson, a very affable man, and senior member of the Defence Security Office, became a friend of mine and very helpful in my task of setting up a Section V network.

Austin Baillon OBE, a friend of my father who was in Special Operations Executive (SOE) on Gibraltar, has described the Rock and a little of its history. Hopefully this will also help underline the importance of having Desmond Bristow from Section V set up his network of agents there.

"The 1895 edition of Chambers' Encyclopedia describes the inhabitants of Gibraltar as "a motley agglomeration of English, Genoese, Spanish, Jews and Moors."

'Rock scorpions' was the inking term applied by some when I was there, but I never had any reason to consider or call them so. Gibraltar has been in British hands since 1704 when a combination of Dutch and British forces took it from Spain. Several military attempts to recapture the rock have failed and the Spanish have for the last hundred or so years tried diplomatic dialogue to recover the isolated mass of rock; 'jaw jaw, not war war', as Winston Churchill once said.

In April 1941 I and seventeen other Spanish speaking officers arrived. Not expecting to be in Gibraltar for very long as our mission was to enter Spain ahead of the expected German forces and to interrupt their communications behind them. Ours was operation

Relator, the Germans' was Operation Felix, neither of which took place.

Gibraltar was bracing itself for an impending attack. General Eastwood was replaced as the governor of the fortress by the more charismatic General the Viscount Gort VC, just as Crete was taken by German parachutists; the first use of such troops, and seen as a prelude to a similar attack on Gibraltar.

By then the Rock was a seething mass of activity night and day. It was the base for Force H, the Mediterranean fleet. The dockyard worked around the clock on repairs and refits. The original polo field and small airstrip were being extended into an important military airbase with the materials excavated form the bowels of the Rock by the Royal Canadian Engineer Company. Construction of an alternative city, with power plant, water storage, hospital and living accommodation for siege conditions was well under way.

Whatever else Gibraltar lacked at that time, it was certainly not bars or booze. At midday Main Street, Irish town and Castle Street would be crammed with servicemen of all ranks, many in transit from passing convoys or naval ships. Desmond, one such passer-by composed an amusing verse unrepeatable in polite company, except for the opening lines: Symbol of the British Empire, Haughtily Gibraltar stands, never will this proud erection, be reduced by axis hands."

As you can see, Gibraltar by the time I arrived was well established; it had become the victim of sabotage, and a potential den for Axis spies to send information about all sorts of Allied Military Movement in the Mediterranean. Besides being this it would also be a potential source of information.

A room had been reserved for me at the Rock hotel where I stayed for two weeks.

The office was in a building just off Irish Town, near Mackintosh Square. The larger space was occupied by the four members of the Defence security staff headed by Major John Medlam. A wide balcony, covered recently to create extra space, led to the MI6 office headed by Lieutenant Colonel Codrington.

Just to clear up any confusion, Father was part of MI6 but Section V was very specific about being actively involved in counter espionage and deception as opposed to straight forward spying (gathering information).

Donald Darling of MI9 had a small office next to that and in a corner sat Brian Morrison, one of the most intelligent and unused heads that I met during my time with the Secret Service.

You will see in some of the following how dedicated and successful both of these men were in their work during the war, but when they were no longer required the Government discarded them in that thankless British manner both financially and morally. Brian who spoke German, Chinese, Russian, Spanish and French fluently was stationed in Finland as an SIS officer at the beginning of the war when the Soviet Union attacked. Towards the end of March 1940 when all others were recalled, Brian remained hiding in the woods operating wireless communications. He was the last SIS officer to leave Finland.

The remaining staff consisted of the chief clerk, Sergeant McNeff , and corporal Kevin Kavanagh, an interesting Irish man, jokingly known as Red Kavanagh because of his communist tendencies before the war. O'Shagar and myself had an obvious space problem which none of the above were going to help with since my appearance on their turf was upsetting for them. Codrington and Medlan made no effort to hide how much their noses were put out of joint.

I decided the best place for my office was on the covered balcony; this would put me in the middle of the two other departments, enabling me to eavesdrop and pick up information received by either one. O'Shagar used his Irish name to befriend Kevin Kavanagh who, being the secretary of the others, knew exactly what was going on at any given moment. Kevin helped us gather a couple of old desks and chairs and had the telephone hooked up. On 18th June Section V opened their first official office on the Rock of Gibraltar.

John Codrington soon realised I was not the threat or bogey man he had anticipated, and showed me around Gib and gave me free access to information running through his office. On the other hand, Medlan was a pain in the rear end; but realizing I was now working with him and from a department of the Secret Service he knew nothing about, he forced himself to be amicable and within a short space of time I was gathering information on local activities gleaned by his field security staff. Besides the information coming via these departments, I needed my own agents. David Thompson told me of Antonio Joseph who occasionally worked for the Defence Security department. David took me to the small office in Irish town where Antonio ran his transport company.

Antonio tried to be suave and sophisticated and always had his slightly receding black hair brushed back and wore the latest designer suits. After half an hour of listening to the details of his company's business, and taking note of his affable attitude, I realised he was going to be very helpful.

'David tells me you have been more than helpful with certain lines of information and I am here to expand those lines.'

'Good,' he said. 'At least you English are realizing how much information is flying around here. And there are some very willing Spanish friends of mine who don't like the Germans much.'

He told of the network he used for his business, and over the next two weeks I had information coming in from Cadiz, Estepona and very detailed accounts of German and Italian movements in the immediate area. He was my first and most helpful head agent and during my time in Gibraltar I liaised with him at least twice a week, usually in his apartments for safety reasons. The help he extended to me far exceeded what was expected. He gave me the use of his car, and acted as paymaster for the little money my agents ever received.

If the Germans had taken Gibraltar, people like Antonio would doubtless have been executed. Perhaps they did it for the excitement value, and their hatred of Nazi Germany and their belief in freedom.

Now settled into the routine of the office I needed to find alternative digs. Staying at the hotel would draw too much attention to my presence on the Rock.

One evening while chatting over a glass of vino with Donald and Brian, they invited me to move into their apartment on the third floor of Plaza de la Verdura, a short walk up from Mackintosh Square. A more central location would have been hard to find, and more suitable room-mates impossible.

When my father told me about his exploits in this apartment shared with Brian and Donald; I wondered how he thought he received less attention from the others living and working in Gibraltar. Perhaps he felt that the more fun and games he appeared to be having the less anyone would take him seriously. But less attention from whom? I would often ask.

We each had our small room set off the front central living room which had a piano in one corner and four rather broken but comfortable chairs around a low oblong table. The two large windows had big sills covered with cushions where I often sat and watched the tops of people's heads as they walked in the square. When I sat against one wall of one of the windows I was able to see the docks of Algeciras and the battleships moving in and out of Gibraltar. Every now and again Donald would put up an escapee for a few days, until their passage to England was organised.

On the second Saturday after I had moved into the apartment I arrived later than usual. Jazz music filled the stairwell, growing louder as I climbed the steep steps. I was puzzled, as curfew was strict in Gibraltar, but not being too familiar with the exact laws was intrigued as to the source, and being a fan of jazz wanted to join in. When I reached the third floor, the door to my apartment was open; the piano and clarinet sounds were coming from the living room. Donald greeted me at the door looking rather nervous as to how I would react and started to explain,; every fourth Saturday he invited Cyril, a jazz pianist from the dockyard, to come over with any other musicians he was able to muster. He started a lengthy apology, which I interrupted.

'Donald, I love jazz music; all I need now is a drink, you silly fool.'

Besides the odd escapee and the Donald Darling jazz festivals our cozy apartment became a safe house in which we three Gib Musketeers discussed and plotted our activities. This apartment became the centre for MI9, MI6 and Section V without the officials above Brian or Donald realizing. I was my own master. The office was certainly not the place. John Codrington, Brian's boss was not very interested in socializing in the lower social circles,.

Occasionally he would venture to Spain to visit Jill Alvarez, whom he has been known to describe as his best agent! (She was an aristocrat who gave cocktail parties and tea parties privy to a certain flow of information. Medlam just did not belong).

To outline what we were all doing in Gibraltar. MI6 (John Codrington and Brian Morrison) watched Spanish army movements in the campo areas and gathered any other relevant information which had a bearing on what Spanish intensions were or might be, not only against Gibraltar, but regarding the Axis and Allies in general. The Defence Security office (headed by John Medlam) maintained the Security of Gibraltar against espionage, sabotage and any other activities detrimental to our war efforts on the Rock. MI9 (Donald Darling) dealt with the escapees and refugees whom he screened before forwarding to London by boat or plane. Section V went to Gibraltar to build up records of German and Italian personnel and their agents operating on the area and establish a network of agents to help in monitoring and developing lines for deception purposes.

Sixteen thousand Spanish people crossed into Gibraltar every day to work. These were all potential agents for the Germans or Italians and I started the area watch so we could possibly prevent some if not all sabotage and espionage as far afield as Malaga, Cadiz and Seville. The area being such an open book made work on espionage almost pointless, so most of my work was to do with sabotage detection and to monitor movements of Spanish Police and Guardia Civil.

Jazz parties living in an apartment often shared with escapees and refugees, dangerous liaisons with my own agents, being my own boss: this was "my Jolly Old Gibraltar". Yes Gibraltar was jolly in every sense; joyful, slightly drunk, festive, and with the comings and goings of naval personnel I at least felt as though I was involved with a real war. It was good to be in or at least close to a battle arena.

My father was unwilling to share this before, but information had arrived from ULTRA about money and support being given by the German Administration to Spain.

Until October 1942 there was a strong possibility that the Germans, aided by the Spanish army, might invade; or so it was thought by those who did not know the Spanish very well. As a result of this threat during the course of my stay on Gib, MI6 and Section V were instructed by London to organise a stay-behind network in the nearby southern Spain area. (A stay behind policy is the term used for the preparations of a network of agents to operate after the enemy has occupied territory).

Early in July my agent in Cardiz sent a report to Antonio who passed on the message to me:

"SPANISH ARMY ON MOVE HEADING TOWARDS GIBRALTAR. TRANSPORTING TWO 15 INCH NAVAL GUNS. THEIR PROGRESS, SLOW".

Ironically, the guns were made in Britain.

In the San Roque area, the hills surrounding the Gibraltar basin, gun emplacements sprang up like mushrooms. Large gasogene driven trucks struggled up the slopes as far as they could, then their cement and brick cargo was taken further on by mules and donkeys.

Kevin gave me a copy of a London Sunday paper. On the front page was a large cartoon showing the Rock with the monkeys looking down the barrels of guns of all shapes and sizes, dominated by the two 15 inch naval guns arriving from Cadiz.

A staff meeting was held at Government house. Brian and I had a hard time containing our laugher when they came up with the devastatingly bright idea of monitoring the movement of these two guns.

Often you will pick up on my father's rather cynical attitude towards the authorities who were often old fashioned and had very little idea of espionage or the possibility of MI6, Section V, or anyone having agents working for them. Antonio and his network kept my father informed of the progress of the Guns and the trouble they were causing. It may seem strange, but my father or Brian could not inform the others at the meeting of this fact. I realised that often Secret Service information gathering was kept secret from outsiders.

With the information from Antonio, and knowing the roads myself, I knew that the roads had always been terrible and had been damaged further during the Civil War. About five days after all the excitement I obtained passes, for Brian and myself from the very helpful Spanish consulate, to take the diplomatic bag to the British vice consul in Cadiz.

I posed as Brian's driver; he sat in the back being important. The security at La Linea was tougher than usual, and at the San Roque checkpoint I was a little worried. Having made it through, I was driving the 1936 Cadillac casually towards Tarifa up a bumpy road lined by oak trees. Suddenly four Civil Guards, rifles at the ready, jumped out in front of the car. They were nervous and looked suspiciously at Brian as they ordered me to turn around. Brian started to get annoyed with them, swearing in English. The youngest was ready to get heavy handed; and I started to fear it could get nasty. Brian noticed the attitude was becoming rather aggressive and stopped his rant. I stepped out of the car with my hands up.

My Spanish stopped them, as they were surprised how well I spoke native Andaluz. One of the older Guards was curious. I explained that I had been brought on the mines of Sotiel Coronada and gave him my name. The older Guard issued the order; guns were lowered and safety catches engaged and hands were shaken. My nerves, shaken but not too stirred, relaxed. The older Guard was a football fan and supported Club Real De Huelva. My father had been an administrator of the club back in 1921 and 1922, and he remembered how influential the British miners had been in setting up the first Football Club in Spain.

When I explained how important Senor B. Morrison was, he was invited to shake hands with every one and to accept their apologies. They explained how the army was transporting two guns to defend La Linea from any attacks that may come from Gibraltar; to which we all smiled. I showed our passes out of formality. After some more conversation about my childhood and Huelva, they all expressed their hope the war would end soon.

On we went, hot and dusty, bouncing around in the large Cadillac belonging to Antonio. Brian expressed his surprise at how well the British mining companies were regarded. He could not believe how my father had been involved with the local football. We laughed about how nervous we had been, as at one point I actually thought we were about to be shot.

Our journey continued slowly due to the size of the car and the condition of what was not much more than a paved track. The countryside was quite spectacular; the dramatic hills and mountains almost desert like, with the odd green patch of olive trees. I started to laugh as we crossed a little old stone bridge spanning a small stream. Turning to Brian, I said,

'I'm no engineer but I am sure of one thing, the bridges between here and Vejer will not take the weight of those guns.'

Brian sort of nodded and ignored me.

'I'm ready for something to drink.'

We stopped in a small village; the little square with a small dry fountain in the middle, next to which were four chairs and a table belonging to the one and only bar. We sat; a glass of vino and tapa de jamon arrived without a word being said. Brian kicked up a conversation. Again because we were British, and the village being close to Cadiz and Jerez, was a very pro-British area; the old boy with one tooth left in his mouth explained that many more Civil Guards had been around recently because of some gun or other.

On we went. As I turned a corner, heading toward the coast, and headed down the hill, Brian noticed a large crowd of soldiers ahead.

'The bridge has gone! Look, traffic is being diverted!' he exclaimed.

'Yes,' I replied 'and there is the first naval gun with its huge barrel sticking out between the rocks and a patch of mud down there.'

We took the diversion. I slowed up and Brian took a photo of the broken gun at the bottom of the gorge. It was pointless to continue to Cadiz since we had achieved our mission. After lunch in Vejer we returned to Gib passing through the same road checks as before. The Guardia Civil, recognizing the car, saluted and waved us by.

The next three weeks brought in reports of Civil Guards and soldiers moving around Seville and Malaga. During that period of Spanish military activity we noticed how much building had started to happen. A house here, a storage shed there; La Linea was growing from the supplies of army cement and bricks. The gun emplacements didn't seem to be happening anymore and had been washed away in the recent rain storms. The Spanish were using the German money supplied to them to establish gun emplacements to build houses and improve the roads.

With regular reports from Antonio's network and Francisco of the Spanish Consulate of Germans and Italians visiting the area, which were also confirmed by friendly local police from San Roque, meant we all had to be much more alert. The Germans were setting up watch stations along the coast to spy on Allied shipping movements. One of our tasks was to find out where these were. According to the information I was receiving from my informants; all lead to the same conclusion. The Italians arriving were engineers and seamen. One was of special interest as we knew him to be a submarine expert.

The Italian ship Oltera had taken refuge in Algeciras at the beginning of the war on the pretext of needing repairs. These recent arrivals with large pieces of equipment, which were being put on board, were making the deadly two-man submarines responsible for damaging a number of our merchant ships. Had the crews of these little subs been Germans, I am convinced the damage to our ships would have been much greater. Fortunately the Italians preferred to stay on board the Oltera, eating spaghetti and dreaming of their wives or mistresses. Nevertheless the threat of limpet mines from these subs being stuck to the bottom of ships made us work very hard at preventative measures. On information I fed through, the navy laid many nets and regularly depth-charged the harbor.

One morning in June O'Shagar walked into the office with a message from London instructing me to meet with an SOE officer, Austin Baillon. On a need to know basis as he needed my network of agents to spread stories to negate any information the less friendly Spanish police or army might have heard about this operation so they would stay out of the way.

Austin Baillon sent me a second letter explaining Operation Musson more clearly. Operation Musson was named after Peter Runciman Musson, born in Argentina, educated at Rugby, serving at one time with SOE's Special Section in Gibraltar. He was entrusted with the setting up of the clandestine activity of infiltrating SOE agents into Spain for onward passage to enemy- occupied territories. Organizing the safe passage for escaped or withdrawn SOE agents was also part of this activity. The concept was the product of the agile mind of Leslie Humphreys of SOE's DF section, with the active co-operation of Victor Gerson; an English Jewish businessman who lived in France for many years. This was known as the 'Vic Line', and operation Musson became the tail end of this very successful SOE escape route.

Peter Musson was one of the eighteen Spanish-speaking British officers trained at Arisaig in Scotland and sent to Gibraltar in April 1941 in anticipation of a German advance through Spain (operation Felix), which as we know never occurred. Austin Baillon was one of the two men who served directly under Peter Musson, the other being Arthur Fletcher, also born in Argentina with previous army service in the Blues. Operation Musson was created for the exclusive use of SOE agents.

The quickest means of infiltrating an agent into occupied France was by parachute or landing from Lysander aircraft, or MTB (Motor Torpedo Boat). If the weather over the Channel impeded this type of operation, the fastest alternative and perhaps the safest was to fly the agent to Gibraltar, then he or she put en route through Spain to the Pyrenees. The initial part of the journey was with the help of Spanish Tobacco smugglers. In Spain, where injudicious tariffs and the Royal Monopolies encouraged the smuggling trade; smugglers were regarded as benefactors to the generally deprived population. In order to survive the Guadia Civil patrols and prosper, it was imperative that the matutero (smuggler) and his whole organization followed a rigid code of secrecy and security.

Gibraltar sitting on the southernmost tip of Europe was always a unique platform for smugglers, especially of tobacco; picadura as the chopped black leaf was called. Due to the war the shipments of commodities were reduced to bare essentials and picadura was not one of these. While scheming to open new and safer routes for the many agents trained to set Europe ablaze, Leslie Humphreys hit on the idea of using smugglers from Gibraltar. Musson was briefed and ordered to develop the operation.

The Seruya brothers who conducted a prosperous business from their premises in Main Street, Gibraltar, could not have failed to be impressed with, and to realise the importance of, the suggestion that they be allowed to import quantities of picadura. Musson having obtained Seruya's promise of secrecy and acceptance of the proposal, asked him who he considered to be the best and most trustworthy smuggler in Gib. Seruya suggested Heredia Saavedra, a 50-year-old Andalusian who had been smuggling since the age of 10. Having met, been amused and very impressed by Jose Heredia Saavedra, Musson asked him to take or pick up a limited number of passengers on occasions, in exchange for the opportunity to smuggle. Suitable craft would be made available for these exclusive smuggling trips and passage through the British naval controls around the Rock would be arranged on each occasion when they would be accompanied by at least one Spanish-speaking British officer. Jose subsequently codenamed Jay accepted the proposal and requested to be allowed to use the services of two of his most trusted men, also Spanish refugees resident in Gib. One was Manuel Pena, a marine engine mechanic and the other an able-bodied illiterate sailor named Nicolas. Both were screened and found to be safe and more than suitable for the work at hand.

SOE Gibraltar had obtained three vessels suitable for the job. The favorite and most used was a low-profile twin Perkins Marine engine launch named Calpe, some 25 feet long with good storage space below decks and, more importantly, fast. They obtained moorings and the airstrip where a Nissen hut was made available. Each person was provided with a special identity document signed by the Defence Security officer, the senior staff officers from the navy, the army and by the civilian Commissioner of

Police; a document James Bond would have been glad to possess. Arrangements were made with the naval authorities in 'the tower' to be informed of the recognition signals whenever required. The signals were for use when challenged by the naval patrol vessels constantly on guard against the approach of small craft like Italian subs and frogmen, and boats, coming from Algeciras. As an additional precaution against these mini-subs and intrepid frogmen, the navy lobbed anti-personnel depth charges at random into the sea off south Mole. On more than one occasion we were uncomfortably close to these detonations, bringing up shoals of dead or stunned fish and frightening poor Nicolas out of his skin.

Two dummy runs involving smuggling without passengers were made to familiarize the crew with the drill and test the system. Having arranged with Jay a time and date for an operation, the procedure was to meet in the night at Seuya's warehouse at the lower end of Irish Town. Here the bales of smelly tobacco, already bought by Jay would be loaded onto an SOE three ton lorry. Each bale covered with sacking weight about 70 kilos (155 lbs). Two 6-inch ears of sacking at each end of the bale would facilitate handling. On the reverse side two strong straps of the same material provided loops through which the bearer of the bale could pass his arms once safely ashore and carry it like a large haversack.

About 70 bales would be loaded onto the lorry, conveyed to the jetty and loaded into the hold of the Calpe, where soon after the 'passengers' (in case of infiltration) would be delivered. Jay by then would have arranged a time and date for a rendezvous; usually in the eastern coast of Spain near Estepona or Marbella. The contrabandist on the Spanish side would have made arrangements for the Guardia Civil to make themselves scarce. The launch would either tow, or carry a small flat-bottomed boat called a patera.

They would approach to within half a mile or so from the coast; as familiar to the Spanish crew as the palms of their hands. A pinpoint of light from a torch held by the expectant smuggler from on shore was the signal. As soon as the light was spotted the patera was pushed into the sea and loaded with three or four bales and the SOE agent. Nicolas would then row ashore guided by the occasional pinpoints of red light. As Nicolas beached the patera on the sand a single man would meet and conduct the agent to one of the several local safe houses from where they would be sent on their way to the Pyrenees.

This happened while a small group of men would appear from the darkness, grab the bales and move as quickly as possible to the waiting lorry or often mule train. The SOE agent returning home would jump into the patera for the return trip to launch. One golden rule was that an incoming passenger should never meet an outgoing passenger. The procedure was always safe and sound except for the occasional close shave with a British depth charge. It never failed our end, and I have been told no casualties were ever suffered anywhere en-route.

Over the course of many months hundreds of agents went successfully en-route until the Allied armies in France

*made Oparation Musson obsolete. Musson won the
Military Cross. Arthur Fletcher after demobilization
joined, of all things the Customs and Excise department in
England. As for the smugglers; until the end of the war
their activities continued but were interrupted. No sooner
was the war over than Jay Jose was deported from
Gibraltar as an undesirable alien. Fortunately news of this
came to the attention of SOE which was able to get the
British government to award Jay a medal in the Legation
at Tangier and organise his return to Gibraltar. After
which I hope Jose was able to resume the activity in which
he was such a master and again become the benefactor to
his overtaxed and deprived countrymen.*

One night in late July I drove across the border to the little
bar in Algeciras where I used to meet with one of my
agents. I parked near my destination and walked through
the narrow streets. I remember it being a clear summer's
evening. The Mediterranean was very calm and peaceful;
there were even little fishing boats out catching squid and
prawns amongst the battleships and cargo boats. Someone
was playing a soulful flamenco song which echoed
through the streets. As I passed a donkey loaded with
sacks of white flour, Frederico my agent caught hold of
my sleeve indicating we must meet in our second
rendezvous spot. I turned and followed behind the donkey,
walked past three intersecting streets and ducked into the
hole-in-the-wall bar belonging to Frederico's aunt. I
waded through the usual crowd of bandits, smugglers, tarts
and off-duty Guardia Civil and secret police often there to
buy black tobacco.

Pinching the bum of one of the tarts, who shrieked with delight, I went into the smoke-filled kitchen rich with the smell of frying sardines and said 'ola' to auntie. From the kitchen I went into the men's loo where the hole in the floor politely known as the Turkish plate mellowed the smell of sardines. Asphyxiated, I opened the little side door relieved to be entering our tiny meeting room. Frederico excitedly spilling his sol y sombra down his jacket told me,

'Amigo, one of the Spanish guards of the Oltera, you know the one who fancies my sister, has just told me that a submarine is due out at midnight tonight. He also told me he overheard reference to a British ship that arrived yesterday; I think it has oranges on board. Novo submarino was also mentioned.'

Thanking Frederico I scooted out of the back door onto the street near the police station. I looked at my watch; the drive back would take too long. There was enough time to catch the ferry so I walked quickly down the cobbled street leading to the nearby docks, jumped onto the last ferry and 20 minutes later was debating with Captain Monday (the head of port security) the possibility of taking his launch, himself and two submachine guns to have a go at the Italians. He agreed subject to my clearing it with his boss, Tito Medlam. I picked up the phone. Luckily Tito was still in his office and readily agreed. Nevertheless he had to clear it with the navy. Lieutenant commander Pyke-Knott thought it a good idea in principle but felt forced to refuse clearance due to the dangers involved which I really had to question. After a rather heated discussion where I expressed my outrage, informing him I would have to report this to his superiors, I hung up.

Disillusioned with our navy I went to the Embassy bar to recover from my disappointment; there I found Biaggio Damato, the Maltese owner with tears in his eyes.

'Captain Britow! Oh, Captain Britow, Malta, Malta, Malta! All the convoys to Malta are being sunk, what a tragedy!' He then took a deep breath, grabbed a glass, smiled and said, 'Have a John Collins!'

Not being able to tell him my own tale of woe, I asked if he had seen Brian. He shook his head. There was nothing to do, so I sipped on the John Collins, ordered a sandwich and wondered what the outcome of the ship might be. Not feeling very hungry I left half the sandwich, said goodbye to Biaggio and wandered around the port area. Captain Monday had at least been able to advise the ship's master to move into shallow water and closer to La Linea. I watched the big boat slowly move across the bay and drop anchor.

Brian came up behind me and clapped his hands, almost making me jump into the sea.

'Biaggio told me I might find you down here; he said you seemed a little preoccupied.'

When I had finished telling Brian about the night's events, all he could do was laugh and swear at the same time.

'Bloody red tape and the bloody fools who always seem compelled to follow it. Come on, Desmond; let's go in here for a drink. I need one.'

Despite Brian's efforts to cheer me up I found it hard to respond. We left the bar and slowly walked around the port again. I kept on looking at the clear moonlit surface of the water in the hope of seeing the sub before it submerged to attack the ship. At 2.50 am there was a dull explosion as a limpet mine went off; a big spray of water erupted from the side of the ship. Brian and I waited for five minutes expecting a second explosion. Nothing happened. The following morning we heard there had only been one mine and the ship had received very minor damage.

About two days later the excitement continued. O'Shagar returned from the signals office a coded message from London:

"Our impeccable source (meaning Ultra) has picked up reports of new sabotage operations being mounted against Allied shipping in Seville."

I should point out that the port of Seville, despite its distance inland could handle ships up to 10,000 tons. The ship most likely to be the target was identified and the Seville vice consul was asked to organise a strict watch. For two days I received messages from Ultra in London who were picking up German reports to Berlin saying that technical problems were making it very difficult to be effective against the British ships. The tide was too strong, and then the technician became ill, most probably from the dirty water.

It was clear however the sabotage war was becoming more sophisticated and that limpet mines were not being used. Extra vigilance was placed around the ship. The watchmen were vetted and given strict instructions to be very discreet so the Germans would not know we had any suspicions of what they were up to. The problem for the Germans was they wanted Spain to stay neutral as much as we did, and therefore had to come up with a device that would not blow up in the river and cause a navigational hold up which would upset the Spaniards.

Two days after the first ship sailed safely away with apparently no devices on board we received another Ultra report:

"Our impeccable source reports the sabotage operator (V Mann Rodriguez) has been successful and with the help of a friend has fixed the devise to the bilge keel. He assures Berlin the device will not blow up until the ship is well out of sea."

I duly told the Admiralty in Gibraltar of my section's findings. In order to cover up the possibility of this discovery coming from Ultra I was careful to imply that it was one of my agents in Seville who had discovered the German operation. The ship's master, having been advised of his problem, set sail down the river as normal but when he reached open sea, instead of joining the convoy he headed for Gibraltar where he dropped anchor in shallow water near no-man's-land. No man's land stretched between the Rock frontier port and the Spanish frontier at La Linea. Naval divers were waiting for the ship's arrival and soon established the sabotage device was nothing less than a torpedo, five feet in length, with three propellers, one at the front, one in the middle and one at the back.

On shore it was nerve-racking watching the procedures. Eventually three frogmen appeared on the surface with the device which they tied to the back of a rubber dinghy. All three climbed carefully into the little boat and gingerly started to row towards the small crowd of us standing in no man's land. Every stroke they took made us wince in anticipation of a loud bang. Their journey with the deadly catch took about fifteen minutes; for me it seemed to take hours.

I can't imagine what it must have been like for them. Once on land two of the frogmen were relieved by an engineer whose name I do not recall, and George Berry, an ex-Scotland Yard detective now with Defence Security staff. The third frogman was lieutenant Commander Bailey, the bomb disposal expert. They placed the torpedo in an old trench left over from the Civil War, and started to dismantle it. Hot tea was served for those of us watching. The second time around, the tea-serving sailor asked me what I was doing there. When I explained his response was, 'with all due respect sir, since you don't have to be here you must be bloody mad.'

The torpedo was a distance time bomb. Very fine wires connected to a shaft driven by the propellers would trigger the large explosives when the ship had travelled a certain distance; luckily for us, that point was not reached while they were rowing the thing ashore.

Sir Samuel Hoare, the British Ambassador in Madrid, issued a protest to the Spanish government based on the information we provided to the Foreign Office about the German operation in Seville. The Spanish responded by increasing security activities in Seville. Ultra informed us that V Mann Rodriguez's activities soon stopped as a result of this action on the part of the Spanish port authorities in Seville.

7   In Case of Invasion

During July and August 1942, Brian Morrison spent considerable time organizing the limited stay behind set up, which he formed from Gibraltar. He would recruit my assistance as often as he could. London kept insisting that we recruit avidly anti-Franco people, a policy with which both Brian and I strongly disagreed since in those days such people tended to be rather unreliable and basically anarchists. Besides a combined military attack by the Spaniards and Germans on Gibraltar would have meant Spain falling into the hands of Germany. I knew even the pro-German Spanish would not have allowed themselves to be taken over to that extent. We sat up into the early hours and watched many a sunrise while debating various courses of action. After consulting with John Codrington we decided to hide only one wireless set and distribute 300-400 lots of instructions on how to frustrate the enemy.

Kim Philby had passed information onto me about some proposed Allied landings in North Africa code named Torch and I assumed this preparation was in case the Torch landings failed and Spain fell to the German side. This information was for me alone and as far as Brian or anyone else on Gibraltar was concerned the operations were defensive due to Franco and his seemingly close friendship with Hitler.

Through Antonio Joseph I established contact with a retired Spanish merchant ship's captain called Luis Miguel Garrido who lived in Cadiz, and to Antonio's knowledge was neither pro- nor anti-Franco and certainly willing to cooperate against the Germans. For some reason I never discovered why he also strongly disliked the Italians. Luis Miguel was able to recruit one of his old shipping wireless operators, and also agreed to distribute a few dozen instruction leaflets amongst his friends and associates.

We created many sets of instructions, all containing general information for our agents in certain areas. None of it was very specific, it just informed them who they could trust and to try and form a communication network back to Captain Luis Miguel. We typed these instructions onto paper; all had instructions to eat them if there seemed any chance of being found out. How to hide and distribute these pieces of paper became our next problem. For two or three days we tossed around ideas, none of which were very practical.

Brian and I felt we deserved a break, so we took up a Spanish friend's invitation to a downtown bar in Algeciras where the alcohol company Negrita was giving out gallons of free drinks as a promotion for their new rum. All along the bar sweaty people clamoured for more than their share of the very tasty rum. Juan came back from the bar with three full glasses and four or five pencils. These pencils had the company name down the side and a rubber holder at the top; you know the type. It was the first time advertising material had been used in Spain since the Civil war. Brian's pencil had a loose top and the rubber came straight out. We smiled at each other and said in unison,

'Now doesn't that make a nice hiding place for small pieces of paper?'

We pushed to the bar and filled our pockets with pencils.

The next evening I came back to the apartment to find Brian nursing a badly cut finger.

'What the hell happened to you?' I asked, looking at the drips of blood on the floor.

'The fucking knife slipped.'

He had been taking the rubbers out of the tops of the pencils and cutting them in half. Brian had very large fingers, which made holding a small rubber rather difficult and he had almost cut his finger in half.

Our hiding place was in the top of the pencil under the rubber. To make space for the paper we had to remove most of the rubber by cutting cut it up, and then putting the rolled piece of paper into the top and push the remainder of the rubber back in. We did this in shifts. For three days in our spare time we cut the rubbers, and our fingers, and put rolled up pieces of paper into four hundred pencils which then had to be distributed amongst our agents and their friends.

We set off to Cadiz in the old Cadillac, which was becoming quite familiar to the Guardia and consequently they very rarely stopped us. We felt they would not stop and search us, even so we hid the pencils and the radio set under the back seat. About an hour outside Cadiz we took a diversion, carefully noting landmarks. For fifteen minutes precisely we made our way up a small road, and then stopped by an old twisted olive tree on its own next to a clump of rocks. We buried the wireless set at the foot of the tree, and for extra security I cut a small V into the bark just below the first protruding branch. We set off to Cadiz and found Captain Luis Miguel. We explained where he would find the wireless and gave him a number of pencils to distribute amongst his anti-German friends. Our next stop was Estepona where we visited a fisherman friend of mine, Paco Churro, my agent in that area. We gave pencils to various others, and told the owner of the Miraflores bar to issue pencils to his gang of potential agents in the event of a German takeover.

During this time there was a consistent flow of reports coming in from Antonio's agents about Italian and German movements in the area. By August I felt it imperative to extend my line of agents.

On a hot sweltering evening I strolled into the Embassy Bar. Biaggio, who was cleaning glasses, looked at me in surprise when I ordered a coca cola with ice and lemon, a refreshing rare beverage in those days.

'What's wrong with you tonight Captain Britow?' he asked.

'Biaggio, do you have somewhere we could talk in private?' I asked.

'Yes! I have a little office at the back, but can it wait for five minutes? My brother Angelo is finishing the accounts with Bianchi.'

'Yes of course.'

I went outside to the large terrace with its spectacular view of Algeciras and the bay. It felt strange to have this moment's peace. The sea was red under the setting sun and the bay sparkled with the reflections of the dockyard lights where they were repairing ships and building the lovely Spanish fishing boats. It was hard to imagine the death and destruction that was taking place in many other parts of Europe. Two days before, a refugee who had been staying in our apartment under Donald's care, had told us about the Gestapo, the firing squad and something about concentration camps; a concept I did not really understand at that time. Sounds of flamenco guitar and castanets coming from the mainland were interrupted by a married couple arguing tooth and nail about her mother coming to stay. Mule hooves clipped along the cobblestone streets taking their owners home. The palm trees on the terrace rustled in the warm summer evening's breeze.

'Well Captain Britow, enjoying this beautiful evening are you?'

Biaggio continued talking as he walked to the far side of the terrace.

'Come this way. Angelo has finished the accounts and can look after the bar for me.'

He led me through a gate into a well finished, well organised little office shared by him and his brother. He already had a John Collins and another Coke waiting and offered me a seat.

'Biaggio I'm not sure how to ask this delicately, but I need your word that you will repeat nothing of what I'm about to say outside of this room. If you do it will be the end of our friendship. Um, what I am about to say could be dangerous to you, but I would like, and need' your help.'

He shifted in his seat sipped his drink glanced out of the window which looked to mainland Spain.

'Captain Britow. I don't read or write very well but I own this bar and the hotel in La Linea. I like to take risks and if it will help you win the war I am at your service.'

Biaggio had become a good and trusted friend.

'Well actually I want you to become my agent and find out what you can about the Italians and Germans. Listen in the bars, or more importantly your hotel lobby on the mainland.'

I had imagined it was going to be a lot harder to recruit Biaggio, but he was always full of surprises. He looked at me and nodded.

'I thought you were more than a Captain. Yes of course I will.'

Conversation continued on about the extra movement and evacuation of some more British Civilians, as the realization of my asking him to become a spy registered.

'I suppose you have already worked out the possibility of me recruiting others. I cross the border every day to and from my hotel.'

He and I went through methods of his asking his friends and associates questions out of curiosity so as to not actually recruit them. Two of his friends offered to dig around on a regular basis as they were very anti-German and quite anti-Franco.

Due to Biaggio's added line of information I was able to confirm the existence of a German monitoring set-up which enabled the enemy to watch all the shipping coming in and out of the Mediterranean. It was thanks to this monitoring station that the Germans were so successfully sinking convoy after convoy. Biaggio especially excited about this discovery gave a small party for Donald, Brian and I. He thought we would be able to get supply ships through to his beloved Malta more easily. Previously, a similar German monitoring post had been discovered and dealt with. London suspected the Germans had some other position for monitoring the ships, which was now confirmed by me, just no information on where and how.

Biaggio received information from one of his Hotel staff in Algeciras about a Villa; he thought as being twelve kilometers west of Algeciras high on the cliffs overlooking the Straits of Gibraltar with a good view of Morocco. It had recently been occupied by a German bird watcher and his partner. This was a possible location for the monitoring of shipping coming and going. My papers were in order so I crossed over into Spain in the Cadillac with no problem. I picked up Jose, one of Biaggio's staff, who agreed to watch the place for two days. We made our way towards Tarifa. Just short of Tarifa was the house high on the knoll overlooking the Med with a very clear view to Morocco.

After a few hours and not much activity taking place, I left Jose with my camera some supplies and a bed role. The fact a German birdwatcher moved here was enough for me to be convinced; still I needed evidence. Jose returned with some photographs of a much younger German gentleman than I was expecting; with a very military style haircut and way about him. With this confirmation I passed the information onto naval intelligence. Obviously they needed to blow up the site, but since it was on Spanish territory the foreign office were forced to negate this possibility. It was out of the question, perhaps more importantly because our findings had coincided with the last preparation period of Operation Torch (the allied invasion of North Africa). It was at this time the Rock of Gibraltar was to receive General Eisenhower who was in Command of the up and coming Operation Torch.

His visit was top secret and was kept very low key by all of us on Gibraltar.

Being such a small compact area it was quite hard to make sure that any rumours which started were quickly negated; denying it was Eisenhower. On the rare occasion he was seen it was apparently in a Captain's uniform or mufti.

Personally I never met The General, I had no reason to. My job was to keep agents ignorant of his presence and very alert on and off the Rock.

The unfortunate fact is to have blown up the villa would have attracted too much attention, although, it would have taken only a small shell or small amounts of explosives placed near the house by friendly Spaniards to destroy the equipment. So unfortunately for the Navy and Biaggio and his beloved Malta convoys still sank at the hands of the German U-boats.

It was around this time that I met a friend of Biaggio's, Stephanos Ioseph, a Greek who was on his way to Casablanca to become the Consul there. He informed me of how he narrowly escaped the Germans and had joined the exiled Greek Government in Egypt. Due to his good French and diplomatic ability he was on his way to Casablanca to encourage the Greeks there to join the war. His appointment as Consul would enable him to help the Allies as much as possible. Many of his resistance friends had been captured and shot. He hated the Germans with a Greek passion. I saw him a couple of times before he left for Casablanca on a British boat.

8   Eisenhower and Canaris

Not long after the arrival of Eisenhower, while extensive preparations were taking place I received information of a pending visit by a very important German intelligence officer to our area. This was very suspicious and it seemed as though the Germans knew about General Eisenhower. Following up on this scoop, all my agents in the area were told to pass information on without hesitation. I passed the warning onto the officers in charge of the General's security. It could have been a ruse, via one of Biaggio's Spanish police friends, Commandante Molina, whom I suspected as being the head of the Spanish security police in the campo area. News kept coming in of the visit but never the name of the visitor. I asked Biaggio if he could find out the intelligence officer's name; shortly afterwards one evening he indicated for me to follow him into his office, where he gave a crumpled piece of paper which bore the name "CANARIO".

'This man will be staying at the hotel Reina Christina from this coming Friday to Monday,' Biaggio stated looking pleased with himself. He had every right to be.

I promptly telegraphed London asking for instructions and suggesting that if indeed it was Admiral Canaris (head of the Abwehr) we have a go at capturing him. London's response confirmed it was Canaris, but said that on no account should he be threatened in any way whatsoever.

On thinking about it I realised the foolishness of my suggestion, because had we captured him the Germans would have changed all their message codes, rendering Ultra useless; and after all Ultra was telling us everything the Germans were up to. Not only that Admiral Canaris was very anti-Hitler but during the early stages of the war he had informed us of the some of the Nazi's brutal tactics, especially in Poland.

This is quite revealing if one knows the history. Again this is not in my father's original text from the book. He mentions how.

"Menzies sent a message via the MI9 line of communication. Suggesting not to meet up with Canaris but to pay ones respects and leave a message of thanks. I never knew what the thanks were for but since Menzies asked I followed his instructions. Canaris' name was not mentioned which is why Donald had to come to the hotel, unaware of why we were there. We paid for Canaris' drinks when we left leaving a thank you note. My observation of this distinguished man was that I did not feel threatened by him at all; yet he was the boss of our enemies Secret Service."

Brian and I decided it would be rather amusing to have tea at the hotel Reina Christina that Sunday. I managed to persuade Donald who, unable to resist the temptation of cucumber and tomato sandwiches, had strangely never crossed the La Linea frontier before. Donald would invariably make trips by plane or boat to Lisbon but had never crossed over into Spain.

We cleared the frontier with no problem at all. The guards were used to the Cadillac and my face. Some even greeted us in English every now and again.

In the grand hotel Reina Cristina we wondered through the slightly threadbare but luxurious lobby to the terrace, which was unoccupied, despite the sunny Sunday afternoon. We sat at the corner table on the raised terrace, from which we had a view of the garden which sloped down and overlooked the Bay of Gibraltar with all the ships.

Brian ordered tea and sandwiches. Donald started to tease us.

'Well I can see why you two don't do any work. How often did you say you came here?'

It was not often the three of us sat and relaxed; Donald especially. He now allowed his wonderful sense of humor to have Brian and me in stiches, about what I don't remember. The tea with an assortment of sandwiches and shortbread biscuits arrived. While Brian was playing host and pouring the tea, I noticed the waiter laying a table for three just two tables away from us.

Casually Admiral Canaris walked onto the terrace with one henchman in front and one behind him. In that polite German manner he acknowledged us as fellow tea drinkers, obviously unaware of our nationality; or maybe he knew exactly who we were. I indicated to Brian that the visitors had arrived. Brian who had his back to their table turned around to look at the Admiral and nodded. Canaris was a smallish quite thin man with greyish hair and distinguished facial features. He looked a kind gentleman in the true sense of the word, not what I expected the head of Germany's secret service to look like at all. But then he was not a Nazi.

Donald quite oblivious of who was about to drink tea on the same terrace as us, was almost euphorically enjoying the cucumber sandwiches the view and the Chinese tea. With rather a full mouth he said,

'Desmond I can't thank you enough for persuading me to join your Sunday tea party; these sandwiches are absolute perfection and the view makes Gibraltar seem like a different world altogether. I wonder why we are doing what we are doing and when will it be all over?' he asked rather despondently.

'Well, for while it lasts this beats being in the infantry.'

Thinking about what he said I leant forward and whispered.

'By the way, do you realise who is sitting at the table over there?'

'No! And why should I?' he asked rather indignantly.

'Does it really matter so long as they behave themselves and don't disturb us?'

Out of a sense of fun but actually rather irresponsibly and not able to hold back a smile, knowing he would be very disturbed by what I was about to tell him, I whispered again.

'The one in the middle is none other than Admiral Canaris.'

Donald, unable to contain himself spitting bits of sandwich everywhere exclaimed,

'Don't be such a bloody fool, Desmond.'

Not wanting to create much of a scene I admitted it was a joke. Pointing out, my joke was in very bad taste, he went on about me having spoilt the flavor of the cucumbers. He turned to the three gentlemen and apologized for his outburst explaining it had been my fault.

Admiral Canaris seemed to be amused by our presence since we were the only other people on the terrace. I wonder what he thought of us. Did he know we were agents? He certainly must have known we were British as we did not disguise the fact.

We finished our tea and paid the bill. As we walked past his table I nodded to the Admiral and Brian followed suit. Donald smiled and apologised again for his outburst. The Admiral acknowledged us and smiled back.

Pale and somewhat shaken, Donald got into the back of the Cadillac.

'Tell me Brian was that really Admiral Canaris?'

Brian answered positively. Donald, not amused, but fully recovered, commented: "The Admiral seems to be a very civilized individual considering who he works for, until you idiots revealed his identity to me I found his presence on the terrace very amenable a generally superior to the likes of you two."

While the conversation about the War, the Abwehr and General Eisenhower absorbed us, Brian and I made a detour to the Miraflores bar near San Roque. Donald still rather bemused by what had just occurred, calmed down and was able to appreciate the comfortable bar where many of the escapees stopped on their way to Gibraltar; sometimes staying the night. Jose, the owner, came over and I introduced Donald.

Jose was a jolly character who took endless risks for the British escapees; if he had ever been caught by the Spanish secret police there is a chance he might have been shot.

9   News of the Camps and Smuggling

I received news from all of my Spanish agents, Biaggio, Fruity, Jose, etc. that the Iberian government had decided to change the policemen around. The present police force around Gibraltar had apparently become too tolerant of, and even friendly with, the British; at least that was the rumor. Donald, Brian, David Thompson and I analysed the change of the location of police personnel was due to corruption, and friendly attitudes the police had towards the smugglers and local councilors.

For the first few days of that very hot August we watched as the local Guardia Civil (police), with their friendly Andaluz faces, were replaced by hard northern Spanish faces wearing German sunglasses. I must admit when we saw the arrival of these obviously hardened police with their German vehicles a feeling of anxiety crept through the Rock. Our security and army patrols were all increased as the threat of a Spanish-German invasion of the Rock seemed to becoming a reality. There was some concern that the presence of Eisenhower had slipped out. Perhaps Admiral Canaris had spoken with Franco and asked for a more forceful looking presence to be maintained on the border. Still finding it hard to believe, I decided to go across the border and do some spy work myself.

Slowly I drove up to the frontier at La Linea. There was an air of efficiency about these unfamiliar faces and clean uniforms, but I did not get the feeling they were about to attack. Next was the check at San Roque, always more daunting than La Linea. I noticed the brand new BMW motorbikes lined up outside the frontier cabin, and a new German transport wagon parked at the back. Three policemen with new Germanic-style uniforms and Zeiss dark glasses sauntered over to me. With a northern Spanish accent I was ordered to get out of the car; when I hesitated one officer opened my door while the other two stood either side of the car.

A distinct feeling of submission came over me and I followed their orders. As soon as I stood up two of them grabbed me and pulled me away from the car with an unnecessary amount of force, whilst the third searched the car. When they had finished showing off and demonstrating their control of the situation, they duly handed me my papers back and ordered me to proceed. The car decided this was a good time not to start. For a few minutes I tried, but the engine was not going to fire. The policemen helped push the car to the side of the road. I opened the bonnet and one of them, intrigued by the big American engine, immediately stuck his head in and started to fiddle about.

'You seem to know a lot about engines', I commented (all this was in Spanish); 'very good of you to help'. He made some remark about the expertise of American engineering. I could not help noticing that his accent was Andaluz not northern Spanish at all. Pausing for a moment, not wanting to seem too inquisitive, I informed him that I knew the area well and asked him where he came from as he sounded Andaluz not Basque.

'Valverde del Camino, it's in Huelva; you won't know where that is,' he replied.

'You don't think so?'

I laughed and told him, I came from the mine of Sotiel Coronada, ten kilometres from Valverde.

His father had worked on the mine for my father, and he himself attended school on the mine and could remember when I was given the donkey on my birthday. A remarkable and lucky coincidence,, as I found a new ally amongst the Germanophile Guardia Civil police. From conversations with him and some of his fellows I discovered these new police had been trained and had served for two years on the northern and the Portuguese frontiers. He and many of his fellow officers were glad to be in the warm climate and to be eating good healthy food.

From him I was able to discover there was no threat of an invasion; Franco was more concerned about Spanish bandits in the surrounding mountains, the smugglers and about basically tightening up on his own people. When he told me the Germans motorbikes had been brought down from the north to facilitate high-speed chases, I laughed. The idea of a high-speed chase after the speeding donkeys used by the aforementioned criminals along the bumpy tracks amused even him. Despite his amusement, he made it clear the smuggling would soon be stopped as these new police arrivals, including him, were going to be very tough.

The engine started, he closed the bonnet. As a token of my gratitude I gave him my half pack of Craven A cigarettes. We shook engine oil covered hands and agreed to go out for a drink sometime; which we did as I needed to keep him on our side. He proved to be invaluable and always facilitated my crossing over the border; and unwittingly would give me information which just confirmed Franco had no intention of joining the war.

In my messages back to Philby and Cowgill I always included an update of what the frontier situation was. After this last visit I was able to confirm my belief that under no circumstances was Franco going to allow German forces onto Spanish soil or become involved in the war.

The last few messages between us had brought up the need for an agent to be stationed in Tunisia. I recommended David Thompson as he spoke very good French and had a good understanding of the Arabs.

Within two weeks these tough northern policeman started to enjoy sugar white flour, fresh tobacco, and other more refined essentials which they had not seen since before the Civil War. Smugglers again crossed the border to Spain quite freely. The threatening atmosphere transformed overnight into one of smiles, salutations, ola amigos, chats over the odd cigarette. Our would-be foes allowed the Green Line to continue and any number of Brits crossed the border whenever we wanted.

All those hours, and Brian's damaged finger, so gladly contributed to the stay-behind plans had been a waste of time, apart from generating a few amusing anecdotes. Now we were confronted with the task of collecting all the messages up again. I asked Fruity to take the bus to Cadiz, call on Captain Wenceslas and help him collect all the pencils and instructions in order to destroy them.

Two days later I met Fruity on our usual meeting place; a bar at the end of a little square full of palm trees in La Linea. Looking around furtively he pushed his hat to the back of his head, took a sip of wine and began to laugh.

'What's the joke?' I asked.

He explained he caught the 7.00 am bus and on arriving in Cadiz he walked to Wenceslas's house. Francisca, his wife, told him that just before he arrived, Wenceslas was shaving in his pyjama trousers. Suddenly he let out a cry and ran out of the house.

Fruity looked at his empty glass. I took the hint and ordered again. The captain arrived back still only wearing his pyjama pants and with shaving soap all over his face. He sat down obviously relieved about something and exhausted from running.

'Oh, Santa Maria, last night I took my suit to the cleaners,' said the captain. While he was shaving he had suddenly remembered he had left some pencils in his suit.

Fruity took another sip and chuckled. For some reason Fruity could not stop laughing about the scene of Wenceslas running to the cleaners, past his neighbours wearing only pyjamas with shaving soap on his face, to save the pencils and messages he was there to tell him to destroy!

The following week started another amusing day. David Thompson invited me to Four Corners, the frontier post. I walked down the high street of Gibraltar and crossed over the large runway and met David there. I had passed a caravan of donkeys on my way.

'Desmond I have just discovered the new method they are using to smuggle tobacco.'

At midday the caravan of donkeys and carts taking the garbage to La Linea approached. David walked up to the first donkey, lifted up its tail and grabbed a fine piece of rope.

The donkey kept walking; David stopped and held the rope tightly. Slowly out of the donkey's rear end emerged a string of eight black sausages. Condoms filled with black tobacco, to be more precise. David then ordered the donkey caravan to stop. He and I found four more donkeys similarly stuffed. He had to stick his arm in the last one and fish around a bit; I looked up as David who pulled out this string of black tobacco. The congenial customs officers all laughed.

At this point I asked David to meet me in the office that afternoon. Luckily there were only a few of the other occupants in at the time of David's arrival. I informed him, on my recommendation to HQ, that he was going to be taken on by Section V. Kim Philby and Felix Cowgill had agreed to make him our man in Tangier. He was delighted. I had O'Shagar organise the necessary papers as he was due to leave for Morocco in a few days. David and I went for a whisky to celebrate his appointment.

Feeling warmed up I went back to the apartment having promised Donald I would be there at 6.30 pm. He had some special quests arriving to stay with us. Brian and I waited for a short while; then Donald arrived with two chaps dressed in RAF uniform who did not speak a word of English. They were Russian escapees whom Brian could translate for, being fluent in many languages including Russian. They told him how they had escaped during their exercise period in Hanover POW camp by pole-vaulting over the fences and running like crazy, somehow escaping the dogs and search parties. They managed to get to Belgium where they were picked up by one of the escape organizations and given passes and clothes, following which on bicycles and by train, they made their way down to southern France, where they were put on a boat (the Tarana captained by Nobby Clark) and brought down to Gibraltar. Now they were depending on Donald to get them to England, so they could fight against the Germans. Donald, through Brian explained that they must stay with him and he would show them the Rock.

The following evening after their tour of Gibraltar, we cooked for them. I was quite good at preparing spaghetti and had picked up some red wine. Chopping the onion and garlic I wanted to listen to some of Donald's jazz records; at one point I felt like leaving the apartment because they would not stop yaberring. Brian, sensing my frustration, explained what all the excitement was about; they could not get over the key ceremony.

In the morning the Governor (then Major General Mason Macfarlane) hands the keys of the fortress over to the civilian authorities. During the parade the General, dressed in shorts, was given a message. As soon as he had handed the keys over he ran off the parade ground. For them to see a general in shorts was very shocking; to see a general run even more shocking; and to see a general in shorts run off a parade ground, unimaginable. Two days later papers ready, their appreciation expressed of Donald's and Brian's and to a lesser extent my efforts, they left. At times I wondered how Donald kept going as these moments would often upset him. Brian had the horrible feeling they would be handed over to the Russian authorities.

Much later when I returned to London I found out that they had been handed over to the Russian authorities, and on their return to Russia it was apparent they had been shot by the Stalin regime.

The following day I went to the runway and saw David leave for Tangier by plane. As the Torch landing date approached, things tensed up on our side of the frontier.

During war somehow we are able to minimize the depressing side of life. For all of us it is necessary, from time to time, to find moments of solitude in a private place, where one can forget everyday occurrences and reflect on friends, family and life in general. For me, in Gibraltar, this place was close to the ramparts near the hotel Bristol. I would sit and look over the bay. Sometimes I walked along the ramparts as far as I could go, sat down and would just stare up at the wonderful Mediterranean sky and think of Betty and my daughter and wonder how they were dealing with the war and the bombing raids. I would think about the terrible destruction going on all over Europe. I was privy to information which I could not tell anyone about, which in a certain way made one feel very important. After all I was the only person in Gibraltar who knew anything about Ultra and at that time (September 1942) was most probably the only person who knew why Spitfire and Hurricane planes were arriving in Gibraltar to be assembled. Everyone believed they were to help Malta and it was my job to maintain this deception. They were in fact for the allied invasion of North Africa, due to happen in November. I realised working as a spy was a lot of fun basically; nevertheless, internally, it often made me feel separate from others, especially friends and family.

The sound of the sea washing over the sand always reassured me that the world was till spinning around and I was not all that important.

In mid-September our department was put under investigation for bad practices. Thyl Vischer, a naval lieutenant attached to John Codrington's staff, quite often acted as courier for the Special Intelligence Service (SIS) to and from Tangier. Sometimes he would carry the diplomatic bag. On one occasion he decided it would be a treat for the staff to enjoy a meal of suckling pig. So the silly bugger bought four little pigs in Tangier, put them in a large canvas bag similar to a diplomatic package. As he walked through customs, the pigs decided to squeal. The customs police confiscated our meal and reported the incident to the Governor. Importing live animals was a very serious offence. Thyl received a severe reprimand and the office was investigated in case we might be up to other smuggling antics. Fortunately the Governor was blissfully unaware that much of my information came from smugglers, or friends of. And certainly 60 percent of SOE and the escape operations were so successful due to the help of smugglers, pickpockets and assorted criminals.

Shortly after the investigation I received a message from London advising me that three new Section V officers, fluent in French, would be arriving. They were to remain in Gibraltar where Brian and I were to teach them coding and decoding, and generally help them to visualize their future. I decided to tell Brian why we were coaching these spies about field operations.

We were on the terrace of the Embassy bar. Biaggio served us with the normal John Collins. I made sure we were alone, and leant over the table.

'Brian, I've got something to tell you which can go no further than your ears. The allies are going to invade North Africa in early November, that's why we are teaching these bods about coding, etc. They are to be SLU (Special Liaison Unit) officers,' (in other words they were going over after the landings to infiltrate and gather information about the feelings of the native Arabs).

Donald in the meantime was increasingly occupied by the successes of the feluccas (small coastal fishing boats such as the aforementioned Tarana, used for transporting escapees).

Brian and I walked into the apartment feeling jovial but a little cheesed off with our students. We found Donald sitting hunched up over the table almost in tears chewing on his fingernails. Brian got out the bottle of whisky reserved for these occasions.

'Oh Christ! I think something has gone dreadfully wrong with one of the boats,' exclaimed Donald.

He was supposed to have received a communication of confirmation from the escape organisers on the ground. He had heard nothing from them.

'The boat is apparently on its way back here…empty. I can only assume they have been captured or are stuck and waiting for the boat somewhere in the South of France; or dead.'

Donald, his hands shaking, took a cigarette off me. These moments were very tense and awkward. Donald was a very dedicated man, unable to fight as a soldier; but the battles he fought at times were harder. There was not much one could do other than offer ones company and support.

I poured him a drink.

We sat in silence. Donald took another large swig.

Donald decided to go to the signals office. To encourage him this was a good idea, I went with him. A message had arrived for him saying the rendezvous had failed. He immediately telegraphed London saying he would radio Tarana to return to southern France and London must get the message back to the people in France to organise a new rendezvous.

After forty hours of smoking, nail biting, nerve stretching and radioing, Donald succeeded and the boat turned around and successfully picked up the escapees. They all arrived safely a few days later. The British members were quickly boarded onto an empty cargo boat which was joining a convoy back to Blighty.

Two French Canadians stayed with us. Lucien Dumais had been taken prisoner by the Germans during the failed raid on Dieppe. Lucien Dumais and Ray Labrosse camped on our floor for three days. Lucien was a marvellous cook, so in the evening we would sit around, eat and drink and hear stories of the war in Europe and how tough the Germans were. It made my senses cringe when I heard these accounts of firing squads, shooting French civilians for harbouring allied soldiers. These two had heard of the concentration camps from one member of the escape committee.

My father heard some horrific accounts from these escapees whom Donald took care of. He reported these accounts back to H.Q. where Cowgill, Philby and the rest could compare these reports with all the other information being received; and analyse what was going on inside Germany. It was these accounts from agents and escapees, along with the endless number of reports from the resistance, which informed the government and High Command of the existence and extent of the Jewish selection activities and the cold blooded approach the Nazi's had towards their enemies; civilian or military.

My father told me:

"The information which we received was only small by comparison, but when it was all added together it appeared on a very large scale. At first it was very hard to believe what was happening on such a scale. What civilized country would be selecting a people for extermination? It was very hard to accept."

Anyway, three days after their arrival, Donald managed to organise for them to return to Britain. Lucien was involved in the early stages of the Torch landings. Lucien applied to join MI9 and, with the recommendation from Donald, was accepted. MI9 said that they volunteered to go back to France and help with the escape routes. Lucien and Ray went to France via Britain where they were equipped with a radio and all the necessities for fighting that kind of war with the resistance.

I asked Biaggio and others to spread the stories of the concentration camps and the treatment the French were receiving from the Germans, in the hope this would spread. Coming up with this idea and informing H.Q. they agreed this was a good idea as this had nothing to do with ULTRA. It was whispers and stories received from escapees.

Messages arrived informing me H.Q. and High Command had at last accepted Franco was not going to join the war, and certainly not with Hitler. Despite all Franco's failings he was very religious and I suspect when he heard about the Catholics and the Jewish situation his supposed support for Hitler stopped.

Spain was now recognized as a relatively safe country. O'Shagar received a message requesting me to go to Madrid and talk directly with my fellow workers stationed there. Brian agreed to accompany me; so on 18th October we packed up Antonio's Cadillac with twenty two gallon tins of petrol and the diplomatic bag. Laden down and stinking like a refinery, (we agreed it was not a good idea to smoke on this trip!), we drove along the coast road to Malaga, passing through the little fishing villages of Estepona, Marbellla and Torremolinos. Palm trees were being planted, and the streets and roads damaged in the Civil War were being paved. The port area of Malaga was being rebuilt and modernized. We called in on the consul to pick up his diplomatic bag and I remember we left Malaga at 19.00 hours, having spent more time with the consul than intended.

The mountainous countryside between Malaga and Granada was wild and wonderful and many areas were being planted up with pine trees, almonds and olives. Vineyards were being tended and rejuvenated. The twisty and very bumpy road was terrible and was being repaired in places. With all the petrol sloshing around this section of the journey was very grueling, but despite the hazards by 22.30 we were sitting in the wonderful coffee house in the main square of Granada facing the hotel Victoria. People were wandering around in the warm evening atmosphere, lovers arm in arm, closely followed by their chaperones, gypsies selling their hand-woven lace, flamenco guitarists entertaining us on the streets; this part of Spain was slowly returning to its colorful self. It certainly was not preparing for another war.

Refreshed by the strong coffee we set off towards Jaen only to be stopped by a Civil Guard patrol. They checked our papers and looked suspiciously at the tins of petrol. One of them smiled and told us about the bandits in the mountains just before Jaen, warning us it could be fatal to continue during the night. This was an indication of how orders had come down the ranks that the British were not to be interfered with too much. A few months earlier the reception of the paper work would not have been quite so straight forward. We thanked them for their advice and with a certain bravado drove on.

'We must be bloody mad. One stray bullet and we will light up half of Andalusia!' exclaimed Brian.

'They are not going to shoot us,' I said confidently.

For the first half hour every corner we went around we expected to find a roadblock with rifle bearing bandits. Brian kept on asking what I thought it would be like to be shot by a firing squad? Or even worse, burnt alive due to a stray bullet setting fire to the patrol? As midnight passed our concern about bandits lessened, and staying awake was more of a worry. Brian managed that quite well by discussing the outcome of the car going over the edge and possibly dropping three or four hundred feet. As I edged around a corner he would come out with some stupid comment about how beautiful the stream in the ravine on his side of the car looked and how if I went any closer to the edge we could both benefit from a cold bath; if we did not catch fire on the way down.

Tired and hungry, at 3.20 am we arrived at the Albergue Hotel in Bailen. I remember this so well because I was surprised to find a security guard, and even more surprised to be offered fried eggs and toast for supper. Tired out, I fell asleep with my clothes on and the diplomatic bag tied to my wrist.

Washed and refreshed we were on the road to Madrid by a quarter past ten, and to top our surprise of the previous night we found a telephone in working order. Brian made a call to the Embassy in Madrid and gave our estimated time of arrival at about six that evening. We had lunch at the Albergue outside Manzanares and were thankful to be driving across the flat and arid countryside of La Mancha. Don Quixote and Sancho Panza might well have been attacking the windmills on the surrounding horizon but we were attacking the pot holes in the road.

Feeling as though the worst of the journey was over, Brian opened up the Cadillac only to hit a very large pothole. Rather shaken he slowed down to a crawl as he maneuvered in between the patchwork of hundreds of large holes in the road; a hangover from the Civil War. The Messerschmitt's and Stukas now fighting in Europe had used this area as practice ground and left torn up tarmac and shot up vehicles as an indication of their expertise. Despite our caution suddenly a loud crack came from the rear right hand wheel which immediately locked up. I crawled underneath the car and looked. Realising there was nothing for it I told Brian to pass me the pliers and screwdriver. The rear spring had broken and the axle was jamming the brake cable. After two hours, with the brake cable tied around the axle to stop it from moving around too much, we were back on the slow move.

This journey sounds all fun and games; as I am sure that is how my father took it. Actually at the time Spain had many bandits who would have shot them without any compunction what so ever. A father being a spy is not quite so action packed or even so glorious as a father in the Air Force, Navy of Army. Actually they were on their own so much of the time; unlike the forces. Their own resolve and cunning pulled them through what may seem rather non-threatening circumstances. Now, when I try and imagine what I have just read it frankly seems ridiculous on the surface of it; when in reality it was very dangerous.

Our arrival at the Palace Hotel looking like tired out grease monkeys was not welcome, and they refused to give us our rooms. Swearing at the manager and anyone else in earshot, I turned to Brian and said, let's break the Embassy rules and go to the Hotel Nacional where I will be welcome.

I cannot believe the hotel would not allow two guests who had been booked in by the British Embassy just because they were dirty. Does this not strike you as odd? My assessment is my father had some reason for staying in the Hotel Nacional, and he invented this story not for my benefit, but for the benefit of the Embassy officials at the time and has stuck to his lie.

Juan the receptionist, remembered me from when I stayed on my way to England in 1939. He put us in the best suite where we bathed and changed, then headed down to the restaurant.

Walking across a dining room full of Japanese and Italian faces felt somewhat strange, considering we were at war with both. It appealed to both Brian's and my rather wicked sense of humor; consequently we spoke in English as loudly and obnoxiously as possible. Juan and the waiters made the most out of it as well, and as we were leaving said how nice it had been to see English faces for a change.

The following morning, Alan Hilgarth, the Embassy security officer and naval attaché sat us down in his plush office and gave us a severe reprimand telling us never to stay in out of bounds hotels again. After we explained to him about the Palace hotel's reception he lightened up. I followed this up with my reprimand of officialdom and how an opportunity of gathering information was being missed due to the number of Italian and Japanese clients in the hotel. On my informing Mr Hilgarth I would make a report about this to H.Q. he seemed rather deflated.

At this juncture Brian made his way back to the Hotel Nacional where Juan apparently served him a free coffee on a table next to some Italian business men.

I made my way to meet up with Kenneth Benton (Head of Section V in Madrid). After all the messages we had exchanged about Garbo, it was good to meet each other and be able to discuss the practices and character of each other's agents, what Gibraltar was like and what Madrid was like. Afterwards, Kenneth took me to the Meson. A short drive out of Madrid and I found myself in a restaurant full of Brits and Secret Service folk. Basic wooden tables and chairs, a friendly atmosphere and, despite the shortage of food in the area, an excellent lunch. Kenneth introduced me to others working in the espionage game, who were having a break. In that homely establishment, on foreign soil, I started to feel as though I belonged to some kind of special club. I informed Kenneth and the others present about the Hotel Nacional and suggested a waiter or porter be given some good gossip of a deceptive nature due to the number of Italians and Japs staying there. It was agreed this was a good idea. When I told them about the hotel being out of bounds; comments were made about the stupidity of normal officialdom and its dislike of the Secret Service.

So what was my father doing in Madrid? It cannot have just been a jolly. I have worked out he had a meeting which was top secret and was to do with information on the shipping of arms from Spain to Ireland. I believe this is when he met Lt Colonel Hill-Dillon to discuss this possibility and that some German shipping from Seville was suspect. Added to this meeting, I believe that Stewart Menzies, head of MI6 was there. Besides the arms issues, discussions were also held over the continuance of deception and the problems being caused by the French Vichy in North Africa. Perhaps this is when a plan was put together leading up to the final decision to assassinate the fascist Admiral Darlan in charge of the French in Algiers and Morocco. It appears from some notes that Menzies also discussed the idea of a meeting with Canaris since Canaris visited Southern Spain on a relatively frequent basis.

On the way back to Madrid, Kenneth told me how they had been watching Frederico, (Garbo's Abwehr connection), for the last year. The German secret service was rather useless in Spain, certainly in Madrid.

Were the Abwehr useless;, or were they trying to bring down Hitler and the Nazi regime? Felix Cowgill my father's boss had a plan to negotiate with Admiral Canaris. It seems this plan was thwarted by Kim Philby. How many lives could have been saved? Why did Philby stop this plan? Because Russia did not want a strong united Europe, they wanted war as they were building up their own war machine with tanks and guns.

When I met Brian later on he informed me of his clandestine action at the Hotel Nacional and how Juan had helped him. The Italians are here to organise the purchase of olive oil in bulk from some big suppliers in Jaen. And the Japanese were apparently there due the amount of Spanish business and influence in the Philippines, and

Wolfram. Wolfram made sense as they needed this for the aircraft engines.

To be English in Madrid in October1942 made me feel rather special. The Spanish always made extra efforts for one's comfort and well-being. Sitting in a famous German restaurant I overheard the group of Spaniards at the table behind us wondering what and who we were. They thought we were Americans or from some other English speaking country. One of them turned around and commented about us being foreigners. I remember distinctly the fellow next to him smiled and patted him on the shoulder.

'They are not foreigners they are English.'

The next morning must have been a Sunday as I remember the people were all dressed up waiting outside the church for mass. Unlike London there were no sandbags, no temporary air-raid shelters, no-one walked around with gas-mask bags; on the other hand there were very few cars, and clothing was in short supply. Basic food supplies seemed good.

Very early on Monday morning, the car full of petrol cans again, Brian driving, the sound of the engine exaggerated by the empty streets, we headed south to Seville. Until we reached Valdepenas the road and country side was almost deserted, apart from the odd gasogene powered truck. Valdepenas famous for its wine was like a different country; trucks, donkeys, mules, people coming and going. It was as though Franco had decided Spain needed to drink wine, and it was all being produced here. We found a very busy bar-cum-restaurant full of truck drivers and muleteers were we had lunch and listened intently to the conversations going on around us.

Money was being invested in the area and Franco was making it easy for these businesses to find funding. Franco had the government set up a cooperative system which would allow everybody involved with the vineyard to profit from its success. Consequently anyone with implements, transport or any other form of agricultural experience queued up to join these cooperatives. Some Italians had been there and turned away.

Back in the car, and on and on, our slow progress making the spectacular trip tedious. We were grateful to be in the newly-sprung large Cadillac, so comfortable it allowed whoever was not driving to sleep.

At last Seville We drove around making a trip to the port area where English and German merchant ships were moored next to each other. We made notes on the German ships there and by asking around amongst the Spanish warehouses we found out they were being loaded with sugar, salt and shovels. The English ships with sugar and oranges. We looked around the rest of the city just to see how the general public was fairing. We picked up the vice consul who took us to a restaurant for paella. We informed him of our findings in the port area and asked him to send this back to London. We assessed the sugar, salt and shovels were destined for the German forces in North Africa.

This spy work was also to find out about arms to Ireland.
An alert was given. Sacks of sugar, a crate of oranges or
shovels could quite easily contain arms. As it was, the one
or two informants on the dockyard who helped the British
had not heard rumours but could not physically search.

Next morning we headed onto Cadiz. We had received
instructions from the vice consul to pick up a marine
engineer who had been seriously injured and was in the
care of a small hospital run by nuns on the outskirts of the
town. We picked him up; he was now suffering from
gangrene. Supplied with some morphine, spirit of the
medicinal and holy kind, and with him lying on the back
seat we drove as fast as possible to Gibraltar's military
hospital. Conversation was in short supply. All I found out
was he had fallen and badly damaged his leg while the
boat was moored up in Cadiz. Fortunately the car had
consumed about ninety percent of the petrol and we only
had a couple of cans left in the boot. Between Cadiz and
Tarifa, about two hours away from Gibraltar we were
stopped by a Guadia Civil check point. While the papers
were being looked over the engine caught fire.

With the help of the Guardia Civil we managed to put the
fire out without it causing any real damage to us or the car.
Quite amazing really considering the petrol we had been
carrying. One of the Guardia noticed the state of our
passenger. When we informed him of our quest, he
telephoned the Gibraltar frontier police and told them to
stay open until we had crossed into Gibraltar. Our
gratitude expressed we set off and encountered no further
problems. As Brian drove up to the frontier to our relief

the two guards immediately opened the barriers and waved us through; by this time our companion was unconscious.

At the hospital we ran into the lobby and taking no notice of the protests from the night duty nurse, grabbed a stretcher. As soon as she realised the condition of the man she ran off to fetch the doctor. If the Guardia had not helped, firstly putting the fire out and secondly by calling up the frontier guards, I am sure our patient would have died.

Back at the apartment, Brian and I collapsed on our beds and slept for a good twelve hours. We were woken by the low throaty roar of assembled Spitfires and Hurricanes being test flown in preparation for the invasion of North Africa.

A few days after the first Spitfires had their practice runs; Brian accompanied me across the border. We spread gossip and rumors of these practice runs being in preparation for the up and coming landings on Sicily and the relief of Malta. We split up, Brian soon returned back to base.

Again, I was surprised about my father wanting the following left out as it helped put so much together. This false information was coupled with many other pieces. As the date got nearer he kept contradicting information coming from Garbo which was true, just out of date. The information given out by them was the 4th November. The message arrived too late and was incorrect by 4 days. This established Garbo as the best source of intelligence as far as the Germans were concerned. This was very important for future deception work.

I returned late in the evening to find La Linea Control in a state of mayhem. Juan Llegado, a friendly policeman, told me 'the Americans have landed and made a mistake'. Apparently they came in too fast. He had obviously heard some of the gossip as he confirmed he thought all this activity was in preparation for Malta.

A squadron of American Lightings had started landing on the Gibraltar airstrip in the early hours of the evening; some had missed the runway and ended up in no man's land between the runway and the Spanish frontier.

I asked Juan Llegado what Madrid would have to say about this.

On this occasion he confirmed my feeling Franco was not supporting the Germans, and in all actuality was quietly helping us. Madrid would do nothing for a few days we just had to get the planes out quickly.

Back in the apartment I found Brian and Donald rather amused by the whole plane situation. Early next morning I went to the office and reported by phone to the Governor's office what I had been told. He told me the American representative on the Rock was worried because one of the planes had something called George on board. Quickly I arranged to meet the American liaison officer as I had news he should know. He was of course working alongside General Eisenhower. On arrival at the U.S. headquarters within the Governor's compound I was escorted in. An American major met me. I informed him the Spanish were happy to leave this situation alone for a few days. Grateful for this bit of intelligence and realizing I was Secret Service; he informed me George was an autopilot device developed by the Americans to enable flying at night. I made some silly comment about it not helping them much yesterday evening. He smiled.

Some SOE chaps and a couple of the American pilots, with the help of a few diversions created by some of my agents and a lot of other people, recovered George from on board one of the planes. The planes themselves were recovered within the day.

Biaggio's embassy bar was full of blue uniforms most of the day; it was the regular hangout for British and American pilots. He was a happy man, and I found it hard not to tell him that the planes were going to North Africa not Malta; he was going to be disappointed.

The dockyard was working day and night. The workers consistently ignored the demands of the union leaders to go on strike. Due to all the extra activity I demanded double vigilance from my agents and their networks as the chance of sabotage attempts was greatly increased. They kept me extremely well informed of any suspicious activities on the mainland and Gibraltar. The security blockades and check points worked so well nothing untoward was reported and indeed no sabotage attempt was made.

The streets were crowded with navy, air force and army personnel wandering around. The white hats of the American military police bobbed up and down, so obvious amongst the other uniforms. Pieces of hurricane planes were trolleyed down the road towards the assembly point near the runway, while engineers rapidly pieced together the planes. I was astounded at how fast these men worked.

It was at this time that General Giraud arrived in Gibraltar to come to an agreement with Eisenhower, which was to convince the French Forces in North Africa not to resist the Allied troops after the landings. General Giraud refused to go to Algiers and had very little influence over the French Army in French North Africa. Admiral Darlan who was disliked by Roosevelt, Eisenhower and Churchill was in command. Darlan's fascist beliefs were of great concern. Again my father did not want this to go into our book, which makes me wonder why? What was he hiding?

One evening around 5th November I can remember going to Europe Point, a viewing area overlooking the straits. Planes taking off and landing, ships sailing in all directions, boats coming in and out of the bay, soldiers drilling in the barracks, and all the people standing around watching; it was incredible to see. Suddenly; bang, bang, bang, bang in rapid succession. Strangely I never did find out why. Guy Fawkes?

Early in the morning on 8th November all the planes started taking off and the ships sailed away with supplies and troops; the drone of the Spitfires, the Hurricanes and

Lightings continued for hours, and the honks and the whistles of ships and boats went on longer still.

On the 8th November the Allied forces landed at Casablanca and on the beaches west of Algiers. Some of our intelligence officers were in at the very beginning doing their bit. Major Trevor Wilson volunteered to ride a motorcycle into Algiers to find out if the natives were going to be friendly or not. The Brits were not involved directly with the landings around Casablanca, and combined forces landed around Algiers. Algiers was taken by the Americans quite peacefully, with some celebrations held in the streets.

Later when things had settled down, my father received an informal message from Philby which confirmed news received from others, but also with a cryptic note about Canaris. What the cryptic note was I cannot say; but there is a reference to its receipt.

The lead up to this landing had stretched relations between Roosevelt and Churchill. General Eisenhower, Commander-in-Chief of the invasion force favoured Giruad. Churchill also had to listen to De Gaulle on this issue; Churchill expressing the idea that Darlan could be persuaded he was the stronger man. Yet Churchill despised the man, and would have been informed of his strong feelings and unwillingness to cooperate. There was certainly strong dislike and distrust between the two French commanders, General Giruad and Admiral Darlan. Eisenhower could not get along with Darlan and mistrusted him, as Darlan was very difficult. Equally

Giraud was very demanding considering his position of being a relative outsider of the Vichy high command, and being on the German hit list due to his non-active support of the German administration.

On 13th November Eisenhower arrived in Algiers for a short period to oversee the establishment of AFHQ and returned to Gibraltar. It had become clear that he and Churchill had some other strong differences of opinion on various subjects to do with the French and their political stance. All this came to my father via Trevor and H.Q. Roosevelt supported Eisenhower and would run up against Churchill over this.

Eisenhower had wanted to keep his distance from us all the time he had been in Gibraltar. It was not until the success of Torch that the atmosphere between the two thawed out. What is quite extraordinary is that from notes in my father's pad it appears Churchill wanted to immediately invade Sicily; which would have been madness. Eisenhower through his own tactics avoided any serious confrontation with any of the British commanders and therefore Churchill. In fact British Admiral Cunningham was Eisenhower's best commander in the naval forces at the time.

10   Algiers and Assassination

On 17th November a trusty DC3 flew me to Algiers airport where Trevor met me and filled me in on all the latest news. Trevor had already settled into the offices on the second floor of number 8 Rue Charras. I could not help noticing some Algerian artifacts he had hung on the wall behind his desk; mostly pictures of rather busty belly dancers and a big poster advertising Molyneux perfume. The building was shared with Field Security. Trevor informed me of the connection he had made with the French intelligence personnel who, according to him, were willing to help as much as they could. I'm sure they could have not been other than charmed by this fluent French-speaking, English skunk shit collector. Of course he had managed to acquire a beautiful Chrysler from the American consulate in Algiers; on the strength of his daring motorcycle trip, I expect.

It was during his time with Trevor in Algiers when my father learned all about the affairs of the French commanders General Giraud and Admiral Darlan. One of Trevor's informants within the American camp had passed on information as to how Giraud had demanded to be in charge of the landings, which Eisenhower could not accept. This was corroborated by Captain Doudot with whom my father was going to work. It would also seem that Doudot confirmed Admiral Darlan was a fascist, hated by the Free French and would always be a serious problem to the Allies.

Both these leading French officers disliked each other. Giraud had been imprisoned and was wanted by the Germans. Darlan on the other hand was wanted by the Free French. Darlan was clearly a liability as he would never gain the support of the Free French due to his open collaboration with the Germans in the early stages of the war. Neither of them was wanted by Churchill, Roosevelt or Eisenhower. Apparently Giraud was the easier to cope with and therefore Darlan had to go. Stewart Menzies arrived in Algiers at this time. Subsequent meetings were held with the Free French. My father mentions this and this alone.

I returned to Gibraltar to pack up my office, as I was to move to Algiers. My last useful action on Gibraltar involved Pilot Officer Butch Gerrard (the fixer). He asked if I could help him out as he wanted Christmas turkey for his lads in the Fleet Air Arm. Having made the necessary arrangements he accompanied me across the border to Miraflores and helped me load the fourteen plucked turkeys into the back of the Cadillac. A very merry Christmas was had by one and all, at least on jolly old Gibraltar. On the 26th December I received a message from Trevor.

"Admiral Darlan was assassinated on the 24th December by a Free French member named Bonnier. Bonnier is up for execution."

Some notes of my fathers, some of which I have been able to corroborate, are on the assassination of Admiral Darlan.

"All sorts of conjecture went around between us. Brian with his dislike for the higher levels of command jumped to the conclusion Churchill was behind this. Donald on the other hand knew of Churchill's deep gratitude to Admiral Darlan. Darlan had commanded that all British soldiers should be evacuated from Dunkirk before the French; thus saving the bulk of the British Army and sacrificing the French. On the other hand Darlan had wanted the French to form an allegiance with the Germans.

Summing this up, and information Trevor had heard from some of his American friends in OSS, it is not probable that Eisenhower was behind it. Although the control of the North African French forces went straight to General Giraud, Giraud had the assassin executed very quickly after he had confessed to the killing.

Do I know for sure? No I do not.

Do I think it was possible for Eisenhower to have had Admiral Darlan assassinated? Yes I do. It was war; and we needed the North African French and the Vichy on our side.

Very soon after this the Germans moved into Southern France and took control from the Vichy. This immediately turned the Vichy against the Germans, thus giving far more support to the Free French and De Gaulle. This led to the conference between Churchill, Roosevelt, De Gaulle and General Giraud in Casablanca January 1943. With very heavy secrecy Roosevelt and Churchill arrived. Apparently Churchill had a double for some of the public appearances which were made for the benefit of the world to show the unification between the two powers.

The secrecy was so high we were not aware of this. Some of the contents were leaked out. The significance of this Conference is the agreement made for an unconditional surrender. There could be no peace agreement, no terms of surrender for the Germans. An OSS officer who was part of the security at the conference, who I later worked with on the Forty Committee, informed me that one of the deciding factors for this decision was the confirmed existence of the concentration/extermination camps. When I heard this I was shocked to the core."

It is this holding back on his story that makes me wonder. Did my father know all about the assassination of Admiral Darlan? As he says, his boss Menzies had been in Algiers at the time of this killing. Did my father collect turkeys as a cover? I am sure my thoughts are just conjecture; but are they? His organizing turkey for Christmas seems reasonable enough, but it seems to have taken up a lot of his time. After all as far as any one of his friends and co-workers were concerned he was in Spain hunting for turkey. Why was he not at the Christmas party? I have a strange feeling he had to cover up some events connected with the assassination. Also he seems to contradict his thoughts on Eisenhower. Frankly, it was mostly in the interests of the British that Darlan was executed. This paved the way for De Gaulle to take control, and who my father most certainly helped on his way to becoming the President. This I suspect was with the guidance of Menzies.

O'Shagar my trusty Irish secretary was to keep the lines of communication going with the network of agents I had built up. I explained my next posting was Algiers. My task was to work with the French and start the deception work. What kind of deception? The French needed to be investigated to find out who was clearly on our side, and who was working with the Vichy. Some Vichy members were still allied to the Nazis and made it imperative to find out who these members were, essentially for security reasons. For the purposes of deception these fascist Vichy could be a prime source of information for us as well as sending deception information to the Germans, who would trust their every word.

From February 1941 to mid-1942 Admiral Darlan was effectively the leader of the Vichy French Government and cooperated with The Third Reich. He was replaced by Laval as the Germans felt he was not reliable enough. He maintained the position of Commander of the Vichy French Forces. Soon after this he visited Algiers to inspect his forces and navy there and to also see his son. This visit coincided with the Free French forces under the command of several commanders including Colonel Jousse taking over Vichy army posts and strategic holdings.

Darlan was arrested during these attacks and handed over to the Americans. General Clark persuaded Darlan to order the all Vichy French forces in North Africa to cease fighting against the allies. Soon after he issued this order he was released and Eisenhower accepted Darlan's request to be made the Commander of the French forces in North Africa, in collaboration with the Americans. This enraged De Gaulle and all the Free French. Churchill was angered by this decision as he felt he should have been consulted. Secondly, Churchill had a serious score to settle with Darlan.

In June 1940 Darlan had been contacted by the British Royal Navy which offered the opportunity to save the French Fleet from falling into German hands. The fleet which was anchored in Mers El Kebir near Oran posed a significant threat to the British navy in the Mediterranean. Churchill had no choice but to issue orders for the destruction of the Fleet. The Fleet was destroyed and thirteen hundred French sailors died as a result. Churchill was blamed for this. De Gaulle fully understood his reasons, and held Darlan responsible for this loss of life and shipping; a very good reason for Churchill wanting him out of the way. Besides Darlan's ability to swap sides as it suited him indicated he was very unreliable, and was always under suspicion of being a collaborator.

Menzies would have had information through Ultra and therefore possibly Canaris. Canaris would have been spying on Darlan. If in his messages he had indicated Darlan's continued collaboration with Hitler, which Ultra would have picked up, Menzies, with the support of both Churchill and De Gaulle, would have had every reason to have organised his assassination. De Gaulle was to benefit from this greatly and therefore Churchill.

My father spoke perfect French and he was based in Gibraltar, therefore could create cover stories quite easily. He was in Algiers in November and early

December when Menzies was there yet he does not mention this at all. *Darlan was shot on 24th December 1942 by a young Free French fighter named Chapelle, who was apparently promised a fake firing squad death; only he was shot by a real firing squad just 3 days later. Hence he never had time to tell anyone who had helped him organise the assassination or who had put him up to it.*

This display of confidence shown by my father in his notes about Eisenhower being a suspect is another indication he was probably involved with the assassination of Darlan and certainly its cover up. From a certain point of view I would like to think so. From another perspective it is quite hard to think of my father as being a part of an assassination of anyone.

On 20th January I made my last trip in wartime across the border to La Linea and Algeciras to say adios to friends, agents and cohorts, including Juan Llegado.

Biaggio, who had drunk a few John Collins to help him recover from his disappointment at Malta not being freed, provided food, drinks and location. Donald had his jazz friends play the night away, and I had a goodbye party to remember my friends and Gibraltar by. The following morning Brian took me to the airport, we shook hands. He started to walk away then turned, coughed slightly as he often did when about to say something slightly emotional, and said,

'It has been fun, hasn't it?'

With that he turned and walked off.

As I turned away from Brian the hot morning sun hit my face making me squint, which was quite painful due to the hangover I was suffering. The American DC3 was waiting, its engines ticking over. On that bright January day in 1943 I joined eleven other passengers also heading for Algiers. The Americans had accumulated so many transport planes in North Africa that they were now responsible for carrying personnel and most of the freight to and from Europe. I made myself as comfortable as was possible on the hard steel bench on the port side of the plane. Flying always made me nervous, and still does.

The engines revved up and the plane slowly taxied along the runway. We waited in line while two other DC3s took off in front of us. I checked my seat belt and smiled at a couple of passengers, when suddenly one of the engines stalled. The high pitched whine of the started motor kept on and on. When the engine fired up, the navigator stuck his head round the door and told the marine sitting up front to pass a message around that all was OK. The plane jockeyed into position for take-off, the engines revved up with a deafening roar, the plane accelerated, then slowly started to climb, thankfully only to a low altitude. We were on our way to Algiers.

The Mediterranean was full of ships rushing around; some heading to Gibraltar, some to Algiers, some, perhaps, back to England. I hoped, for Biaggio's sake that one or two were on their way to Malta.

Although the sea was calm, the air turbulence was terrible and a couple of times when the plane dropped rapidly, reviving my nagging fear that the engine might stall at any moment, I wished I had taken up the navy's offer of a ride on a destroyer. The bumps and dips broke into my reminiscences of how good life and work had been during my seven and a half months on the Rock. What was in store for me? The plane suddenly made a very severe lurch, and I stopped wondering. Thank goodness the reason for the last big-dipper effect was our descent to Blida.

The airfield in Blida was no more than a flat piece of land with a wooden hut at the southern end. The airstrip was muddy and rutted after the rains, so the engineers had laid down strips of steel mesh all over the surface in the hope that these would stop the planes from sinking into the soft mud. The steel strips worked quite well, but there had been so much air traffic that the surface was incredibly bumpy. Two planes that had obviously tried to take off before the mesh had been put down were sitting just off the runway, mud completely covering their wheels.

The airport was mayhem; it felt rather like being at a rugby or soccer game for the army and air force, or perhaps I should say an American football game. The yanks were everywhere. Trevor Wilson met me, threw my bag into his requisitioned Chrysler and drove me towards Algiers, filling me in on who and what was what. At that moment I was not sure what was expected of me, except to be his number two in the rank and file of Section V, and to start up a deception network with the co-operation of the French.

The scenery of adobe houses, Arabs with sun beaten faces in their Jalabi robes talking animatedly on street corners, the donkeys and camels being led by their Arab masters, walking leisurely to their destinations was in stark contrast to the military vehicles and soldiers. Trevor just managed to avoid two camels which suddenly ran straight in front of the car due to two American jeeps racing towards the airfield.

Trevor looked at me over his glasses and said,

'Good to see you Desmond. It has been a little confusing around here recently. The Americans like to do things on such a grand scale and always in such a hurry.'

The looks on many of the local's faces showed their bewilderment and disbelief at the amount of vehicles and military running around.

The French navy, with Darlan out of the way, and despite their bitter memories of the British raid on Oran (then an important French naval port) in 1941, agreed to join the Allies. Members of the Deuxieme Bureau and the Bureau de Renseignements, both well established in North Africa, presented themselves as more than willing allies. Trevor had struck up a particularly good relationship with Captain Paul Paillole, the head of the Bureau de Renseignements du Territoire. This bureau monitored the flow of information between North Africa and France.

Due to North Africa being under the Vichy French this information often included very clear notes on the German movements. His department had about thirty agents. Some Spanish, French and German; working for the Germans but under their control. Before the allied landing it had been relatively easy to give these agents enough low grade information to keep their German masters happy that the build-up of planes and military in Gibraltar was for Malta and Sicily. The invasion by American Forces in Morocco and Anglo-American forces in Algeria was a shock to the German forces. Very quickly the Abwehr were asking these agents to provide information on our troop numbers, the American numbers, and what aircraft and armourments were arriving? We needed to start giving some answers, which made our forces look more substantial than they were. This had been a successful tactic established by Brigadier Dudley Clarke over in Egypt.

Trevor had informed the French Secret Services of my father's arrival and some members of AFHQ and that he was there to read and pass on messages to and from HQ in England and to set up deception networks and develop some double agents. This is when I come to realise how hard it must have been to keep track of what his work was like. Most of it would have been analysing conversations and hearsay on the streets and creating stories that were sort of true but not true.

In short my father was a professional liar. He was never able to share his workload with anyone other than his cohorts in the world of deception. So much of this was without training as who could train him. It was a matter of trying and seeing if it worked with a great deal of thought and follow up on the lies. I am still looking to see if there is any detail, or trip in his papers, which could indicate he was involved in the assassination. If not the assassination; then what?

Trevor explained that I was to sort out the situation with the French.

'You must get Captain Paillole to introduce you to Captain Germain and Doudot, who seem to be involved with the Das (double agents) game. The question of free information is up to you to deal with.'

Trevor stopped talking to avoid an Arab boy who had just run into the middle of the road and stopped; he turned looked at us and raising both fists started to yell at the top of his voice.

Trevor continued in his calm fashion as though nothing had happened.

'Lieutenant Colonel Hill-Dillon will give you all the support you need. He is the British G2 at AFHQ and a very supportive friend of our activities; our man in AFHQ as it were.'

The Military G2 at this time was Brigadier Mockler-Ferryman. Given my father's clear memory of so much it is strange he does not mention him. I know Major Bristow Section V MI6 Algiers (my father) must have worked very closely with Bigadier Mockler-Ferryman and his successor Brigadier General Sir Kenneth Strong; the G2 officers for Eisenhower of AFHQ.? So why the secrecy about them and what was he really covering up?

Lieutenant Colonel Hill-Dillon was also in Algiers at that time, (and this is corroborated in other books written about Algiers at the time). Whilst Hill-Dillon did indeed work for intelligence, (MI5), this was in Ireland, where he had been brought out of retirement by Major General R V Pollock to help him on the worsening problems in Ireland. Why then was Hill-Dillon in Algiers at this time and what was his role there? Did this have anything to do with my father's earlier meeting with him in Madrid or was Hill-Dillon in Algiers for some covert operation?

Up until now I thought my father had told his story only holding back a few juicy secrets, (some to come later). Why then come up with all this smoke around the time when Admiral Darlan of the French Vichy navy is assassinated? Maybe his possession of the German officer's Luger and ammunition was not due to an interrogation? Of course I will never know now. I could not get the truth from him when he was alive. Now with access to so much more information, maybe the truth is there, and certainly less motivated by deceptive protectiveness. All this is where the history of my father becomes one of investigation and what seems to make sense.

With rather fearful thoughts I think my father was probably involved in covering up details of the assassination. More notes will hopefully shed light on this as we go along.

Trevor was right, I did like Hill-Dillon and he was very helpful. It made my life much easier having a friend in Allied Forces Head Quarters as the regular army chaps did not like us supposed cloak and dagger boys very much at all. Eisenhower was very skeptical of Ultra.

Trevor had organised an apartment for me in the centre of town. Having disposed of my bag and taken a shower I walked down the narrow staircase to the street.

The contrast to Gibraltar was one of noise, to start with. In Gibraltar vehicles were not allowed to honk their horns; and the language heard in the streets of Gibraltar was a kind of Spanglish, interspersed with Hebrew and some Arab. In the centre of Algiers it was predominantly French, and anywhere the forces were it was American, English and some French. There were so many soldiers milling about curious about the Arabs. Very few of these men would ever have dreamed of being in North Africa; a very different world for many of them.

The roads were full of honking military vehicles, such as ambulances, troop carriers and of course jeeps. These tough four wheel drive vehicles were the envy of the English as the Austin pick-ups we used were always breaking down or getting stuck in the sand. I often wondered how much manpower was wasted repairing these hazardous vehicles. All this hustle and bustle gave off a tremendous chaotic energy. Being this near to the fighting, and amongst so much military might, victory seemed inevitable; just a matter of time. At times I would wonder how many of these men would die; thankfully I was too busy most of the time to brood on this thought.

Just around the corner and down the hill from my apartment I found a little French bar next to a grocer's shop. A glass of Algerian wine and some goat cheese with French bread made up my first meal in Algiers.

The antiquity of the streets and the faces juxtaposed to the tanks and army vehicles made their normal life seem very tranquil. Algiers was a beautiful Arab town, with the blue Mediterranean to the north; the snow covered Atlas Mountains to the West and the Sahara to the south.

Always useful to watch were the farmers from the very fertile surrounding area who travelled by camel, by donkey or by foot to the souk (market) in the centre of Algiers to sell their herbs, spices, rice goats, etc., as they had done for hundreds of years. These farmers could be a source of information, as well as being a useful way of spreading deception in the surrounding areas.

The large port area was very simple and not mechanically equipped to deal with the destroyers and merchant ships toing and froing. The port's busiest time until 1943 had been in the eighteenth century, when it was the haunt of the famous Barbary pirates. The French Foreign Legion conquered Algeria in the 1830s and Algiers had been an important Arab-European trading point since, but only for carpets and spices, and of course fishing. Now lorries, sailors, mechanics, cranes, large crates, small crates, armored cars, tanks, jeeps, tents, and packages of canned food in abundance seemed to be disappearing in all directions; and not all to the Allies. The Arab workers had extremely dexterous fingers. The passing of information was an old established trade which was also becoming much busier and free flowing in Algiers.

The Arab's distinctive adobe houses made up a large part of the town. Many of these families of Arabs worked and sold their goods in the souk. It was very easy to get lost amongst the labyrinth streets with all varieties of shops, cafes and mint- tea houses. Regrettably these areas were more or less out of bounds to the Allies.

On asking my father he admitted to entering these areas on many occasions. With his near perfect French and not wearing a uniform helped him. At times he admitted he would wear a blue Berber head scarf to try and blend in. The influence of Brigadier Dudley-Clarke encouraged the wearing of disguises to infiltrate areas to spread deception.

Again why did my father not readily admit to entering these areas? Perhaps he had an Arab girlfriend? Or perhaps some of his best agents lived within these quarters. Algiers did have a resistance force that helped during the occupation; perhaps he was more involved with this group than he cared to admit to the authorities? This again would indicate he was involved in some cover up.

I am sure that every conceivable crime in the world happened in those tiny streets. The women, hidden behind their yashmak (burkas) face masks, walked around in groups, constantly haggling. Many of the men wore

French clothes, and seemed very European in an Arab way.

11   Free French and De Gaulle in Algiers

Getting back to the day of my arrival.

Trevor drove through the Arab section at the southern end of town, and we slowly climbed into the upper outskirts where beautiful palatial houses, built by the French, with tree lined drives and grassy rose gardens revealed the rich colonial elements of Algiers. He turned into the gateway of one of these grand houses.

MI6 HQ. He looked at me over his pince-nez specs and added, in answer to my unasked question,

'Yes, we are going up in the world.'

Another contrast to Gibraltar became apparent; here everybody wore uniform most of the time. We needed to be recognized in Algiers and our presence needed to be felt. The British army was on the move and counter espionage was playing a very important role in the decision making of the generals. Due to our success in transmitting confusing and wrong information to the Germans, which they believed, (e.g. we were going to save Malta), the Torch landings in North Africa had been very successful and not very expensive in the loss of material or life. This success had convinced many of the generals of the importance of good deception work. Now, with counter offences being planned, every false piece of information the Germans believed would help us win the battles and consequently the war, hopefully more cheaply, and with as few deaths as possible.

The gardens at MI6 HQ were beautifully laid out. Small pools with fountains in the middle fed small canals, which flowed through the shaded gardens that extended around the house; pepper trees, pine trees, mimosa trees and a couple of olive trees.

We walked into the tiled lobby, where marbled stairs led to the upstairs section, and through a brass handled door down into the basement. Trevor's introductions were interspersed with the usual idle chat, and swigs of Algerian vino.

'Captain Cuthbert Bowlby, Desmond Bristow, Cuthbert used to be head of station in Cairo; took over here a couple of weeks ago.'

Cuthbert, an ex-naval officer had joined SIS just before the war. His quiet discreet manner made him popular with the French and his easy way went down well with the Americans. All in all he created a co-operative and congenial atmosphere. His staff consisted of three assistants, several secretaries and a signals unit, handling MI6 signals.

'Desmond I believe you already know Lieutenant Morgan, Head of Signals. He's waiting for you to find some good agents to operate the radios for us so he can retire and spend a few years on the beach.'

Lieutenant Morgan smiled as he shook my hand.

'Good to see you, Desmond, I hope this is good reading.'

He handed me my first message, which had arrived that morning addressed to me by my new codename of Tap water. This made us all laugh. I remember wondering who in London had decided I should be Tap water for my duration in Algiers.

Knowing how many pundits there were amongst the SIS members, significantly, Tap water was very rare and very important in North Africa and the desert.

After lunch, Trevor dropped me off in the Rue Charras.

'I'll see you at seven in the main office,' he yelled as he drove into the thick traffic.

Where did my father go during these 3-4 hours? He gives so much detail on other occasions, why not here?

Back in the office, which was shared with Field Security, there were five messages on my desk, all unimportant, from various chaps inviting me to meet them. Amongst them a brief note from Brian and Donald wishing me well.

I sat at my desk thinking about Trevor introducing me to the French Secret Servicemen I had heard so much about. So! How to play the game with them? How many were truly on our side and how many were involved with The Vichy.

From my understanding of my history of that time, the French in North Africa were not to be trusted. Giraud and Admiral Darlan had been Vichy and it seems as though the French Forces in North Africa had little knowledge or

165

real concern of what the German's were doing in France. De Gaulle mistrusted most people; and was quite open about his concerns of the Vichy French in control of North Africa. They were fascist and very old fashioned. Their control had to be taken away.

My father very rarely talked about the field battles. He did mention to me about the fiasco and arguing of the American and British High Command in the early days; especially when the British forces failed to take Tunis due to bad organization, bad communication and bad planning; and the unexpected strength of the German resistance. My father on the other hand seemed to get along with the Americans very well. The only people it appears he usually had issues with were the English. Why? What did he have to hide from the British officers? On the other hand the British officers for the most part were very stuffy and old school.

How my father would feel at that time is any body's guess. He was about to work directly with the French Secret Services.

Some were for sure still very ambivalent about their loyalties. Much to my bewilderment he did not express that he had any feelings of doubt or worry. Nor did it seem to bother him at the time.

It must have been around this time that he gained some of his German Trophies which had so worried me as a child after finding them in his wardrobe.. His story to me is as follows; although I am not sure if this account is the truth.

Just after the notorious Battle of Kesserine in Tunis a British force had captured a small German patrol. Since the German officer spoke no English but very good French I was asked by the G2 officer to question him. He was a very relaxed Captain, not what I had expected a German officer to be. As it turned out he had lied and did speak some English. He offered me information concerning the strength and resolute attitude of the German forces in Tunis. He realised the war was over for him and gave over information about the type of man Rommel was; and that the German's biggest concern was Malta and therefore supplies.

Over a period of two weeks I and two Army officers gained a lot of information, which we duly passed on. At the end of the two weeks I accepted his pistol, his dark sun glasses and various other bits and pieces. Highly irregular of course!

On my asking why, he informed me that the English pistol would jam, the sunglasses would let sand in, and the German equipment was just so much better. He told me he never used the gun, if he had I am sure he would not tell me about it. With my new suspicions of him being partied to an assassination I have other thoughts concerning the Luger. If at any point he had wanted to kill one of the French, he could easily have used the German gun. He would never have been suspected.

Trevor had built up a very positive relationship with the French enabling me and the Allies to utilise their network of agents quickly. It became clear I was in Algiers to take over and enhance Section V's liaison with the French specifically for the purposes of deception operations; at certain moments I was indirectly operating thirty double agents with the French. Despite my reservations and trepidation due to the unknown quantity, the French seemed to be anti-German and I can honestly say they were wonderful people to work with and certainly knew what they were doing. They understood the locals and Vichy mentality very well indeed.

French HQ was very near MI6 HQ and the houses were quite similar. Captain Paillole, Captain Germain, (an unfortunate name I thought), Colonel Rivet and several other officers were at this first meeting. Captain Paillole was one of the most striking characters I met during the war. He was one of those people who could walk into a crowded room and everybody would notice him; tall, quiet, very good looking, cool, calm and collected, he was in charge of the French double agent operations. Captain Germain was a shortish, balding, fair-haired man, who prior to the war had been a professor at Metz University. Colonel Rivet was an affable man in charge of the overall Secret Service proceedings. He appeared to be very overshadowed by Captain Paillole.

The following day I was introduced to Captain Doudot. Captain Germain took me to Doudot's little office in a side street off the main Algiers Boulevard, introduced us to each other and left.

My newly found cohort and I gave each other a brief life history and then started a conversation which did not finish for nearly eighteen months. There were a few intermissions but from then on he and I saw each other almost every day to talk about agents, troop movements, messages to and from Cairo, London, Gib, army camps, bars, street corners, and how we would make plans for agents and where they were geographically and consequently structure information to be fed through to the Germans.

Closer to home he was there to investigate who on the French side was working for the Germans. Perhaps he did not remember this or perhaps this is just my conjecture. There has been so much conjecture around Captain Paillole, as to whether he was a double agent or whether he was as loyal to De Gaulle as he has been portrayed. This is when I think my father was in a potential vipers nest.

All the political maneuvering amongst the British and Americans, the different game plays they had going with the French was at this time potentially very dangerous. The balance of power within the French of North Africa and the exiled government in Britain under De Gaulle was fractious. Their loyalties were very divided and complex. After all, the French suspected Churchill, or Roosevelt/Eisenhower of being behind the assassination of Admiral Darlan. Some notes I have found recently indicate that Captain Paillole, and Captain Doudot were quite pleased about the death of Darlan. According to the notes it appears it made life much easier for them and cleared a path for De Gaulle and the Free French government.

Captain Doudot was in his early forties; he had gingerish hair, a freckly face and stout build, and wore very strong glasses. He was from Alsace, which gave him an understanding of the German mentality, and his stamina gave both of us the strength to deal with our forthcoming task. Luckily he had a very lively sense of humor, very much like my own, so we were able to laugh at the frequent times when the intensity of the double agent game might otherwise have broken us.

Realizing that, besides having to work with each other, we genuinely liked each other, Doudot offered to take me to lunch at a little restaurant out of town, which he thought I might enjoy. Indeed I did! It was owned by a Spaniard whose specialty was fish with mimosa eggs.

It is strange how the fortunes of war could take one down a road which might have death at the end of it; or might turn into an exciting journey. During the very first trip we were followed by a local. Doudot recognized him as being the owner of a shop near the office. The local Arabs were not so happy about our occupation as the Axis forces would pay over inflated prices for goods such as spices, carpets, and foods. Many local Arabs could make extra money from feeding information out to an Axis network. Being followed happened on a regular basis. For the few who worked for the Germans as many again helped us; consequently we could always find some way of losing our tail.

Doudot who knew every side street, and every other French Policeman, managed to lose him near the outskirts of town.

The Spanish restaurateur, Jose, could not believe I was from Huelva; or I spoke such good Spanish. Ola Hombre, a very hearty embrace, so usual for friends in Spain. Of course it became a favorite eating place for us. It was on the outside of town, easy to watch who might be following and very good food. To sit amongst the lush palm trees, planted in large pots with Arab designs. Punka-type fans rotated in the ceiling creating a cool breeze. At the exclusive end, high backed wicker chairs formed four seat private tables.

On this first visit, Doudot and I took a table in the back corner near the kitchen, affording us a good view and privacy. The chances of us being overheard were less than in the office. We discussed the fragile political situation for the Free French who were pro the allies and those devout Vichy members. How strong was the French Foreign Legion, and where was their alliance? Doudot reminded me of The Battle of Bir Hakeim where a very small force of Legionaires had resisted the German forces for six days during Rommel's attack on Tobruk in June 1942.

He told me about a French air force officer who had abandoned the Vichy. He came to us with a plan and, with Captain Paillole's agreement, volunteered to become an agent for the Germans. He was sent to Tunisia by the Lufwaffe, parachuted in, landing somewhere South of

Tunis behind the British lines, with a radio and receiver. The Germans trust him implicitly, Doudot said. I could use him to feed the Germans with what we called chicken feed.

Chicken feed, what is it I asked? It was a continuous line of irrelevant information about troop movements, uniform arrivals, and so on; stuff the German's would most probably have information on already. This way it would convince them this agent was in a good position, and could be trusted. When the time came to feed some real deception messages the Germans would not doubt their sincerity.

This was very important.

'What type of information could we send, and how often without jeopardising his position?' I asked.

It was essential that he worked his cover and kept fairly quiet until it became clear that he was entirely trusted by the Germans, and we in turn could continue to trust him. We created a fictional agent as a Lieutenant with a notional post in the French liaison department in AFHQ.

With the right handling this man was to become the best agent for our purposes. Most of the agents then working for us as doubles had direct contact with their German or Spanish employers, which was a very dangerous situation especially for deception work.

Doudot was convinced of this man's loyalty to France.

'We must build him up very slowly and carefully for the next few months,' I said. 'Since he is supposed to get info from AFHQ the information we give him must be very selective.' I quickly added, 'We must not be too ambitious yet.

This daring air force officer was known to us as Gilbert.

For the next three hours or so we discussed the strengths and weaknesses of many other agents, and how best to use them. It became clear to me these few French Secret Service men had been working against the Vichy, the Germans and Italians in North Africa in depth and in a masterly fashion for some time, without any defections. I felt elated and surprised at the end of this meeting that the French should be handing over this intricate network for us to use. The fact there was a certain lack of trust towards the French strangely seemed to work in my favour and certainly in favour of the deception tasks at hand.

Just another strange fact my father did not mention in our book. In his notes he mentions how Doudot revealed how he himself and Paillole and some of the Police had instigated the riots and fighting against the Vichy army just prior to the landings. This meant they must have had inside information of dates and times of the landings in advance; unless it was sheer coincidence??

Doudot and I arranged to meet the next day and left. Trevor was in our office looking through telegrams and organised a meeting with Hill-Dillon the next day.

12   Deception

In those relatively easy days, when ideas were abundant and untested, and no definite plans could be made, my first task was to analyse each agent the French presented to me. It was imperative to reduce the possibility of detection by the Germans to a bare minimum, while maximizing the potential of each informer.

I had dinner with the French refugees who owned the local grocer's shop. This became a regular stop off and where I bought my food when tired of bully beef. It was also a good gathering place for the local French and some Arabs. These two refugees, in 1920, had been professors at the Sorbonne University, teaching foreigners French. *(What a coincidence.)* I had spent six weeks studying French at the Sorbonne in 1937, so we had some things to chat about, such as La Coupole and other fine restaurants in Paris; which again, was one of those coincidences which proved invaluable.

I remember going back to my apartment and studying the names and characters of AFHQ staff. It was an important part my job to obtain cooperation from AFHQ for the information we needed to pass on. At this early stage, it seemed that the military could be persuaded to give us information on troops, their badges, movements and general activity. The G2 was a great supporter of our work and had very high regard for Ultra and spies. On the other hand the naval element, under the command of Admiral

Sir Andrew Cunningham was very reluctant to bless any kind of information, even non-consequential chicken feed.

We knew an enemy plane had been doing reconnaissance over Algiers and Bone, and had without any doubt spotted the destroyer and merchant ships in the port. Cunningham would not allow us to confirm through our potential agents what the Germans were looking at photographs of. If the agents were informing their masters about ships in the port and when an airplane could take photographs, what good were they? This had to change for us to be able to build up the Germans' trust in the agents we were using as doubles. I realised our department was going to have to put pressure on these elements of resistance to deception and persuade them how important it could be. After all, we were trying to make life easier for the likes of Cunningham.

I made up my mind to suggest to Doudot we take a tremendous risk and give some chicken feed to Gilbert to radio over to his German masters.

Lieutenant Colonel Hill-Dillon had big bushy eyebrows which set off his aquiline noise and the permanent twinkle in his eyes. He walked as though he had been in the saddle of a horse from birth. As Trevor had predicted, I liked him and he was very supportive of us. He listened to our makeshift plans with great enthusiasm; we told him very little about our work, but he understood our need for information about army activity and that it was for deception and it would be going to the Germans.

He realised there was a great deal of mistrust towards us amongst the main part of the forces. In his words, more or less,

'A lot of chaps neither trust nor like what you are doing, but I shall see what I can do. You know, if it wasn't for you chaps I'd get awfully bored around here; you give my brain something to do. Besides that, it tickled me how stupid some of the people around here can be, and you make me feel as though I'm not one of them.'

He smiled.

'By the way, I reckon if you are seen with us army chappies often enough the old naval boys will get jealous and want a bit of the attention as well.'

He showed Trevor and myself around the enormous complex of AFHQ. It was a large building on the eastern end of town. There were constant comings and goings of personnel and vehicles, naval, air force and army. I took note of some apparent new arrivals. Hill-Dillon confirmed they were new, and not important and could be used as chicken feed.

I then called on Doudot in his tiny room. Papers and books were everywhere. He was sipping coffee out of an enormous cup, and poured me some, strong and black.

I explained about the skepticism existing in our camp about the value and effectiveness of deception. Part of my job was to convince those bods that deception with a network of agents could prove very worthwhile.

'I thought if we could send a little something to the Germans via Gilbert it might help.'

The risk I was taking was very high and if it had gone wrong would have potentially been the end of my work with Section V. I knew any message Gilbert sent to the Germans would be picked up by Ultra in England.

On informing Doudot of the new arrivals at AFHQ he agreed to contact Gilbert. He understood it was essential to start some activity to help me convince the likes of Admiral Cunningham how vital our operations could be to the war.

Doudot and I worked on the wording of the message for hours in his little office; we ate sandwiches, talked, drank copious quantities of coffee and smoked cigarette after cigarette. It was vital this first message gave enough to the Germans to make them trust Gilbert, and even more vital we did not over-indulge our German friends, and thus get into trouble with AFHQ.

Doudot sent the message to Gilbert, who in turn sent it to his German masters. Doudot and I continued to make plans. Over the next four days I began to understand his hatred of the Germans who had killed several of his friends and had taken several Jewish friends away to what he was realizing were these concentration camps.

My father remembered these following events very clearly. For me, listening to them as his son I felt a certain edge of pride; yet also felt how crazy he was as he really took a risk of incalculable scale. Had he been wrong I have a feeling he might have been shot for being a traitor or God knows what?

At the end of the fourth day I walked into my office and sitting on my desk was a triple Z envelope from St Albans. I opened it quickly thinking that it must be confirming the success of Gilbert. It started:

"ACCORDING TO US AND OUR FRIENDS HERE (ULTRA) WE FEEL YOUR MAN IS SUSPECTED OF MAKING BREAD IN THE WRONG BAKERY"

In other words the Abwehr suspected Gilbert of being under our control. Of course I could not believe it. I did not want to believe it.

What would have happened to him if this had been the case? He explained nothing at this juncture but Gilbert might have been a potential agent for the Germans and this made life more difficult.

I must have re-read that telegram twenty times. My heart sank through the floor. After an hour or so of deliberation I called up Doudot who came over straight away.

How my father built up the confidence to do what he did next I do not know. Again he seemed to regard it as having no choice. He was flippant about it. Maybe by now Ultra had lost its power. Brigadier Mockler-Ferryman got into trouble for sticking too strongly to Ultra information, concerning The Kesserline Pass incident, which is partly why he was replaced by Brigadier General Kenneth Short in March 1943.

As he walked in he exclaimed,

'Mon Dieu Desmond, what's happening? You look as white as a sheet. Some brandy perhaps?' he said offering me a silver hip flask.

I refused as I gave him the telegram and translated for him. My previous deliberation had been over the dilemma of whether to show Doudot the telegram. By giving him evidence of England's ability to intercept German communications I was informing him about Ultra, one of our great secrets to the war. I had decided that if we were going to work together efficiently and freely we could afford no secrets from one another.

Quickly Doudot had assessed the existence of our ability to intercept German messages.

'I assume from this that England can intercept everything. Do you realise what a risk you have taken in showing me this telegram?'

'Yes, I do realise and I thought about it before I called you, but if you and I are to work together like this and we cannot trust each other we may as well stop here and now.'

He agreed with me, and was quite clearly flattered and impressed by my show of complete trust and obvious understanding of our situation.

I explained some of the details of Ultra and other aspects of British Secret Service capabilities. He reciprocated my trust, and divulged secrets which I'm sure the French authorities would not have been too pleased to have me know at this early stage of our relationship. This mutual trust enabled us to discuss, to plan and to operate more quickly and clearly. From that moment on our work relationship was never questioned by either of us.

Doudot left the office and returned an hour later. He asked me to telegraph London and request they thoroughly check their findings of the discrepancies, which had made them think the Germans were controlling Gilbert.

He knew the Germans called their wireless transmitter operators 'piano players' and thought some confusion had occurred over this code used by them. He felt sure a mistake had been made. He had checked all the details of his agent's message and the call signs, and had found nothing odd at all; and believe me he had been reading and sending messages for a long time.

That sleepless night went on forever. I tossed and turned, got up, made coffee, smoked, paced the room, listened to the traffic, and I worried a lot. I had run a risk by having the message sent by Gilbert, but nothing compared to what might happen if HMG found out I had let Doudot in on Ultra.

Early next morning I received a phone call in my office from HQ to say a triple Z telegram had arrived for me from London. I borrowed Trevor's car and rushed up there. I ran into the telegraph and radio room and grabbed the telegram which read something like this:

"FOR TAPWATER, REGRET ERROR MADE ON OUR BEHALF. V MANN REFERED TO AS PIANO PLAYER CONFUSING, ALL A-OKAY."

What a relief.

Gilbert went on to become our best agent and extremely important in our game of deception.

Apparently upon examination of Abwehr records after the war some historians have compared Gilbert with Garbo. His story still remains a secret, there is some doubt about him and his loyalties as he died at the end of the war when he was suspected of being a triple agent, and consequently was never able to tell his story.

I have researched Gilbert and cannot find any readily available information relating to him. Some historians confirm what my father has told us about this agent.? It is at times like these I wonder how much of a spies world is locked into continually deceiving people, convinced for the need of secrecy or due to the regular practice of deception. Was my father deceiving me? If so, why? Perhaps out of habit.

By early February messages were continually being sent by Doudot and I, through Gilbert and other agents; my knowledge and comprehension of his network grew every day. We spent hours sifting through snippets of information, formulating a message to be sent by one agent, usually Gilbert and supporting messages to be sent by others; that is, the important message would be sent by one agent, then we would put together subsequent information supporting the contents of the first. With a time set plan we would have other agents transmit the supportive information a day or two, sometimes a week later. As we became visibly successful in confusing the Germans, our department was able to put ever-increasing pressure on AFHQ and Cunningham. We were also able to persuade Brigadier Dudley-Clark, who visited us regularly from Cairo, to apply some highbrow pressure in the right places.

Official clearance was obtained, and the reporting of anything which Field Security sections overheard in the camps, town, or wherever, proceeded. We studied carefully all indiscretions which came our way, and worded them in such a fashion as not to tell the Germans anything of real consequence. We now had a steady flow of information being sent by our various agents. Sometimes we had to send something meaty but we always managed to phrase it so that the Germans either reacted too late or, when the wording was really vague, ignored it until after the event. Then they most probably sat down and told each other they should have listened to the agent.

I was now attending regular meetings with the French; Captain Germain, Captain Paillole and others. I was also attending regular meetings with Hill-Dillon and field security officers in order for the flow of information being fed to the Germans to relate to the needs of the military. All this information became too much for me to cope with. I was to all intents and purposes a lone committee for a short period. Thank goodness Major (later Lieutenant

Colonel) Michael Crighton arrived from Cairo with his A Force experience. He became chairman of the committee and brought in Colonel Golbranson of the US general staff. He in turn brought in Lt. Arne Eckstrom, a member of the Office of Strategic Studies (OSS). Michael Crighton had Captain Thomas as his aide. I was the MI6 representative at these meetings, during which we decided what information I should run through with Doudot and send via the appropriate agent. I insisted that either Doudot or Germain be present at some of these meetings and I would translate for them.

Doudot and I were essentially the joint controllers of about thirty agents at this point – around the middle of March 1943.

It was at this point when my father and I were working on 'A Game of Moles' a subject came up which he did not want in the book or to be revealed at all. Something I discovered one night when he and I had rather too much wine and he was trying to explain to me the complexity of running agents, and how all information had to support other information which was being sent from London, Madrid, or anywhere else.

My mother in her wisdom had realised my father must have had an affair or at least a lady friend. In her words, 'Oh for god's sake! You were away for 18 months are you trying to tell me you never slept with a woman the whole of that time." To which my father would reply, along with his dismissive chuckle. 'Of course not.'

I brought up the subject when he mentioned a French speaking Yugoslav named Olga, who was working with Captain Germain and would often help Captain Doudot and my father with secretarial duties.

On his admission he had an affair with Olga, he became very guilty and angry with himself; frankly more for admitting it than having the affair, although he made it look the other way around. I tried to persuade him to put this in the book; as well as talking to my mother about it. He flatly refused. Which indicated to me this had been a serious affair not just some casual sex partner. I have not revealed this to any other family members to date but they will now know.

Of course my mother knew she just wanted the truth; sadly my father never told her, which strangely hurt her more. My respect for my father also fell a few notches due to his lack of honesty. I mean, at this point in his life at 80 years of age what the hell was going to be done? Possibly, a big invisible rift might have been closed. For some time after this I found it hard to talk with my father, other than in a very factual manner.

The Americans in the committee were not so familiar at deception. How to persuade them to co-operate as much as we needed? Arne Eckstrom fully understood our predicament, since he well knew how stubborn many of the American generals could be, especially General Marshall. Arne kept chipping away at the US delegates, and eventually we had the authority to start sending

American chicken feed through our network in conjunction with OSS.

The relationships having been established with the French and various hurdles having been dealt with, it was time for me to visit our man in Oran, Captain Bobby Barclay.

I acquired an Austin pick-up, and went to the grocery store for basic supplies. When Albert heard where I was going, he asked if I could do the shop-café a favour. I owed them a few meals and other favours, so of course I said yes. He asked me to get eggs.

'Where do I go?' I asked.

My instructions were, "approximately three kilometers after Tenes, the road leaves the lie of the coast. About two kilometers on I would find four huge straw stacks on the left, were I was to stop and press the hooter three times."

This I did and after about two minutes, out from one of the stacks crawled two young boys who approached the car timidly. They asked what I wanted in their Algerian French.

On my response of eggs they looked at each other.

'Are you American?' I remember the taller one asking.

'No, English.' I replied, smiling at their interrogative methods.

The short one observed I was not French on account of my uniform.

'Good, now what about the eggs? I don't want them today. I will be back in two days.'

'How many eggs do you want?' The tall one asked.

I asked for five hundred expecting them to laugh at such a quantity.

Much to my surprise they did not bat an eyelid. It was agreed.

As I was leaving the boys ran back to the stacks to dive under the straw. Immediately about twenty heads of men, women and children appeared from the inside of the stacks to take a look at the Austin pick up and me. Where on earth were all the chickens? I wondered.

I arrived in Oran late in the evening. It was not such a busy place as Algiers, and luckily I found Bobby's apartment near the centre without any problem. The European influence was not as strong here in a cosmopolitan way; there were a few French Foreign Legionaries wandering around.

Captain Bobby Barclay, a short good looking aristocratic Englishman, had been in Belgium at the outbreak of the war and was the MI6 man in Oran. He had established a very close liaison with the resident French Bureau de Renseignement officer Eduard Douare. There was a covey of French-controlled agents in the pay of the Spanish and Germans, ostensibly working for the Spanish in neighbouring Spanish Morocco, or for the German vice consul in Oujda. Most were doing no more than satisfying inquisitiveness rather than giving information on intelligence targets. Ship movements in and out of Oran had a certain degree of intelligence interest, especially the types of vessels, but this passing of information from here was of very little consequence to the Allies. It was the deception messages these agents passed on which were so useful.

Bobby's apartment was very close to Douare's house and after I had cleaned following my dusty trip across the desert, Bobby took me around to meet Eduard and his delightful wife. We drank some very good Algerian wine and chatted about the war in general. Eduard took us out to a small bistro around the corner. Here we talked and established who we were. As it happened Douare was very familiar with Captain Paul Pauillole. He seemed to have some reservations about him but did not disclose them to me.

The next morning we reviewed Douare's agents and their possibilities selecting the few who could be useful in a future deception campaign. I spent some extra time with Bobby working out which agents would be in the best positions to put out messages or stories to back up details coming from Algiers. A lot of this work was hypothetical, but it was necessary in case the Germans started to do better in the desert war. Also, if at any time there should be a particular tricky piece of information going to the Germans it was comforting to know that an agent in Oran could put out a story to support it and give it further credibility. I quizzed Bobby as to why Douare seemed to have some dislike for Pauillole? He was not sure, other than Douare was not a great admirer of De Gaulle and Pauillole was.

In the late afternoon Bobby took me for a guided tour of Oran and its environs, and of course to Sidi Bel Abbes, just to have a look at the headquarters of the French Foreign Legion. There seemed to be Spais and Goumiers (French Moroccan regiments) everywhere. Moroccan troops under French command marched across the quad and back again; these later proved themselves in the Italian campaign; especially with women, I gather! The prejudice which had been held against the Moroccan/Arab troops by the French prior to Giraud was disappearing slowly. Giraud had issued orders for this practice to be outlawed although he personally did not agree with this. Being politically weak, and trying to regain some trust from us, he had to.

At some point in the evening I informed Bobby of my connection with the Greek consul in Casablanca, Stephanos Joseph, and that he could be considered a friend. I knew he would be useful in sending deception messages to Greece. At this time Bobby informed me that our man in Casablanca had heard of a Vichy controlled bank trying to send gold to the German controlled Vichy in France. The message came through:

"THE BANK OF MOROCCO ATTEMPTED TO SEND ALMOST $75,000,000 WORTH OF GOLD TO GERMAN-OCCUPIED FRANCE LAST FEBRUARY."

This was four months after the American Torch landings and we must not forget that the Bank of Morocco is an official institution in the hands of the French administration.

Early next morning I got back into the Austin pick-up praying it would not break down, and headed back to Algiers. I was egg bound, and after a long and uneventful journey through the northern desert I stopped the car to become involved in a minor black market operation. To my surprise, when I honked the horn three times, the lower part of two of the straw stacks came alive. Fifteen or twenty boys ferried the forty two dozen eggs into the back of the pick-up. When the last box had been loaded, the tall boy came up to me to be paid.

'Just one thing before I leave,' I said.

'Yes, monsieur?'

'Where are the hens?'

He pointed at the two stacks and explained how the chickens lived under the front four, and the family lived under the back two. He turned away on the ball of his bare foot, then tuned back to say, Goodbye, and thanked me, as he held up his hand with the few extra Algerian francs I had given him.

These interludes must have made the war seem rather stupid. It is now when my father talks that he seems to remember so much which must have been quite good fun. It is this fact which makes me realise he was not remembering so much on purpose. He was covering up or was still so emphatically attached to the Secret Service, so even 50 years after he left he could not reveal names or the truth; more to the point, the significance of the truth.

I drove with great care over the bumpy road, and when I made my delivery I was invited to a supper of scrambled eggs, which I gratefully accepted.

13   Deception 2 and Mincemeat

This next section comes from notes; again not revealed to me when he was alive.

The Casablanca Conference brought Churchill, Roosevelt, De Gaulle, and even General Giraud together. Plans were sketched out detailing movements for the rest of the war including the plans for the D-Day landings to take place in 1944. This marked the beginning of the end for the Germans. The first major move was the invasion of Sicily and Italy. The Germans needed to believe it would be the South of France, and Sardinia or Greece.

Brigadier Dudley Clark, based in Cairo, of A Force, thankfully was in charge of the military deception. And he was very eager for us to spread messages of deception. It was now time for us and the OSS to work together. The OSS had solid networks of agents in Spain. Being friendly with the Communist factions, plans were always safe from any fascists, but actually may have got through to the Russians. At some point I was going to have to establish a direct line of communication with them.

Why had my father not wanted this to be published? My father also mentioned his speaking with German Officers who were willingly talking about their armies' plans. More and more it would seem my father was unable to express his liking of the Germans, even his respect. He would question them about the concentration camps and believed their acts of disbelief. He said he always found the German prisoners very polite, and respectful. Apparently none ever showed any willingness to escape.

Doudot and I started to relay messages to our agents that would start to make the Germans think the Allied plans concerning an invasion of Europe would come from Africa. Plans are being made for the primary landings to be in the South of France, with possible secondary landings on Sardinia, with no date set. We agreed it would be a good idea for me to visit Gibraltar and spread rumours there, this would substantiate our messages being sent from North Africa.

Brian had been recalled to London. O'Shagar now on his own, was gathering more information on German personnel in the campo area and keeping tabs on the Italian frogmen. Donald was still hard at escape work. The flow of people escaping had almost doubled, partly because the Germans had to use prison guards to fight on their front lines, and mostly because the escape organisation was much more efficient, and so many more civilians wanted to help defeat the Germans. The success of The Torch Landings had changed the French. They were realising the Germans might well lose the war.

I arranged with Donald to spend the night in my old bed and left the office to walk around the Rock. On my way to Biaggio's, I noticed how quiet Gib was except for the shipyards where vessels were being repaired, or waiting for repairs.

Thankfully, just after the success of the Torch landings, Operation Stoneage, commonly seen as the relief of Malta, took place. Several thousand tonnes of supplies reached the near starving people. In December, Operation Portcullis was carried out when four transport ships successfully reached Malta with food, fuel, military supplies and mechanics to carry out repairs. This was the end of Malta's struggle for survival. In a very short period it became a major stronghold for our air force and navy enabling attacks on Axis supplies to Rommel's Africa Corp. Malta was very important in our deception messages concerning the up and coming invasion of Sicily and Italy.

Quietly opening the door I crept up to the bar and coughed very loudly. Biaggio jumped up from behind the counter.

'Captain Britow!' He exclaimed, arms in the air and big smile. 'You are still alive; you better have a John Collins.'

'Why else would I be here Biaggio?'

'And how are you?'

'Very well, Captain Bristow. Malta is able to eat reasonably good food again and my family is healthy again. Supply planes are there, and supplies are getting through.'

He started to mix my drink.

'Nice little party you are having with the Americans in North Africa.'

He placed the John Collins on a tray and led me to the office. I apologised for having had to lie to him about Malta, he clearly understood.

'I assume you are here to ask me something, or have me pass some information around,' he said with a smile.

He had guessed correctly. Having thought about all the agents who had worked for me in Gib, I had decided Biaggio was the best person to spread stories around Gib and La Linea and beyond. The contents of the casual conversation in bars and markets would gradually reach the Spanish Police and any Spaniards working with the Germans.

I informed him of the plans to invade the South of France and Sardinia. I explained how the Free French were gaining in strength and how consequently we felt much more confident they would prove to be a good fighting force. I talked to him about all the activity in Algiers and how some of the French Vichy were now working with us. All this was to support the concept of the invasion destiny being the South of France.

He informed me how he had donated £2000.00 to the Spitfire fund, as a result of these wonderful aircraft being so badly needed in Malta.

Biaggio was arrested by the British for passing on this gossip (information) in his hotel. Whether or not he tried to get hold of me I don't know, but I did not learn about his arrest until after the war. Amazingly, he was not very upset as the authorities released him when Donald and Brian explained just who he was.

A week after my father's return from Gib, Captain Paillole called for a meeting with all the members of Le Bureau de

Renseignement du Territoire, (The French Secret Service in North Africa.) My father was also invited.

Captain Paillole informed us of General De Gaulle's arrival in Algiers which I already knew, but had been told not to pass this onto any of the French. At this time there were still some Vichy members in Algiers who might assassinate De Gaulle. For the first time he clearly explained the dislike De Gaulle had for General Giraud and the Vichy members. These French Secret Service members were clearly on the side of De Gaulle. Captain Paillole was asking for my help. Of course I needed time to assess this as my duty as an MI6 officer might be compromised. I was being asked to interfere with French internal political affairs, which was highly irregular. On the other hand if this helped unite the French and therefore win the war, what option did I have? They were asking me to help them topple General Giraud. With my being a regular visitor to AFHQ and attending meetings with A Force meant I could easily pass on rumours about the feelings amongst the French Police and some members of the French army directly to the British and American Commanders.

Being more aware of the problem between De Gaulle and Giraud than they realised I was cautious not to commit to anything at this first meeting. When the meeting ended I wanted to talk with Doudot but felt wary. He had obviously presented this idea of me spying for them. I was in a prime position to keep tabs on the feelings of High Command concerning Giraud and De Gaulle. After two more meetings that week I decided to throw in with my

French friends. I did not inform HQ back in the U.K. It seemed to me they did not need to know and they might not understand my motives. The Free French were gaining ground politically, and would have greater support from the North Africans. This in turn would mean more willing troops to fight alongside the Allied forces.

So I set about spreading rumours about Giraud and his continued prejudice against the Arabs. At AFHQ I would casually mention how unpopular Giraud was with some police forces, how some members had been arrested on his orders for being too friendly with the Arabs. How his leadership was keeping North Africa divided even amongst the French population. Paillole would inform me of Giraud's dislike of both the British and Americans. How disagreable he found working with Eisenhower. When these rumours started to take effect General Giraud realised he was losing ground with Eisenhower. In a public display he awarded the Legion d'Honneur to the Allied Commander, The Liberator of North Africa.

Following this I informed the High Command just how much of this was a public display as Giraud felt it would help his cause amongst the Free French, nothing more.

Captain Paillole, a friend of De Gaulle's, fully explained how The Free French were giving their lives for the fight against the Nazis as well as the Vichy French. I was aware of most of the details. Before now I had had my suspicions about Paillole, and felt a little nervous about my having divulged the secret of Ultra to Doudot. He asked me to gather and pass on any information I received from Ultra and from the AFHQ meetings, concerning Giraud and the Allied plans for him and for De Gaulle.

From all the time I had spent with the local citizens and some police in Algiers it was clear Giraud needed to be replaced.

I agreed and became a French spy working on undermining General Giraud and promoting General De Gaulle as the best man for us to support.

Bobby Barclay was moved from Oran to join me. He moved into the spare room of my apartment and the two of us moved the office from rue Charras to the consulate general which initially was shared with Brigadier General Kenneth Short.

It was a great relief for me to have Bobby as my co-worker; my workload was growing to enormous proportions. Confidence in deception had grown and the preparations for the next big push were under way. The deception from this point on included the misinformation concerning the up and coming landings in Sicily, the South of France and even the Normandy landings. The counter espionage was essential to aid the advances to the end of the war. Russia was becoming a concern as to its final intentions, as more Russian soldiers who we came across reported the terrible acts of brutality carried out upon them by the Stalin regime.

Added to this, the extra work needed to gather gossip on Giraud was more involved than I had anticipated. Whenever Giraud was at AFHQ, I had to be there. I had one of my local Arab agents follow Giraud to see who his friends were and if he was having any affairs.

I was invited by General Short and Dudley Clarke to attend a meeting at AFHQ with A Force and some OSS members. (OSS being the America Overseas Intelligence Service) This was when I received formal confirmation of the plan to invade Sicily and Italy. Dudley Clarke wanted us to up the deception work and emphasized Greece was to take priority as the invasion destiny over the South of France. He had a lot of connections in Greece and perhaps underestimated the flow of information we could pass through to the Germans via the French. The day before the meeting I called all my co-workers for a meeting.

Bobby agreed with me that in order to maintain the validity of the deception we had to keep France as a potential option, emphasizing how many of the Vichy were now collaborating with us. In our messages Greece became the favoured destination with high command, because of its close proximity to Russia and the support we would receive from the Turks. Of course it was logical for our agents to be aware of what was happening within our area of North Africa.

We analysed in depth the potential of Doudot's agents being able to come across the sort of information we needed to send which would be believable. Some were Greek speakers. It was for Doudot to come up with the French forces' activity. By spreading rumours and sending messages with mixed information; we hoped it would keep the Germans guessing. We had to include casual conversation; information that agents picked up negating the possibility of Sicily. This was usually along the line of the Italians being too strong. Or the fact their espionage was too efficient.

At the end of May General De Gaulle arrived in Algiers. During the period just prior to this I went to all my friends in the bars and the cafes. Captain Paillole and the others did the same on the streets, and involved the local police and the French armed forces. Our efforts succeeded in encouraging vast crowd of Algerians, Free French and even Vichy French to come out on the streets. He received an enormous welcome.

On 3rd June Giraud and De Gaulle formed The French Committee of National Liberation. The very acrimonious relationship between the two was obvious to us although in public it appeared quite amicable. De Gaulle wanted to free France from the Germans and the old fashioned Vichy style government.

While all this was taking place, Doudot elaborated on the importance of the increased enlisting of more locals and Moroccans into the French forces as a result of De Gaulle's arrival. This was excellent material for the purposes of deception messages being fed to the Germans. We could show this activity by the movement around Fez, Mostaganem, Rabat and Sidi Bel Abbes.

By talking about this in detail with Brigadier K Strong, Dudley-Clarke and others, they in turn would pass this on to Eisenhower, General Alexander and Admiral

Cunnigham and therefore they would see how much more effective De Gaulle was as an ally.

By my father playing this double role, I can see how it helped with the war effort. Why could he not talk about these acts with me? This makes me feel quite proud of his work and the more of these secrets I find out about him, the more interesting it becomes. I can now see why my father was awarded the Croix de Guerre with Palm and the Legion d'Honneur two of the highest medals that can be awarded to a Frecnchman let alone an Englishman. Why they were hidden away in his handkerchief draw along with a disused condom packet and some cuff links and other things men kept in drawers has always bothered me.

My Algerian friends and the local community within the civilian population rapidly changed. They wanted the Germans defeated. They wanted De Gaulle. The same was true of the police, and many of the Vichy supporters within the army were starting to support the very powerful figure of Charles De Gaulle.

While continuing with my activities to promote De Gaulle amongst the Allies, the deception of the Sicily Landings needed serious attention. In actuality the fact that French North Africa was becoming more united made the deception work easier and more effective.

Sardinia, South of France and Greece continued to be our deception destinations. The conversation covered all the details about the French networks and the possibilities of using Douare's network in Spanish Morocco. I suggested we use the Greek consul in Casablanca, Stephanos Souliotes, who would be a natural source of information. He could send messages to the Greek resistance asking them to start preparing for an Allied invasion. I would send small details every week or so. This was supported by Dudley-Clarke.

The next day I attended the committee meeting with a breakdown of our discussion and our ideas of how to implement our programme of deception, which included notices in Arab newspapers and transmissions on the French/Arab radio.

OSS man Arne Eckstrom agreed and offered to support any of the deception messages through their network in Spain, which would penetrate through to France and be picked up by the Germans there, if not before. It was agreed by the committee one of our jobs was to convince the Germans of a big build-up of supplies and combat forces training in Algeria. Their destination could be one of Sardinia, the South of France and/or Greece. From week to week the emphasis would change thus making the Germans have to physically analyse using their agents on the ground. By now we knew who most of their agents were and we were therefore able to convince them. One primary agent was to receive information from us that Greece was the main objective with the secondary force objective being Sicily which was made up of mostly French troops. From this we hoped the Germans would assume the South of France was a strong possibility also.

That evening Bobby, Arne and I met Doudot to tell him of the committee's approval. The task of designing misinformation for our double agents began.

To start with one needs to find a person who is in a position of free movement around the public places, such as bars, restaurants, repair shops, newspaper vendors. The Germans tended to choose barmen, waiters, mechanics, etc. The Spanish were keen on journalists on local newspapers. Doudot had spent long hours following and watching such people, looking for one who was obviously making extra money somehow, and assessing whether this money came from being an agent for the Germans or Spanish. When sure of his man or woman, he would allow some time to go by and, choosing the moment very carefully, perhaps when the person needed even more extra cash. We would then have a friend approach the person and give them information which would go to their paymasters. From then on we would feed deceptive information to them. These agents often did not realise what they were involved with so long as they received money. For them it meant receiving two paychecks, tax free.

Some agents volunteered their services, which added an extra worry since they may have been triple agents, as they had the freedom of meeting their German or Spanish masters in private. It did however mean they could reply to the Germans or Spanish questions with the answers we wanted the enemy to receive. The fact that the French had thoroughly researched these people's loyalties reduced the risk considerably. Also, we could put in the reply message a small piece of information over and above whatever they were curious about. Yes, it is nothing more than lying. But very creative lying!

For example:

Jean the waiter is asked by the Germans to find out about the shipping movement going east from Algiers port. We would tell Jean it was headed towards Alexandria, when in fact it was bound for Malta. Hopefully this would ensure the Germans would not attack the ships until they had supposedly passed Malta; which of course they never did. This information would always be close to the truth. Then we would add some information about new tanks heading south. The Germans would then start a line of questioning about the tanks and they would obviously assume there was a build-up of forces in the south. With luck, they would send troops south, and our troops could then attack from the north and meet less resistance.

The need for constant clear communication with the Military was fundamental as our information would aid them. But if wrong it could cause problems. I was directly involved with the Ultra information which lead to a supposed misunderstanding of the German troop movements which lead to serious losses and defeat at the Battle of Kesserine Pass. When I received news of this, and the outburst of Eisenhower which pointed towards the failings of the espionage information and the deception, I was glad I had not been involved directly. In actuality it was not the fault of Ultra or the G2 Mockler-Ferryman.

When information came through of the inexperience of the American troops, and ultimately a victory albeit at a high cost; Eisenhower's reaction was none other than political. He had to save face and blame the British. He should have known better than to place inexperienced troops up against the Africa Corp. According to him he had not received information of Rommel being there. Well he did. It is true that Rommel did make some very unexpected moves catching the French, American and British forces unaware; which explains why he was called the Desert Fox. Field Marshal Rommel was the best tactical General in North Africa, possibly in the war. One fact I was certain of, he was the most respected and admired by his own men. Not one German I interrogated had anything but praise for him.

As a result of this Brigadier Eric Mockler-Ferryman, the G2, was replaced by the amicable and very proactive Brigadier General K Strong. There is no doubt he was the better man for the job. As a result of Eisenhower's accusations about the lack of information coming from the British Intelligence network; Strong encouraged MI6, Section V and other Secret Service sections to work very hard with the Americans. Like my father, he was rather against the stuffy attitude the British high ranking officers suffered from.

During this time in Algiers, information put out to the Germans by the agents had to be coordinated with A Force in Cairo and the XX committee in London. Since AFHQ was a joint US-British organization, A Force Algiers incorporated joint American and British deception planners for the first time in the war. As I have mentioned the French also became part of this committee.

Arne Eckstrom, Bobby Lloyd, Doudot and I had our first meeting in Doudot's cramped office. Bobby sat on the corner of the old French desk, Arne on a wooden packing case and I on a tiny chair; Doudot went on smoking, filling the room with the aromatic smell of black tobacco.

I explained to Doudot that we needed to convince the Germans of our next attack being on the north-eastern Mediterranean.

'We must put over the idea of Greece and Crete. Turkey is on our side and will help. We must give the impression of military interest in the Peloponnese area in general. Added to this information we should add, that theoretically we could attempt to cut off the German forces in Italy, by attacking the north east and the north-west in the Ligurian Sea, and around Venice. We will have more instructions coming in during the next week or two. For the moment we should allow agents to be quite negative about our future intentions and the significance of the military movement going on around Algiers, and eastward towards Tunis. All agents are to spread the word; the big build is for Greece.'

'Yes that coincides with how we Americans feel,' said Arne, who spoke perfect French.

'We ought to involve Douare from Oran in our next meeting,' suggested Bobby.

Of course realistically all this movement was going to be engaged in the final liberation of Tunis, and then on to Sicily and Italy.

Subsequent meetings were concerned with the deception leading up to the Sicily landings. Douare attended several of these and Captain Germain began to add his intellectual abilities attending a couple of times a week. I am glad to say not many of these meetings were held in Doudot's office. I don't mind the smell of black tobacco but when one started to feel as though one were sitting in the Black Hole of Algiers, the smoke did not help.

A-Force meetings were now receiving regular visits by Brigadier Dudley- Clark from Egypt and Brigadier Short, (G2 of AFHQ), as the build up for the Sicily landings needed more deception. The date of the landings was a constant subject of conversation; it kept changing. This was partially influenced by what we in deception were able to get the Germans to do with their forces. For a short time the committee wondered if we had too much true information slipping through to the wrong places, and I was concerned by the Spanish consulate general, for no specific reason other than not being able to recruit or control them. I had failed to recruit one of the Spanish consulate officers. As we left a meeting together Brigadier Dudley-Clark said,

'Desmond do you think you could find out what our Spanish friends are up to, if anything? This business of the girl going out with the lieutenant may be harmless;

nevertheless I for one would like to know, not about her especially but what the Spanish are up to in general.'

'I'll see what can be done by the time you return,' I replied.

Walking through the crowded streets I formulated a plan. Doudot had recently taken a professional safebreaker into his employ. This man had been one of the top safe mechanics in Madrid before the war, and since being in Algiers had made good use of his abilities. Doudot had heard about him from a rich French lady who, having lost the key to her Louis XIV bureau, employed Carlos to open it. He did so without leaving a scratch on it. Doudot employed Carlos for information and safe cracking if needed. As it now was. My plan was to break into the safe house in the Spanish consulate and take copies of all their cypher codes.

So on a moonless night, while we watched from a safe distance, Carlos slid through a window and one and a half hours later slid back out again.

'Where are the codes?' asked Bobby, wanting to photograph them very quickly and have Carlos return them.

Carlos handed over the cypher books and we photographed them. Meanwhile he pulled out another package from his large pocket. Twenty five pairs of silk stockings and six Omega watches appeared.

'I found these in the other safe, which I must say was very easy to open.' His eyes twinkled as he held up the ill-gotten gains.

What follows quite surprised me as it was nothing more than theft; but I suppose I would have done the same.

We distributed the booty amongst ourselves. I received a watch and some stockings for Olga. The cypher books were returned to the safe, and no more was said or heard about the break-in, not even from the consul. I expect he thought it was an inside job; the chances were the stockings and watches were stolen goods anyway.

After that, the Spanish consulate general appeared to stop making intelligence reports. This indicated that they were probably using their diplomatic bag, so we kept a flow of deception material going their way.

Not long after this episode I was in the bar around the corner from my apartment chatting with the local carpet trader who was also selling camels for his brother. We had talked on many occasions; he thought I was the regular British army. On this occasion he told me how his brother had been to a monastery near Boufarik and had heard strange noises, like a wireless set or something. He thought the Italians might be involved. The next day Francisco my newly acquired driver, with my newly acquired Chenard Walker from the Americans, took me to the monastery.

The fact that a major in British Intelligence (MI6) received a car from the Americans and had a driver indicates my father was rather more important to the Americans than just a friendly Major in British Intelligence. I have some more of his notes to look through on this subject. It would appear my father worked very closely with members of the OSS such as Arne Ekstrom. The OSS became the CIA, and my father certainly worked very closely with them at a later stage in his life.

The Abbot received me very politely and showed me around. He did get a little upset when I asked him directly about the radio set, which of course he denied all knowledge of. I remember my footsteps echoing on the stone floor and how cool the air was in the passageway; when we passed a door which he ignored and did not open.

'Monsieur this door needs to be opened as well,' I said with as much authority as I could muster.

He nodded and tutted a lot. I continued.

'If you refuse me I shall return with some army chaps who like nothing better than knocking down doors in monasteries.'

After a few moments he unlocked the door to what appeared to be an office. Amongst the papers I discovered hundreds of Bordeaux wine labels. Further on, in a small yard full of wine bottles, were two monks pasting labels and another carrying the labeled bottles into a room. It was a bottling plant turning Algerian wine into French. No radio set was discovered but I did return home with a case of very good Algerian Bordeaux, a couple of bottles of which I took to the next meeting as a gift and example for Doudot and company. It was a safe assumption this commercial enterprise was making money by selling to the Germans; subsequently this group of monks proved very useful for a period. By one of us visiting them once a week to purchase a case, we used them to pass information on to the German officers, maybe Rommel. I tried to have the camel train followed but was told we lost them overnight. I was never sure if this was true or not. On further consideration I realised it was not a good idea to have them followed as this would lead to suspicion. For now we had a very good message carrier who was going directly and very innocently to enemy officers.

A few days later I was invited by Sacha, a good friend of Doudot's, to take a trip into the desert near Hassi Messaoud beyond Ghardaia to visit a Sheik friend of his at his palace. This would enable me to see what was going on in this southern area of Algiers.

From his notes he also worked very closely with the American PWB (Psychological War Branch). This was set up in London in October just before the Torch Landings. The Americans were very new to deception and intelligence and the role it played in war. The PWB officer, Colonel Hazeltine, according to some notes, approached my father and asked him to advise on the contents of radio transmissions and the wording of pamphlets put out to the locals. It seems that Arne Ekstrom from OSS worked with him on this. It also seems that my father placed a radio in the Monastery with the French

Monks upon the agreement their secret wine business was kept secret. They agreed to transmit and receive messages.

The following piece of information explains his next exploit was not some friendly expedition. The G2, on behalf of Eisenhower, needed to know what American Cat men were doing so far south in Algieria without any registered Military clearance. When my father informed Brigadier General Strong he was taking a trip south into the desert to gather some information on the people of this area, and acquire the assistance of the Sheik, Strong told him to check on any rogue Americans down there.

And so...

A jeep was assigned to me; the friendly American mechanics who had just repaired the Chenard Walker, pointed out this was quite unusual. After this they were often very helpful in return for a few cans of bully beef, the occasional meal at the British mess at AFHQ and bottles of Johnny Walker, or bottles of Algerian Bordeaux, which I acquired every now and then. They would give me information on vehicle movement and any unusual orders from American officers.

We set off early in the morning driving further and further into the desert, where it got hotter and hotter. The jeep was proving a great vehicle; fun to drive, quite comfortable considering how basic the seats were and with the added security of four wheel drive, there was much less fear of getting stuck. The only interruptions on the first leg of the trip were the crossings of camel trains. We rolled into Ghardaia with very little petrol in the tank, dust-covered, tired and hot. We stayed at the only accommodation available. The shower was greatly appreciated. As was the tagine, couscous and the cool water from the well. The desert fleas and very uncomfortable beds were not. The next morning we filled up with petrol and drove for three hours to the well of Hassi Messaoud, where there was a supply depot with petrol, water and coffee.

The water was discovered by Massoud in 1917. According to some of the locals the first dig brought up a strange smelling thick liquid, with a strong unpleasant odor.

Hassi Massoud is the area where vast oil wells were discovered in 1956. Not strictly true! Oil was known to be there from about 1920, just never officially. I believe that Paillole had found out about this from one of his camel herd informants. Sacha, who knew Paillole and was good friends with the Sheik needed to establish a firm relationship with the local tribesmen and their leaders. Frankly I also believe my father knew about this as well.

About half an hour out of the desert town we came across an American personnel carrier heading in the opposite direction. We both stopped on the narrow desert track, creating a large cloud of dust.

'Hi,' roared a large sandy Texan sitting in the back seat smoking a cigar.

'Do you know the neighborhood well?' he asked. 'We need somewhere to stay tonight not having seen or felt a bed for two days.'

He lifted his arm and sniffed his armpit. 'We could do with a shower as well.'

Returning his rather overbearing attempt at humour, I described the rooming house in Ghardaia as having marvellous French beds and it being the best hotel between here and Algiers.

After a quick exchange of Anglo-American ruderies, I explained, this is a restricted area and asked what they were doing out here?

'We're sort of lost. We've been driving along this sandy road for the last few days, from Libya,' the Texan drawled. 'We are cat men.'

Looking them over, and not liking the arrogant attitude of this man, I replied,

'Oh of course; but you won't find many cats around here.'

According to his notes he was trying to get them to explain who had sent them, not because of the military law they were breaking; more importantly he needed to know about these American oil explorations being undertaken as he could then pass this on to the French and the British.

Laughing the Texan explained,

'We have been sent out here to look for oil and are returning with soil samples. That's what cat men do, look for oil. And I used to think it beat the hell out of fighting for a living, but after a few days in this desert I'm not sure.'

He leant forward and tapped the driver on the shoulder.

'Well nice meeting you guys. Maybe, we'll see you at the end of the war somewhere. Au revoir,'

My father's notes:

He stopped them before they drove away and informed them that it was against military regulations for them to be there without a pass. He did not explain this to me when alive. Why Not? This does not seem to be of national interest or a need for secrecy.

They could quite easily have been Germans even though all German forces in North Africa were supposedly captured or had evacuated. Rommel was known to have rogue troops to operate behind the lines. He took their names and looked over their paper work and found out they were working for Standard Oil. He informed James Slater the Texan that they all needed to report to AFHQ and to speak with Arne Ekstrom and Colonel Hazeltine.

He could have arrested them there and then and advised them that if they did not report in they would be put on a black list, be arrested and possibly shot. They all apparently understood the severity of their position and realised they might be suspected of black marketing or spying for the Germans. They agreed to report in and left. As my father says; 'With a lot less of their swagger and bravado.'

Bedaux was a well-known French Vichy business man in prison in Algiers for trading with the enemy. He also had connections with some of the American oil companies which is why there was a suspicion about oil men. Apart from that I would imagine the French would want the oil for themselves.

We arrived at the Sheik's palace, where we were shown to our rooms. Water and a large fruit bowl were brought to my room. It was strongly suggested we take a bath in the large pool set inside a beautiful Arabian courtyard. After the bath and putting on some clean Arab robes which had been laid out for us; we were offered mint tea and dates. The Sheik was out riding. On his return Sacha introduced me to Abdoul Hakim, a most hospitable host.

It was marvellous to relax in such simple yet luxurious surroundings; Persian rugs everywhere, a cool breeze in every room, and a stable of fine Arab horses.

When it came to meal time I enjoyed the couscous and lamb, but the lambs eyeballs set in a garlic sauce were a bit hard to chew on. The wine served was the very same Algerian Bordeaux from the monastery. Amusingly enough Abdoul Hakim knew of the monastery as it was housed within the walls of an old Arabian fort which had belonged to one of his uncles. He willingly agreed to inform his men about the victories of the Allied forces and any messages would be passed onto the outlying villages, the tribesmen and camel herds. I informed Hakim of the change in the French administration. He knew of the assassination of Darlan and the agreement between De Gaulle and Giraud to jointly govern. During our conversation I emphasized how Giraud was not very strong and was still very prejudiced. My story of De Gaulle was just the opposite. Hakim very quickly worked out he needed to convince his powerful friends and followers in Algeria to support the leadership of General De Gaulle. He would consider organising a small uprising to demonstrate this and call council with his equals and suggested they have an audience with the Generals. I agreed to organise this through Captain Paillole.

In the morning I agreed to go for a ride on one of Hakim's fine Arab horses, with Hakim. It took me back to when I used ride in the rough terrain of Andalucia as a child. Besides the fun of riding in the wide open and arid Algerian desert area, all this enabled me to build up a very good friendship with Hakim.

On my return to Algiers I attended a series of important meetings held by A Force. We went through the plans being made for the Sicily landings. I was informed of the deception activity consistently working in northern parts of Europe and was successfully keeping many German forces in that area. We were instructed to indicate to the Germans that southern France was to be the Allied forces' target which hopefully would divide their forces in France and keep them out of Italy. We were to play down the possibility of an invasion in Italy as much as we could without it appearing suspicious. In our deception messages we emphasised the Italian force's unwillingness to continue with the war and how quickly and easily they surrendered in the desert battles. Many of our messages gave accounts of conversations between the prisoners who were expressing great relief at having been captured and how misguided they had been by Hitler and the Nazis stomping around their country expecting them to fight or die for the fatherland and fascism.

This was all part of the work in coordinating military espionage with (PW) Psychological Warfare.

Messages of this type were starting to work very well as many of the Germans who were reading or hearing them were realising the evil elements of the German political machine which were controlling the military and the war.

The successful pincer movement coordinated between Admiral Cunnigham and Eisenhower brought the fall of Tunis, quickly and without bad losses to our forces. The Germans lost a large number of planes and ships and were starting to lose the war. Their moral dropped rapidly as a result of this defeat. It put 250,000 prisoners at our disposal, some who needed questioning; and created a great opportunity for the use of (PW) Psychological Warfare tactics. We immediately made sure the Prisoners were well treated and raised questions about why they were fighting.

This was something very hard to answer for the Italian soldiers as they were not great supporters of Mussolini. The Germans who had been under the command of Rommel also had misgivings about the war. We encouraged letters to be sent home explaining how they were being well looked after and would definitely see the end of the war. All this helped create the feeling that the war was lost. Under the circumstances did Hitler want to lose many more troops in an Allied invasion on Italian soil? Added to this we made sure the letters going home would include gossip that prisoners would pick up about some military plans to invade Sardinia.

We judged that the Germans would be inclined to believe an invasion would take place elsewhere; with the Italians about to surrender, why would the Allies invade Italy? While all this misinformation was being received by the Germans the Allied troops were preparing for the invasion of Sicily.

In early May the well-known Operation Mincemeat took place. This involved placing a dead body dressed as an officer of the Marines off the coast of southern Spain near Huelva. It was discovered by Spanish fishermen, who handed it over to the Spanish authorities who in turn handed the documents in the briefcase over to the Abwehr.

Amongst the documents was a letter from Sir Archibald Nye to General Alexander (commander in the Middle East), detailing London's wishes for a planned attack in the eastern Mediterranean with a hint that Sardinia was a possibility. The letter also implied that the Germans might think that Sicily was the target.

It has always puzzled me why my father was awarded and made a Chevalier of Legion d'Honneur and The Croix De Guerre with Palm; two of the highest medals to be awarded in France. *The Croix de Guerre with Palm was awarded for notable acts of Bravery.* The title and award of being a Chevalier Legion d'Honneur was given for acts of political importance, civil honour, and even great works of art.

When Rommel started to move his troops and Panzer tank divisions in preparation for an attack on Greece, and other German troops massed in Sardinia expecting this and the South of France to be one of the targets, we knew all the mis-information we had been sending had worked. Rommel himself was highly suspect but was forced to follow orders from Berlin and Kesselring.

The Abwehr certainly forced the idea of the Greek Invasion in a very convincing way. Admiral Canaris made sure this was understood to be one of the prime destinations of the major attack. In these notes my father refers to his realising Admiral Canaris seemed to be a major asset to the Allies intentions, whether this was intentional or not no one will ever know. Personally, the more I investigate about World War 2 espionage the more I am convinced the Abwehr under Admiral Canaris were helping the Allies.

On 10th July the Sicily landing was successfully executed with token resistance from the badly shaken 15th Panzer Division, the Hermann Goring Division and the Italian 6th Army. Unfortunately after the landing our troops dug in at the beach-head instead of pursuing retreating German forces, which enabled the latter to regroup and put up a very tough fight which was to last for a long time. If it had not been for General Patton and Montgomery forming plans amongst themselves, the invasion of Sicily and the continued advance on Italy could have been a disaster. The commander of this campaign, General Alexander was dangerously slow and dis-organised with his plans.

For the next few weeks it was our job to supply agents with irrelevant and mundane information to create as much confusion as possible. The A Force committee had decided that for the time being we were to give no definitive indication of future Allied force plans. It was agreed to hover between the two possibilities. Trying to convince the Germans the invasion of Sicily was a mere distraction with the main targets still being the South of France and/or Greece.

Clearly Italy was the next destination; our troops just had to fight across Sicily.

One evening I was invited to see operational training in the basement of our HQ. The lieutenant in charge went to great lengths to explain the details. I was visiting while volunteers were being trained to land in northern Italy and report back their findings. The lieutenant showed me a photograph of an agent; a dark-haired man, who looked convincingly Italian. I suddenly noticed his shirt; the collar had buttons at the tips.

'Who is this?' I asked casually.

'Oh him. He is half Italian and half English; scheduled to leave for northern Italy tomorrow as a matter of fact,' replied the lieutenant jovially.

'Not wearing that shirt I hope, nor with a copy of this picture as his ID,' I said, a little perturbed.

'Why not?'

'That shirt style is only made in Cambridge or America. They don't exist in Italy, so if he was caught with this photo in his papers or he is wearing that shirt he will be for the high jump.'

I was rather angry at this obvious lack of thought concerning dress and when dressing a man about to go into enemy territory.

'Oh God! I'll have to find an Italian shirt and take his photograph again. I shall be up all night.'

'I should bloody well hope so.'

I then asked to see the instructions and questionnaire being given to this poor unsuspecting agent. All the questions were about German troops and their movements. I pointed out that since this man was running a risk of being caught, questions should be added about the beaches in the area. Such questions might make the German interrogators think we could be planning to invade northern Italy. Appropriate questions were added to the papers of all agents going to Italy.

After this distressing episode I went to the bar at HQ and who should walk in but Trevor, whom I had not seen for a while. He told me he was perpetually involved with liaison and sorting out communication problems. He invited me to go to a bar on the outside of town where there were some women of a dubious nature, who, besides anything else could be a great source of information.

We left HQ late in the evening and drove slowly along the desert road, because the headlights were restricted by slit-eye covers. The Chrysler was very wide. We had been travelling for about half an hour on the road leading south of Algiers when an Arab screaming at the top of his voice sprang from the darkness on our right- hand side and ran straight into the side of the front wing. Trevor immediately slammed on the breaks causing the Arab to somersault on the bonnet and land on his feet on our left hand side. He turned around very quickly to look at the car then carried on running and screaming into the dark distance of the desert.

Trevor looked at me rather bewildered.

The episodes of the wrong shirt and the screaming Arab were by no means the only incidents serious or comic, which I vividly recall from wartime.

As I have explained the office in rue Charras was opposite a US army vehicle repair unit, which occupied the ground floor and basement of an old warehouse. The efficiency of this set up always fascinated me. They possessed racks of supplies of spare parts for every single Allied vehicle involved in the war; engine parts, suspension drive shafts, fan belts, radiators, everything. Being Americans they were quite willing to repair our motorcycles and cars in exchange for something they wanted or needed. A bottle of whisky, as I have said, or two cans of bully beef, (they hated the constant American cookhouse supply of lima beans and tinned liver), would purchase a full repair job on a motorcycle, or a transmission rebuilt on my Chenard Walker. The number of vehicles the twelve or so mechanics would get through in a day was astounding. I remember watching one chap take the motorcycle engine to pieces, replacing every old moving part with a new one. On the back wall were crates marked 1st grade, 2nd grade and 3rd grade where each old part would be deposited depending on its condition. The bike arrived at 8 am and was ready by midday looking brand new. The American arms supply to the front was as efficient but not always as effective as hope for. Thinking about that reminds me of a story that went around the British mess that helped keep British moral up.

For those of you who are not up on WW2 history in North Africa; this story is about Green American Battalion which received its battle baptism at Kasserine Heights. After a few days of fighting, with ammunition running low and machine guns starting to malfunction due to overheating, the supply chain kicked in. Whenever guns got too hot they were replaced. Fresh Arms kept arriving, and the American casualties kept mounting up. On the sixth day the losses were bad and they had to pull back. They were replaced by one of our most experienced fighting unit, the Scots Guards, who, within twenty-four hours, had forced the Germans to surrender.

Another story that springs to mind is of medical interest. The 1st Army hospital was in Algiers for a time. I used to visit a friend from Cambridge. Robert had been badly

223

wounded in the leg. The flow of ambulances to and fro was horrifying and some of the poor chaps I saw arriving- well it was bad. The smell of putrifying flesh in the ward was enough to make one want to wretch. The second time I went to see Robert he was lying on his bed,. The wound on his leg pegged open and a seething mass of maggots were wriggling around inside the bloody gash. I was repulsed and fascinated at the same time as. I knew why this was. Robert started to come out of his deep anaesthetized sleep. He was rather taken aback by the sensation and the sight of his leg. I explained how during the Civil Was a Spanish medic, Dr Trueta, had discovered that the best way to prevent gangrene setting in was to allow maggots to eat the dying flesh and bacteria. A medic confirmed my story and we were able to convince Robert to accept the treatment. In the heat many men lost limbs due to gangrene. Two weeks later Robert was limping about with both legs in tact.

Here is a story of circles, which is a reflection on how efficiently records were kept during the war. After the Sicily landings, my American Friends had some jeeps to spare, and kindly asked if I wanted one. I duly signed the papers and used the jeep for a while; then it was taken to Italy and used by SCI (Special Counter Intelligence) unit which later took it to Trieste. This vehicle had been in the thick of some very heavy fighting and had travelled extensively through southern Europe. Despite the number of flat tyres, boiled radiators and other hazards it must have suffered, ten years later, in 1954 I received a letter from the War office enquiring how I had obtained a jeep in Algiers; when I told them they informed me that it was being auctioned in Oxford and asked if I wanted to put a holding price on it. I didn't. I should have; but it is amazing that they tracked me down.

Now an ironical story, which started when I employed a Spanish driver, for nostalgic reasons. He was a refugee from the Vichy concentration camp in northern Algeria. His name was Francisco and he reminded me of the chauffeur on the mines who had taught me to drive the old Model T Ford when I was a child. Not long after he proved himself a competent driver but a lousy mechanic, he told me he was a Communist and that the Russians had approached him and asked him to work for the NKVD. Two days later I walked into the office in the British consulate, where Kenneth Younger a political warfare rep, (I think), introduced me to two Russian officers who were supposedly aiding lost Russian citizens in the desert who had been released from the Vichy concentration camp.

The Russians at this time were spying on the Allied forces to see how well they were doing and seemed to know where some of our intelligence officers where. I am convinced Philby would have passed this onto his Russian friends and this is how they knew where my father was. Although my father never seemed to put this together for himself. Why would the Russinas have been there at that exact time? And with all the coming and going it seems a very strange coincidence to me that they should have been at the Consulate at the same time as he was. I am sure they must have followed him. Maybe he knew about it but he made nothing of it.

After Sicily there was a lull in our activity and many of the small-time agents were paid off by the French. Changes in staff took place, essentially people leaving. Malcolm Muggeridge came for a spell, taking up a glorified liaison position, and graced us with his inimitable amusing and cynical manner.

My main work load as the MI6 Section V man in Algiers was now down to monitoring the French and following up minor deception messages. I was now able to concentrate working with Captain Paillole for De Gaulle. Paillole had suggested I meet De Gaulle over a dinner, in order for it not to look official. De Gaulle was a big man, gentle, quite humorous, very strong willed and a quiet man.

As the meal progressed it became clear how incredibly Nationalistic he was. He held incredible anger towards the Vichy members, and hated their treacherous acts towards the French people by collaborating with the Germans. De Gaulle had a few Jewish friends who were part of the resistance. At that time he was not anti-Semitic at all.

I had several meetings with Captain Paillole and De Gaulle, always informal and off the record. Invariably at these meetings I was asked to spread some rumours about Giraud. On several occasions I was given information which lead to the military arrest of Vichy French police officers and some prominent businessmen. The arrests were made by British forces, who, handed the men over to the French Police working with De Gaulle.

226

It was during one of these meetings I mentioned about the willingness of Abdoul Hakim to help me. I made it clear that the ruling Arab classes would support General De Gaulle over Giraud.

For those of us remaining in Algiers the front line war had moved on. The port was almost back to its picturesque and primitive self. No more jeeps, trucks, tanks, ambulances, large cases, small cases, soldiers or sailors running around. The French language was all I heard in the streets, at the bars and in the restaurants.

Doudot took me for a stroll around the souk. For a while I was sure we were being followed. Since my deep involvement with internal French affairs I was possibly watched by some Vichy French who still were on the side of Giraud.

Added to this there appeared to be some Russians around. When I informed Doudot about Russians, he confirmed they had been hovering around the area with the story they were looking for Russians from the camps; and Russians who had been conscripted by the German army and were now prisoners. Doudot, knowing the souks, took me on down many narrow streets until we ended up with a carpet trader who was obviously very well acquainted with Doudot and even seemed to know who I was. He was one of Doudot's agents. Whoever had been following us was well and truly lost.

Besides this little bit of excitement, I remember the rich smells and colours of all the spices, cinnamon, vanilla, pepper, saffron, paprika, and aniseed. With all the dark alleys and tiny doorways it was no place to get lost. Many people waved at Doudot and many of the more wealthy traders invited us to sip mint tea with them. We sat on Moorish carpets with our legs crossed and talked about the war. One trader told us he had made the same money in that year as he would normally have made in three years. Before you, the Germans would buy everything, and now the Americans buy everything, but they haggle, he said in his broken English. He had lost a lot of camels, either shot or taken by the army at a price below the value. Besides all this he was glad the Vichy French were no longer in total control as they and the Germans were very unpleasant.

In November 1943 De Gaulle had ousted Giraud and became the sole leader of the Free French in Algiers. This was the beginning of the new French Government. De Gaulle immediately placed his supporters in ministerial positions which they would hold when France was liberated.

Well this answers my question of why my father received the Croix de Guerre with Palm and Legion d'Honneur, (with a personal letter from De Gaulle). It also explains why he was not permitted to accept them publicly. He acted on his own, not under instructions, and obviously took considerable risks. He was obviously passing information from Ultra onto De Gaulle which helped him gain insight as to what Churchill and the Allies were planning and gained their full support. I feel quite proud of his action here, however underhanded it may have been. Frankly the whole spy world is underhanded, and thank goodness it is.

It was amazing how quickly the military forces moved out of the town, leaving very few signs of their occupation. The road from Algiers to Tunis, once seething with army vehicles, was now deserted apart from the occasional truck or staff car, or camel or donkey rider who would wait to be honked at before moving out of the way. The closer one got to Tunis the more conscious one became of the recent battles. Vehicles mostly German, some American and English, were strewn along the roadside having been either deserted or blown up. There were tanks, armored cars, trucks, troop carriers, guns, helmets and other war-torn metal objects all starting to rust and be covered with sand, as though time and the wind were trying to hide the destruction.

As things were so quiet, I decided this was a good time to take some leave. I visited my good friend Mr. Stephanos Souliotes, the Greek consul in Casablanca and stayed in an apartment near the beach. I swam in the turquoise Atlantic, ran along the beautiful white sandy beaches, and ate freshly caught tuna and sardines at the beach side restaurants. Stephanos offered to drive me to Fez via Rabat. The hundred kilometer road from Casablanca to Rabat was empty and very straight. The 200 kilometer journey from Rabat to Fez was also empty but not so straight or flat. Some of the bomb holes left in the road could have hidden a camel train without much difficulty. The two of us stayed in the famous Hotel Palais Jamai, and languished around the superb gardens, swimming, drinking, eating and talking idly about nothing, and about the war of course. It was very hard not to, although one often wanted to talk about something completely different.

Stephanos informed my father of the presence of Russians in Egypt who had been hovering around the Greek Government Offices. They were obviously investigating our intentions of invading Greece, as this would have helped them with their war. Again the whereabouts of the Greek exiled government officials and identities of the some of the other Greeks must have come from Philby.

Refreshed by the week of pleasurable nothingness, I was able to get back into the routine of constructing messages for the Germans with a new verve; telling them southern France and northern Italy were very strong possible invasion points. This was reinforced by the Allied occupation of Corsica, where a large contingent of French troops was garrisoned. The coastline round the Ligurian Sea became very important for deceptive purposes. Many of our agents landing in northern Italy to spy on German troop and supply movements would have leading questionnaires about gun placements, building construction, minefields and points of interest which might concern our armies if they were to invade the area from the coast. These questionnaire sheets would be left on the floor of a café frequented by Germans. Or left on the seat of a taxi, or just left lying in the street. Agents were often taken to their drop-off points along the Northern Italian coast by MI6 naval personnel in boats called feluccas.

14   My Feluccing Friend

A felucca looked like a fishing boat typical to the area it was operating in, usually the Mediterranean; fitted with very large inboard engines and Bren guns instead of fishing nets. These boats would drop off or pick up agents in enemy territory often carrying explosives and supplies, and taking tremendous risks. The amazing fact about these non-fishing boats is that, for all the risk involved and the 150 or so operations undertaken, not one was ever caught.

One evening someone walked into the office who initially I took no notice of. I was aware of this person standing by my desk but, wanting to finish my paperwork, I continued writing without looking up.

Suddenly a loud voice said,

'Ola, cono!'

I jumped up, recognising the voice of my childhood friend Fergie Dempster. He and I had shared many trips to and from England as school children. My destination had been Spain, his Tangiers.

'Good God! Fergie! What the hell are you doing here?' I asked, unable to control my laughter of delight.

'Well, I've been meaning to try some couscous and this chap told me that someone stationed in Algiers called Desmond Bristow is an expert, so I stole a fishing boat and here I am.'

Then he stood on one leg stuck his head in the air as though trying to touch the ceiling with his nose, and made the cry of the male stork when wanting food; an old ceremony we practiced when we were thirteen years old. He stopped and stamped his foot.

'Now where's the couscous?' he demanded as we embraced.

I took Fergie to my favorite couscous house arriving early so we could talk without the bells and drums that accompanied the belly dancers. Pierre, the French-Arab waiter, presented us with the usual hot scented towel and warm water to rinse our hands and faces with, and then brought over the best bottle of Bordeaux Algerian wine and took our orders. I told Fergie about the wine and the Monks which made him laugh and admire their business sense. Fergie was the first friend who I confided in my real work. That I was a Major in British Intelligence, as the uniform said, and that I was the Section V man for MI6. Mind you my life and story seemed rather dull in comparison to what Fergie was up to.

Fergie explained how he had been recruited from the navy by MI6 to become second in command of a felucca. He recounted some of his crazy adventures; of course all were near fatal. Fergie tended to be overly dramatic.

'Here Desmond read this little ode written by my skipper, Lieutenant Commander Letts; that explains who and what we are,' he said very seriously as he handed over a crumpled piece of paper and looking around making sure no one was watching us. Instead of a list of instructions or missions, the following is what I read:

Special Service

We are not just common seamen,
We are above that sort of rot,
We are hand selected he-men,
A tough and desperate lot.

If we have a thing in common,
It's that little daily tot,
We are Special Service Sailors; Special Service - What!
(Dei gratia in Slocomotion).

Our lives are fraught with danger,
And our deeds are frightfully hush,
We are awfully Lone Star Ranger,
And all that sort of gush.

We seldom see a harbor,
For us no guilt and plush,
We are Special Service Shoeflies; Special Service Slush.
(Sic transit Schickelgruber).

We explore the Riviera,
In our quaint old fashioned craft,
And cry Bueno Sera from a twin screw rubber raft,
To make them think we're friendly or simply rather daft.
We are Special Service Sleuthhounds in Special Service craft.
(Pro bono Benito).

Our engine rooms are smashing,
We can speed at nearly nine,
While the chiefs and chaps are dashing,
Valves and pistons into line.

And the whole thing's tied together,
With lengths of binder twine,
We are Special Service Speedsters; Special Service Swine,
(Floreat Meccano et Gibb).

When this bloody battle is over,
Will they send us silly suckers,
To the old white cliffs of Dover?
No: they'll very quickly chuck us.

Crying eastward ho, my hearties,
In junks or Jap feluccas,
Pukka Service Sahibs; Special Service Fuckers,
(Per ardua ad Norman).

We can spin a spiffing story,
And spin it frightfully well,
Of how we rolled to glory,
On a rough and ruddy swell.

But there are precious few among us,
Who won't roll down to hell,
We are Special Service Sinners; special Service? . . . Well,
(Requiescat in barque).

After the meal Fergie and I went to the notorious Hotel Alletti for a nightcap. The Alletti, a large modern hotel close to the port was the meeting place for many officers engaged in non-orthodox warfare. The large comfortable lounge bar, decorated with French can-can posters, witnessed some very shady conversations and dealings as well as ridiculous party behavior. This night was potentially one of those nights.

I don't like to lead the reader on, but for me to write any more about this night would mean recounting events which are somewhat personal and any man who has gone to an establishment of relatively ill repute will know; it's best for you to use your imagination as to what we did. We drank a bit, and had a lot of fun.

Frankly, Fergie and my father had a very good time with some very friendly women, and I am quite sure along with his affair, this was not the only time he would be in the company of women. My father genuinely liked the company of women.

15   Russian Agents in Lisbon

As the Allied armies advanced slowly northward through Italy, they captured the Adriatic port of Bari where an SCI unit was set up and required staff.

I was in my office packing up files and writing to my wife and parents when the telephone rang.

'Major Bristow please.'

I recognized the voice of Captain Monday, the port security officer in Algiers.

'Speaking. How can I help you, Monday?'

'I was wandering if you knew anything about two signals corporals who have just reported to me, having just arrived with the convoy from Gib?'

Monday sounded rather concerned.

'My guess is they should be on their way to Bari, we need signals operators there. Put them back on the convoy headed for Bari. Don't worry, I'll take responsibility.'

'Desmond, the convoy set sail about five minutes ago.'

He radioed the escort convoy commander who instructed a destroyer to slow down and the two signalers boarded safely.

That same afternoon I received a ZZ telegram:

"TAPWATER, PLEASE MEET SIGNALS CORPORALS ARRIVING BY CONVOY NO 37 AND FORWARD TO BARI."

My reply read:

"LONDON, CORPORALS ALREADY ON THEIR WAY. PRESUME YOU SENT TELEGRAM BY SLOW BOAT AND THE CORPORALS BY WIRELESS. TAPWATER."

I was reprimanded for this by our new man handling administration of Section V in London, Major Roland Adams, a lawyer by trade with no sense of humor. In all actuality he had sent the telegram too late; when I reported this back to Cowgill, Adams was seriously reprimanded. This mistake could have had disastrous consequences all round. Consequently his approach to me was far more professional after that.

The end of 1943 and beginning of 1944 was a dull time from a work point of view. AFHQ was disbanded; Trevor left in early '44. The French friends went back to their normal routine, and I kept a spattering of liaison going, sending messages every now and again. I would spend evenings with Paillole, Doudot and Germain. We would take trips to various parts of Algeria. They now explained to me how complex the problem with the Vichy French had been.

In February 1944 I received a ZZ telegram instructing me to pack a bag with civilian clothes and to board the next DC3 bound for Lisbon, where I would receive further instructions from Charles DeSalis, the head of Section V, Lisbon.

Lisbon remained blissfully unaffected by the war compared to other European cities. I stayed in a little Victorian hotel called the Europa.

Before my arrival I had established that I was to pretend to be a tourist, and that the work was of a very clandestine nature. This was the closest I ever came to being James Bond. Although, or maybe because it was just an act, I enjoyed being a tourist for a few hours. I asked the concierge about the gambling at the casino in Estoril, fishing trips, the museums and other local tourist attractions, making sure the policeman sitting in the corner reading a newspaper heard my loud enquiries. The only evidence in Lisbon of stressed circumstances was the shamefully obvious policing by the over-zealous Germanophile Portuguese secret police, the Policia International do Defensa do Estado (PIDE). There seemed to be a member in most hotel lobbies, and certainly a large number had been hanging around the airport.

That first evening I toured several hotel bars to try and pick up on the current topic of conversation on Lisbon. As far as I could tell it consisted of the news reports of the Allied advance through Italy, and how well the Germans were fighting back. There was a definite Germanic slant to the reports received by the Portuguese people. After leaning on four or five bars and chatting with several bartenders I went back to the hotel to dinner and bed.

The following day I made some loud enquiries about the location of the British passport control office saying I had to renew my visa. The concierge very kindly drew me a map which I followed, occasionally stopping to ask someone to confirm my directions, for the benefit of the secret police who were following me. To have tried to lose them would have been pointless and would have created too much suspicion.

I reported to Charles DeSalis at the passport control office in Rua da Emenda. Charles told me of several agents who were in touch with the Abwehr, and how I could get in touch with their controllers. One occasionally visited the office under the disguise of being involved with shipping. Another, Rita Windsor, was an experienced operator in the Firm working at the Embassy as a personnel assistant.

'As you know, Desmond,' said DeSalis.

'But I don't know,' I replied.

DeSalis continued,

'Well there is a much more pressing engagement for you here in Lisbon. MI5 have lent us and asked us to look after a long standing agent of theirs who is due to arrive in the next few days. This chap is a German expert, who I understand fought for the Germans during the First World War and has worked for '5' for some time. He is on his way to make contact with some old pal of his, a member of the anti-Nazi group, so it seems. His name, not the German's but the agent's, is Ustinov and you are to make sure his back is covered and everything runs smoothly. It's very hush-hush so watch out for the PIDE; they are devil.'

Charles went on to explain that I had a secretary at my disposal. My God, what luxury, thought I. Mrs. Jenkins was an American volunteer, the minister's wife no less, who obviously enjoyed being part of the cloak and dagger department and was extremely efficient. She will inform you of Ustinov's arrival, said Charles.

On leaving the office I watched for followers and footed my way around Lisbon to familiarise myself with streets, bars, hotels and restaurants further away from my hotel. It was indeed great fun playing the tourist and playing spy, looking in shop windows, admiring the architecture, taking bus rides, train trips and one short boat trip up the river.

On the third morning the hotel receptionist gave me my train reservation to Estoril, and a note from Mrs. Jenkins:

"Your friend arrives at Hotel Avenida Palace at 6.30 this evening. Table for two reserved at his hotel restaurant in your name."

After breakfast I set off to the gambling casino of wartime Europe.

The casino at Estoril was grand, with red velvet curtains and sparkling chandeliers everywhere. One of the English croupiers was very helpful in showing me around. After getting his name and address and chatting about clients and the problem of the English nannies left behind by their employers at the outbreak of the war, he showed me the short cut to the bar where Garbo had met Gene Risso Gill. I ate a seafood lunch, chatted up a couple of abandoned English nannies and continued to behave like a tourist for a few hours before the train took me back to my Lisbon hotel. There I put on my best clothes caught the tram down the hill to the centre of Lisbon and walked into the Palace Hotel restaurant to meet this Russian-German MI5 agent whom I was to help rendezvous with a German.

A gentleman of forty-five or so, with greying hair, a smiling face and an interesting air about him, was already sitting at our table. As I approached he stood up and held out his hand. 'Iona von Ustinov'.

We made polite conversation about his trip to Lisbon and drank a glass or two of vihno verde. Ustinov had already ordered a lobster for both of us. I was glad MI5 were paying and that Iona von Ustinov's visit warranted first-class treatment.

'Klop,' he said.

'Beg your pardon?'

'My friends call me Klop…. I like horses.'

'My friends call me Derry, short for Desmond.'

We laughed and talked and I really enjoyed our first meeting. He told me about his time in the German cavalry during the First World War and how in the early thirties, working as the German press attaché he became an English spy, and then defected. He was a fascinating and amusing man with adventure and culture running through his veins. We arranged to meet the next day, by the river.

After a good night's sleep and hearty breakfast, I caught the tram to our morning rendezvous. With the noise of the boats and traffic, Klop and I could talk freely.

'I was an active member of the anti-Nazi group before I became English, and I'm here to meet an old friend who is involved with some German officials who want to get rid of the Nazis and Hitler,' he told me. 'Apparently there are one or two groups but none dare to talk to the other for fear of being betrayed to those lovely Gestapo.'

Klop stopped walking and looked straight up into my face.

'For obvious reasons I shall not tell you his name.'

We continued walking.

'Thank you, I'd rather not know more than I have to.'

This time I stopped and looked around. Sure enough there was a PIDE standing by the tram stop, where the ferry terminal was.

'I don't how often you have been to Lisbon,' I leant on the back of a wrought iron bench, 'but the police are everywhere. I have heard they are quite pro-German. My feeling is they are cautious, and don't want trouble. Even so we must be careful.'

'Yes, I was briefed about the police here before I left. It is half the reason why 5 chose Lisbon, because if they have any information about me or about the man I am supposed to be meeting with, they hopefully will assume it is to do with working for the Germans.' Klop laughed.

We continued talking, walking and watching the boats and the horse buggies. We lunched at a table on the pavement, underneath a beautiful old elm tree, then set off walking again, this time up the hill to the Europa.

The famous Lisbon trams were rattling along the very wide main boulevard, O'Rossio, with its lovely wrought iron baroque street lamps on pedestrian islands. We were in no hurry and continued exchanging stories about ourselves and our families. We loitered on one of the islands, tram wheels hammering over the tram tracks on either side. Klop, who was wearing a long Russian astrakhan coat and a wide brimmed black hat, offered me one of his gold tipped Sobranie Black Russian cigarettes. Accepting one, I brought out my lighter and put the flame to his cigarette then my own. The wind blew the flame out a couple of times, and we started laughing, when suddenly two hands grabbed us by the shoulders.

'Senor, please show me the license for your lighter,' demanded a very serious looking PIDE officer, in Portuguese. I shrugged my shoulders, Klop kept quiet.

The other policeman looked hard at Klop's coat and hat, and at our cigarettes. He informed us, in a small policeman's arrogant fashion, of Portugal's law that a person needs to have a license for a cigarette lighter. We found this rather amusing, but could not present a license.

'Passports please, senores; you are obviously foreign.'

Klop and I looked at each other not quite able to comprehend the situation. After examining our passports, the older policeman took me aside, as I had been the one to break the law.

'Desmond Bristow, you are English, of Russian descent, are you not?'

Meanwhile the other officer cross-questioned Klop, who indeed was of Russian descent. They clearly thought they had caught some big fish spies which inflated their ego further. Lisbon during this time was full of spies, hence they came to their conclusion of us being soviet agents?

This was not a good situation to be in. To avoid going to jail we would have to prove our identity, and therefore our connection with the British Embassy. I started to protest very loudly as they guided us towards the police station. Eventually one of them asked which hotel I was staying at. When I told them they escorted us very politely to the Europa where the receptionist confirmed that I was British, and that in fact the Embassy had reserved my room. Not totally convinced the younger more zealous, policeman insisted we all go to the British Embassy.

Finally satisfied of our legitimacy the two officers went on their way, but from that moment on we were never left alone; PIDE eyes followed us everywhere in a very obvious fashion.

Klop and I decided it would be safer and easier to deal with this problem if we moved to Estoril, trains being an easy form of transport to lose a tail on. We informed DeSalis of our run in with the police. He laughed, and apologized for not informing us of this ridiculous law, which existed to encourage people to use matches and therefore support the match industry. DeSalis agreed that Estoril was a good idea and gave us the use of his Embassy car. This would reinforce the fact we were British. The car, a black Citroen, was identical to the cars used by the secret police.

Luckily the croupier I had met at the casino rented out a spare apartment; it was ideal, with two bedrooms overlooking some pine trees on the cliffs above the beach. From the lounge window we could see the access road and the casino, making it easy to spot the PIDE.

For two days the police watched and followed us in a very conspicuous manner. Klop and I made a joke of it, and resigned ourselves to playing hide and seek. This suited us for the time being, since the presence of the PIDE would keep the Germans away from us. Klop tended to stay around Estoril, (secretly gambling, I think), while I made daily trips to Lisbon and around the general area, and tested out the resilience of our shadows.

On the third day it appeared that they had become fed up with watching Klop win or lose, and followed me doing my tourist impression. I would talk about the war and how good it was to have some leave. In the evenings we would go to the town centre and hang around the cafes. No one appeared to be following us, but just to be sure we never stayed in one place for too long. Sometimes I would walk on ahead while Klop sat hidden behind a café window and watch for a follower to appear, or I would stand in the shadow of a tree or doorway, while Klop crossed the road; we did not see any secret policeman or other followers of any kind. Thinking about it now we had a lot of fun and I certainly learnt a lot from Iona von Ustinov in the techniques needed to lose a tail and when you wanted to have them find you.

As time went by the absence of followers bothered Klop. He always wanted to know where they were. Maybe they had lost interest.

Klop's first rendezvous was due in four hours.

As I parked the car I noticed the red of a reflector shining from a car up in the pine trees. I warned Klop. At that moment their headlights flashed, obviously signaling another watcher. We rushed up the stairs and into the lounge to watch the black Citroen roll down the road without its lights on. We went out to inspect the parking space they had used. Klop and I went for a walk, making sure our tail was in site as we went into the casino. They waited outside; I put Klop's coat and hat on while Klop slipped out of a back door he knew of.

I walked home on my own with one of the tails while the other went inside the Casino.

Klop returned at 3.00 am.

He did not have another rendezvous for a few days so we agreed to repeat our movements for the following three nights. I parked the car they flashed their headlights, we rushed into the apartment, lightless they'd cruise down the hill, we went for a walk. What fun they were having, and what hilarity we found in the situation. The last night before Klop's rendezvous was nerve-racking. We sat up and made our plans, repeating the details to each other. It was our hope and the hope of MI5 that this rendezvous might bring the war to an earlier end than could possibly happen without inside help from this German anti-Nazi group. Whether this was the same group which tried to blow Hitler up or not, I am not sure; although I feel sure they must have been connected in some way.

To this day I do not believe that my father did not know the identity of the person or people Klop was meeting. When I think of him spending time with someone in those circumstances why would my father not know? There is no other reference to this in his papers. It seems probable they were acquaintances of Klop's forma German friends from the First World War, when he had worked for the German secret serice. They were now working on an agreement to help rid the world of Hitler. Or Klop was there to check on Tricycle's connections? (Tricycle being the double agent who worked for MI5 and the Abwehr in Lisbon).

Also there was talk about the mistress of a German General who was possibly a friend of Klop's. Any way my father did not reveal any more in his private notes. He clearly enjoyed his little escapade in Lisbon.

We spent the morning in the semi-circular arena of seats overlooking the Atlantic just below along from Estoril station. After two hours of chatting and reading, two gentleman seated themselves to the left and down from us. About five minutes later, two more similar looking gentleman arrived and sat to the right and down from us. The last two arrivals Klop and I had seen hanging around outside the station early in the morning. As I stood up to leave one from each pair got up to follow me. I went to the Tamaris restaurant just next to the station and surveyed the men's room window and the back entrance hoping my followers thought I was just peeing. After twenty minutes, as agreed, Klop and I met in the front of the entrance of the restaurant went in and ordered our meal. Five minutes later a young nervous chap about nineteen years of age, sat at a table near the door and ordered lunch. He had obviously been sent in by the four police who must have realised we knew who they were,. I then went out, as if to the toilet in fact I just checked out the rear exit. On my return to the table Klop pointed out the four policemen sitting in the shade of a tree across the road.

Having investigated the layout earlier I informed Klop of where to go.

'When you go down to the loo, there is a small door next to the broom cupboard that leads to the back garden. At the end of the path is a wrought-iron gate which opens onto the side alley of the station adjacent to platform 3, there take the 1.15 to Lisbon.'

Pretending to have said something funny, I laughed at my own joke; Klop followed my lead. He had an exceptionally good false laugh. While laughing he got up and asked the waiter for directions to the toilet.

I sat quietly sipping my coffee and looking around as if expecting Klop to return. At last I heard the Lisbon train-whistle blow as it puffed out of the station. Klop was on it; otherwise he would have been back by now. I paid the bill, left the table and sauntered out. The young man hurriedly called the waiter. About a minute later he rushed out of the restaurant to find me sitting in the shade of a tamarind tree reading a newspaper while wearing Klop's hat, which he had left at the table. The young man looked at me; I smiled at him and nodded. Poor chap; he looked very annoyed and went rushing off, presumably to find the four others.

I slowly wandered up the hill to our apartment. There was another follower! As I opened the front door the black Citroen appeared, picked up the follower and drove off.

Late that afternoon I sat in the arena to watch the sunset and the fishing boats coming in with their day's catch. I wondered how Klop's meeting was going. Klop did not return until early the next morning, nothing was said about his endeavor other than that it was a good meeting.

The black Citroen and our followers lost interest after this, enabling Klop to have two more meetings without the same harassment or excitement. My watchdog work mostly consisted of sitting around waiting.

At the end of March, Klop and I said farewell. It was difficult for me to implement any deception from Lisbon than was already being sent out via Tricycle. I did spread stories confirming the rumours I had been sending from Algiers; for instance, that the south of France would be a landing place for combined French and US forces coming in part from Corsica and in part from north Africa. The other supportive deception story the Germans received from our agents in Lisbon was that since the Normandy beaches were too well protected the main Allied attack location being discussed, was in all probability Calais and the beaches thereabouts.

It is important to note that the two agents in Lisbon were reporting directly to their German controllers, which meant that Allied intentions became a subject of normal conversation between the controller and agent. The stories needed to be vague since there was no reason for anyone in Lisbon to have particularly good information. It had to be a balancing trick, all of which had to support the deception messages being transmitted by Garbo.

I met with Gene Risso Gill, unfortunately not very often, as it was too dangerous for me to be seen with this well-known British agent. It was at this time that he told me about his meetings with Garbo. I left a few stories with him and Charles DeSalis to pass to the double agents at various dates. At the end of April 1944 I returned to Algiers.

By early May I was back in routine work of sending off deception messages to keep the confusion amongst the Germans. Italy was proving to be a tough battle with the well dug-in German troops fighting very hard. For a short period Algiers was again busy with troop and shipping movement as supplies and reinforcements had to be sent to the slowly advancing Allies. Amongst the reinforcements preparing to leave for Italy were American and French troops being gathered for the real landing in Corsica, to take place in August. Now that this area was the real target for landing, our deceptive messages contained information to mislead the Germans into believing that Genoa would be our next troop landing area. Fortunately the Germans fell for it, and moved troops towards the Genoa area. I remember sending one message about Genoa via Genoa on the 2nd June, mentioning the possibility of a major offensive near Calais on 6th June, which was in fact D Day. This message was sent to add to the German's confusion, and also to make it seem as though Gilbert was receiving information of a very important nature from time to time.

For obvious reasons, we in Algiers were not told very much about the specifics of the D Day landings. Doudot and I often discussed possible dates and places; we actually thought the offensive would take place sooner that it did.

It is clear from his private notes that my father continued to support General De Gaulle. In one part he made it clear in one of his messages sent to H.Q. how essential it was for Churchill to support De Gaulle and The Free

French by indicating how the political situation in North Africa was so much more settled since the collapse of the Vichy. There is also a reference where during one of his meetings with Captain Paillole he informed him of his encounter with American oil prospectors near Hassi Massoud.

During some of our discussions Ricardo Sicre joined in on our meetings. He was being trained by OSS to drop behind the German lines in France with his radio operator, Betty Lucier. He also thought the landings would be earlier, as his departure for France was set for 12th May. I had last seen Ricardo when he had walked into my office in the late spring of 1943, filthy dirty. He had hitch-hiked from Marrakesh to Algiers, and the official in the OSS office would not believe who he was; unable to have Tangiers confirm his identity, Ricardo found me. I knew him from a brief trip I had made to Morocco shortly after I had arrived in North Africa. Betty Lucier, who became his wife after their stint in France, had been flying wrecked Wellington bombers and other planes to repair yards in Britain. It was a nice surprise to them again and between the 5th and 12th May we spent a lot of time together. We truly thought we would never see each other again.

Why does my father not mention his brief trip to Morocco in more detail? His meeting Ricardo Sicre and this trip could well have been part of the cover up of the assassination of Admiral Darlan. Or an investigative trip checking on some of the French he had started working with. It was obviously a covert trip of some kind.

6th June: D Day. Of course we all know this now, but at the time we did not know how successful it had been. As the Allies slowly struggled through France and Italy we were kept busy throwing as much confusion at the Germans as possible. When the south of France was successfully invaded in August, deception work for the Allies and the French became rather pointless so I cleared my office and said goodbye to my French and Arab friends.

In actuality what occurred was Captain Paillole, Captain Germain and Captain Doudot invited my father out for his last night small party. They picked him up from his apartment and took him to a very exclusive restaurant. They were led through to the back by the maître d'. A curtain opened to reveal General De Gaulle with two other gentlemen. My father was a guest of honour. His notes do not tell me anymore of real interest other than he was thanked for his assistance against the Germans and against the Vichy and that his help would not be forgotten. This is confirmation that my father did help General De Gaulle and his supporters which may have been dangerous to him in more ways than one. This confirms why De Gaulle and others felt he deserved the Croix de Guerre with Palm and the Legion d'Honneur.

There were four of us in the steel seats of the DC 3, smoking, looking at each other and unable to talk above the noise of the revving engines. The three others looked quite relaxed and appeared to be as comfortable as one could be. I was very nervous as the captain had warned us that turbulence over the Atlas Mountains would be bad due to a storm. I was especially nervous, as my right hand clutched a bag containing special intelligence military consignment documents.

Considering all the situations my father had been involved in during his time in Algiers why would he be nervous about the bag? The flying I know about; he always hated flying. Unless he had agreed to do something with the bag I am not sure why he would be so nervous, after all he had it attached to his wrist and the flight had a short stop in Marrakech en-route to the U.K. and all the other passengers were military personnel of one kind or another.

No sooner were we in the air when we hit some very bad turbulence. We passengers were jolted around and I must have turned several shades of green. The storm was worse than the captain had anticipated and the route to Oran took us over the eastern end of the mountains, a bumpy ride under normal circumstances. On this occasion the air currents were so bad the plane lurched and dropped like a stone. Suddenly one engine failed; and despite not being very religious, I will admit, I started to pray. For half an hour or more I quite expected to die. Thanks to the cool head and skill of the young American pilot the plane stayed in the air until he landed us safely at our first destination of Oran.

As I was leaving the plane, a US sergeant suggested it might be safer to leave the bag under my seat as the airport canteen was very busy and it might be a while until the engine was fixed. The plane will be locked, he assured me.

There were after all other documents staying on board, and there was a guard.

I telephoned John Fisher, who was meeting me at Marrakesh. The Americans had already informed him of the engine trouble and that my arrival could be delayed by up to three hours. About an hour later, the plane was ready. I stepped on board and headed to my seat.

'This is not the same plane!' I exclaimed, panic creeping into my blood.

'What do you mean, sir?' asked the sergeant, as I kept looking around, not wanting to believe what my eyes were telling me.

'The bag, where is my bloody bag?' I demanded.

The pilot casually informed me that the bag had been put onto a RAF plane flying direct to London. My heart sank. To lose any bag was bad; but this bag! I would rather have lost my life.

Did my father lose the bag? Or was this deliberate? Did he want the Americans to see what was in the bag? Maybe. He was closer to Arne Ekstrom of OSS than he has led me to believe. This I will never know.

On the flight to Marrakesh my fingernails disappeared. I smoked feverishly, prayed, feared and walked up and down the very empty and now stable airplane. What was to be done? If I had only stayed on the plane; if only I had taken the bag with me, my mind kept nagging away.

This does not seem likely. My father was not some junior officer. His cover was as a Major in British Intelligence; when he was the head of MI6 in this section of North Africa. Added to which, what information could have been so important at this stage. Apart from revealing the oil interests in Algiers, or information concerning General De Gaulle and the Free French political situation, what could have been so important?

John Fisher was waiting at the airport; he consoled me as much as possible, but agreed that to trace a missing bag was difficult; even so, knowing I needed comfort and that I was leaving that evening, he undertook the task. He informed London of my dilemma and the probable destination of the bag, since the only RAF plane to have left Oran that day was arriving at Debden air base in Essex.

I left Marrakesh at dusk. The flight to England was smooth and long, and in no way helped appease my worry.

On arrival at Prestwick airport at 9 am I telephoned the office and spoke with Kim, who suggested I go home and report back two days later. He made me feel less worried and did not seem overly concerned about the lost bag. It was good to talk to him, and to be back on British soil, despite everything.

Maybe Kim Philby organised for the bag to be taken off the plane. He would certainly have known my father was carrying it. He would also have access to the names of the duty officers on the plane and on the ground at Oran airfield. Maybe some Russians were there. My father

would not have suspected anything like that. At least I
hope he did not. Perhaps he knew everything all too well?
This is how suspicious of my father I have become.

Who was he really?

I caught the train and headed home; at least I would see
Betty again at the cottage in the country. The English
countryside looked so peaceful as I walked down the
twisty lane from the station. Birds sang in the trees, the
green lush grass swayed in the gentle breeze, smelling
marvelously fresh after a light shower of rain. No more
palm trees and camels. Seeing Betty again was quite
simply wonderful. Her hazel eyes shone and her wavy
brown hair glistened in the sun as she called Rosanne, who
was now two and a half years old. Betty had shown
Rosanne photographs of me in uniform and when she
came waddling round the garden wall she put out her arms
and yelled 'Dad-da!' Gosh, how quickly children grow
when one does not see them for a long time. I think it must
have taken me a while to realise I was home and that the
two previous years had not been some kind of a dream.
The contrast from rushing around the desert sands of
North Africa and the copious amounts of food in the
restaurants and at AFHQ to being back in a domestic
surrounding and in a country suffering from food rations
was a bit of a shock.

Betty had become very strong having continued her work
with the Land Army and was now a well-established
member of that very efficient agricultural unit. She had
two Italian prisoners of war working under her who lived

257

in the cottage at the end of the road; they seemed very happy and willing, if not too good at English. For two days I wandered around getting in the way making lots of suggestions as to how they could improve the farming system, which of course was already working perfectly and generally enjoying myself and being a nuisance. I was able to forget about lost bags, double agents, secret agents, any kind of agent. The war and North Africa seemed so far removed from this simple life.

Those two days went by very quickly. I walked up to the phone box on Kerswell Green and rang the office.

'Philby, please.' I waited for what seemed ages while the receptionist put me through.

'K-K-Kim Philby here,' the familiar stutter. 'Oh! Desmond, you will be g-g-glad to hear that the bag turned up yesterday.' I breathed a sigh of relief. 'I'm s-s-sure you need two more days off; report here on Friday morning. See you.'

I was about to hang up when I heard him yelling,

'Desmond! Don't forget that the office is now in Ryder Street just behind the renowned J-J-Jermyn Street and no longer at S-S-St Albans. Bye.'

The bombing must have stopped, I thought.

I rushed out of the call box and ran all the way back to the cottage to tell Betty the good news. Two more days to relax and enjoy being with my family. Oh, what marvelous medicine.

I have to wonder if he really felt this overjoyed and happy at the prospect of being home. Was being home really that exciting? It all seems too gushy to me. My father always had these rather phoney moments of affection, yet was quite distant, certainly as I knew him.

16   London: The Cold War Begins

The Ryder Street office was totally different from St Albans. For a start the atmosphere was quite obviously much more relaxed. The early days of developing filing systems, creating deception and undermining the strength of the German infiltration in neutral countries was over. Espionage work had become a matter of monitoring movement and helping agents behind the ever decreasing German lines.

I shared an office with Martin Lloyd who was MI6's representative on the XX committee. Robin Campbell, a commando who had been badly wounded during the daring raid on Rommel's HQ in 1942, also shared the office; what he was doing I'm not quite sure. I found out from him that an old school friend had been killed and that another, D. G .Gardner had won the Victoria Cross.

My job was to read over ISOS reports with information about France and the French people as the Germans retreated. Intermittently I attended XX committee meetings and LCS (London Control Section) meetings, now controlled very effectively by Lieutenant Colonel Noel Wild whom I knew from Algiers. He seemed to appreciate the tightrope Bobby, Trevor and I had walked in the early days of the Algerian campaign, when we had formed our relationship with the French. The committee sessions felt more like business meetings and were very informative and open, discussing the details of how various operations had worked. We even discussed whether or not to continue deception. The success of operation Overlord's deception had not apparently gone to anyone's head; perhaps we were blasé, or perhaps we all felt as though the hardest part of our work was over. Despite all the questions, deception work was to continue as a result of the V1 bombs dropping on London.

During the week I shared a flat with Donald Darling again, this time in Ebury Street. We of course had fun, talking about the good old days in Gibraltar and listening to jazz and wondering what had happened to Brian. Ebury Street was also quite dangerous and perhaps the closest I had been to being blown up during the whole of the war. Three nights after I had moved into the spare room, I was sitting up in bed reading when Donald appeared in the doorway to say goodnight. At that very second a V1 bomb landed about a hundred yards away. The flash created a halo of lights all around Donald's plump form.

'Good God, death appeareth,' I said.

At that moment Donald was pushed against the wall, my bed shook and moved around the floor, the loud blast temporarily deafened us. It broke windows, cracked the walls and made powdered plaster fall from the ceiling. Donald shook the dust off his terrified head, and turned into the hallway, stumbling over fallen plaster. He stopped and said quietly,

'I'm having a drink. Can I get you one?' I could not help but burst out laughing, as he stumbled to the sitting room, dust everywhere.

Not long after this Donald came back very late, and upset. He found out the two Russians who had stayed with us in Gibraltar had been turned over to the Russian authorities, and had been returned to Russia where they had most probably been shot. This was depressing when you think of what they had gone through to get back. The war was a very strange experience, emotionally more so than physically.

I was able to introduce him to many of my friends such as Kim Philby, Tommy Harris and Trevor Wilson. In late August the German V1 launching pads at Arras were taken over by the Allies, so I looked for a flat or house around London. A friend's mother owned a house in Kew, just in front of the gates to the gardens; Betty, Rosanne, Betty's mother and I moved in.

That September was a beautiful month; the autumn colours seemed especially spectacular. There were no bombs, I was around the family and old friends, I started rowing on the river again; it was good to be back in England.

Having said that, at about 2 am early in October, one of the first V2 bombs landed alongside the Great Western Road, damaging the Firestone Rubber Company's spectacular factory. This was worrying from my family's point of view. For a few days we debated whether they should return to the country, but my confidence in our department's deceptive abilities convinced me all would be well.

I was attending meetings dealing with the flying bomb problem. The XX committee had several consultations with scientists and proposed they report the place of landing to the Germans, except these reports would not give the true landing places. The newspapers and radio news would put out false reports to the British public. We sent reports to the Germans via our double agents that indicated the bombs were going too far west, or north, and gradually the bombs started landing in harmless places like Romney Marsh.

This was not quite as straightforward as it sounds. Due to the risk of bombs going astray, we had to argue with borough councils, and have meetings with MPs wanting to protect their own constituents. Plans also had to be submitted to the Ministry of Production, essentially in charge of arms and work areas, and the Home Secretary, Herbert Morrison, who was very concerned about unnecessary loss of life. Despite objections full authority was given to the XX committee to go ahead. Political objections continued, but there was a directive that the north-west of London be protected as much as possible.

Early reports given by Garbo convinced the very accurate German launchers to shorten their range; this persuaded the skeptics that deception worked, even in this situation. The success of the D Day landings was largely due to Garbo, (Juan Pujol and Tommy Harris), and now the successful deceptive messages from Garbo regarding the V bombs was working also. Many V Bombs missed their targets; as a result they landed causing very little serious damage. Tommy arranged to have Juan Pujol arrested. A ruse to make the Germans think he had been caught spying on the V bomb areas. This convinced the Germans of the authenticity of this agent to such an extent he was awarded the Iron Cross.

In October 1944 I was posted to Paris. This posting coincided with Dick White's appointment as head of a joint intelligence set-up housed in Baron de Rothschild's mansion in the Versailles area. My particular role was to control the dissemination of ISOS to the various SCI units and to decide how much information any given agent should have. The nearer to the front line, the less they received. By the same token, German stay behind agents, left by the Gestapo mostly, had to be rounded up, turned and used, or simply arrested. The SCI unit commanders had to be given their names and identities where possible and this information was then shown by ISOS so that field security could find them. With the French who had worked with the Gestapo, even those forced to, we had to be very careful as the local French would find ways of executing them. This we did not want as we wanted to use them.

There was some resistance to my passing ISOS information to Ricardo Sicre who, after his brave and successful undercover job in southern France, had become a US SCI man. Despite the resistance I decided it was essential for him to have the benefit of any ISOS information pertinent to his area, and sent it to him.

It was the coldest winter I have ever had to sustain, and with only one log fire in an enormous mansion it was no fun.

Luckily I was recalled to head office in London in February 1945. I say luckily, but as I drew up to the dock at Dieppe and saw the motor torpedo boat and the condition of the weather I did not feel so lucky. The rough sea and gale-force winds, the rain, and a boat that started to flood from the moment we were in the open sea, made me so terribly seasick that the possibility of drowning was not as such an unpleasant thought.

The end of the war was clearly approaching. The office sensed this and an air of relaxation wafted through the narrow corridors of Ryder Street and we started to look for distracting pastimes. Beer being in short supply, some of us deployed our espionage expertise in a serious endeavor. Within half an hour of briefing, Tom and Bertie had learnt how to find out which pub had been supplied with beer in the morning: the secret was to spy on Watney's drays (the horse drawn carts which carried the kegs around London); they appeared more frequently than Whitbread's. Tom, I may say, became the best beer wagon spy in London town. I developed counter-espionage and deception channels to inform falsely those we wanted to direct to the pubs that had not received a delivery.

On leave I would spend my time rowing at London Rowing Club and walking around Kew gardens with Betty and my daughter, which made the war seem as though it had never really happened. We bought our first house; a pretty, lead-windowed house in a cul-de-sac on Strawberry Hill, in Twickenham. We made several trips from Kew to Twickenham in Betty's Ford 8, carrying our bits and pieces of furniture. Betty had to be somewhat careful since she was expecting our second child in June.

In April 1945, Section V became section IX, and many of us hoped Felix Cowgill would continue to overlord the post war counter espionage department within SIS. None of us, except perhaps Tim Milne, appreciated how Kim Philby was manipulating Colonel Vivian, the deputy head of MI6. When Felix was posted to military government in Germany, we all believed it was a temporary position and he would return to take up his rightful post shortly. This was not to be the case and his masterly wartime role, especially in the protection of ISOS, went almost unrecognized by the authorities. Philby took over as head of section IX.

The end of the war, in May, brought about a different requirement for the secret services and lessened the need to have so many invisible people within its visible walls. Some of us were invited to stay on. I willingly accepted the invitation and soon found myself assisting the Iberian G officer, Hamilton Stokes, whose last post had been as the head of station in Madrid. We dealt with Iberian affairs and were in charge of receiving and distributing reports from stations abroad and administering their needs.

In September 1945, Philby made a trip to our station in Istanbul to interrogate a Soviet Union defector who supposedly had names of three British people working for the Russians. By the time Philby arrived the man in question had been picked up by the KGB (NKVD) and returned to Moscow. I suspect he was executed.

Reading about Marxism, and many books and papers on the subject of Communism and the increasing threat from Russia, took up a lot of time. A real war had just ended and something which became known as a cold war was beginning. Many changes of personnel took place, many associates left, and those of us who stayed on became the butt of Malcolm Muggeridge, who described us in somewhat scathing terms in his humorous and highly cynical book Tread Softly, for You Tread upon My Jokes.

Most of us thought it not only a very worthwhile job but very interesting and of national importance at the time. The in-tray was still being filled with aspects of cleaning up Europe after the war. But the coming challenge was Soviet Russia, as its spying branches became the post-war enemy.

Physical sabotage was not part of the USSR's program. Russia resorted to a campaign of upsetting the working capacity of the West. It spread feelings of discontent amongst Western workforces, provoking strikes even if it meant funding certain elements in the trade unions, such as shop stewards, who were potentially susceptible to the 'preachings' of the Communist way.

Without a clearly defined program either politically or industrially it was very hard to grasp the situation and deal with the problem. Britain, a declining world power, entered a long period of apathy when fear was able to get hold. I might add that Britain is still reeling from the effects of that time, economically.

Shortly after I joined Hamilton Stokes, the department received a letter from Madrid suggesting we visit Senor Valverde Gill, who was staying at the Piccadilly Hotel. Hamilton Stokes told me Gill had been our vice consul, or honorary consul in Zaragoza.

On my asking why Valverde Gill was in the U.K. Stokes, informed me how Senor Gill had been acting consul in Zaragoza for us, and had given us a lot of help. At the end of 1941 a priest from one of the local churches reported that the Germans were about to dispatch a mass of propaganda wrapped up in Catholic tracts on the vessel SS Cabo de Hornos, bound for Latin America. Senor Gill took a risk and broke the normal lines of communication to get the information to us directly. As a result, Section V had the ship intercepted in Bermuda and the documents were found and confiscated.

This broke a small German ring in Spain and embarrassed the Spanish Church. Subsequent enquiries made by the Spanish police, rather pro-German in that area, had exposed Senor Gill and owing to, I assume, pressure from the High Church, the Spanish Government labeled him persona non grata and gave him five days to leave Spain or be arrested. 'We brought him over to London where he has been ever since, and he is now at the Piccadilly Hotel,' Stokes added.

On contacting Valverde Gill at the hotel he agreed to have lunch with me. We met at Martinez, the Spanish restaurant on Swallow Street. We ate paella and chatted about his dilemma. Valverde Gill explained how he was waiting to be allowed back to Spain but had not heard anything for a few days. I promised to do everything I possibly could to help and suggested we meet for lunch at Martinez in a few days.

When I enquired, the FO confirmed Valverde Gill's return to Spain was imminent; some minor details just had to be cleared with the Spanish. On failing to get hold of Valverde Gill at the hotel I went straight to Martinez and waited for him in the downstairs hallway admiring the beautiful tiles from Seville. Valverde Gill walked in with a strange smile on his face.

'Ola, Desmond! Why do you think I am late?' he asked.

He went on to explain about the visit from a young third secretary of the Foreign Office who told him he could return to Spain.in a week. The tickets would be organised and all his papers would be ready. Valverde had a coffee with the young Foreign Office worker who informed him permission had only been granted on the condition that he was of good behavior. Valverde Gill was rather taken aback and amused at the same time by this rather arrogant condescending approach to him.

I was rather speechless that someone from the Foreign Office could be that tactless and that anyone in the Foreign Office thought they were in position to dictate anything to Valverde Gill. What a bloody nerve.

As we walked up the stairs to lunch, he told me of the vineyards and bodega he owned. He was concerned that the distillery might have been damaged in his absence. We had another good lunch accompanied by a bottle of very good Rioja. He extended an invitation to me and my family; that if we were ever in his area of Spain to visit him. I of course accepted, adding that I would only visit to taste his brandy not to see him.

His travel documents were organised so there wasn't much I could help him with, but I gave him the Madrid telephone number of David Thompson, then head of MI6 in Spain.

On the mantle-piece in my father's office I always remember an unopened bottle of brandy labeled "Good Behaviour". Valverde Gill had labeled several bottles as "Good Behaviour" and sent some to the foreign office as a joke. He had also sent several as a gift to my father. I still have just one bottle today; never to be drunk.

A few days later I escorted Valverde Gill to the airport and as we said goodbye gave him a tin of Fortnum and Mason's Earl Gray Tea. He grinned and said. This must be vintage; like my brandy waiting in Spain.

On the retirement of Hamilton Stokes's in 1945 to become secretary of the Dublin Yacht Club; I was appointed G liaison officer and administrator of the Iberian Peninsula in England.

As G, I was responsible for the administration of the stations in the Iberian section, and all communications to and from these stations were initially channeled through me. For instance, a demand from the Air Ministry for more information on a foreign air force would be requested through the G Section.

The system worked as follows:

The Air Ministry would request information on the parts of a new fighter plane being manufactured in Seville. I would send the request to the head of station in Madrid who would put a suitably placed agent onto the project. The agent would obtain a job at the place of manufacture as anything from tea boy to whatever his qualifications would allow. Some weeks later the agent would report back. The subject in question is under construction but there are teething problems of one sort or another. Further details will follow. 'One sort of another' often meant quite serious problems; 'further details will follow' often meant there would be a delay before more information would arrive. Of course the agent's message would be much longer, but the head of station in Madrid would edit it, put it in the diplomatic bag and send it off to London. Everything, including this particular message, arriving from the Iberian section would be dispatched to me. I would then mark it for circulation to the Air Ministry, and if appropriate to the Foreign Office.

The report would then be digested by its recipients and returned to me marked with an A, B, C or D according to its importance, usually accompanied by a request for further information. This post-box system was the intelligence side of the G section.

Every few months, I would evaluate each agent in collaboration with the departments receiving his or her reports.

With this promotion came an invitation to join the Seniors' Club. This consisted of a small den in the basement of 54 Broadway, (head office), which opened at 5.30 pm. The atmosphere reminded me of the Snake pit at Glenalmond at first, but I soon realised it was somewhat of a farce and rather boring; most of the conversations were about the war, and about people being laid off due to cutbacks. After all, the war had been a tremendous adventure for most of us, and I suppose the older members found it hard to accept it was over, and would continually recount their stories. Some would talk about the new position of espionage and the centre of interest being the activities of the Soviet Union. Most found it hard to realise the possibility of Soviet Union subterfuge. Much of our concern was the continued activities being carried out by members of the Nazi regime who had escaped trial and were escaping to South America via Spain. An interesting and frightening topic of conversation was the Nuremberg Trials, and the revelations of the extent of the German brutality and cold blooded murder of over 6 million people. We all had known about the concentration camps but not the industrial scale of their operations.

In June 1945 John Charles Desmond Bristow was born. Christmas 1945-46 was a happy one. The house in Twickenham was looking marvellous thanks to all Betty's work. Rosanne was growing up fast and my son John Desmond was a terrific new addition. Oh, and there was

Buzz. Buzz was a dangerous bull terrier who ate chickens and cats and guarded us very well.

Betty, my wife, developed an absolute hatred towards the Germans as a result of the news concerning the concentration camps and the trials. I would often inform her about events which were not in the papers. Even to this day I would wonder why I had not developed a hatred towards the Germans. All the Germans I ever met personally were all very likeable people. I did not associate the officers from the Africa Corp with the camps or any other internal matters.

Being the G meant visiting stations from time to time. In January 1946 I went to Madrid to see David Thompson, and meet Pat Dyer, (a short, tough Irishman), his Basque wife Nina and one of his Basque cronies. I listened to Pat's reports about the goings on in the north of Spain. I don't remember specifics, but I'm sure some of the reports must have been about the Basque problem which was just starting to get serious, though not yet a real threat to Spain.

The stations were working on the strength and activity of the Spanish Communist Party, the Basques, the monarchy and any opposition groups. We were monitoring General Franco's efforts to keep the peace and watching the direction he was taking now the war was over. What industrial deals were being made, and with whom. The amount of ex-Nazi members moving through Spain was quite high at this time. Of course we could not arrest them, but our agents could follow their movements. From this we were able to establish an understanding of the considerable investments the Germans had in Spain.

The political strength was mostly monarchist, therefore army. The balancing tricks the Generalissimo played between the Falange, (the fascist party), the Church and the army (monarchists) were dangerous from his point of view, but he apparently knew what he was doing. The king was in exile and living as a British naval officer in Lisbon. The Falange party, which had played an important part in the Civil War and post-war period, was starting to lose political influence, especially as reports started to come out of the atrocities committed by the Fascists in both Italy and Germany. Franco was making a bit of a name for himself as being a fascist due to the prisons he was setting up for political enemies. This was not helping his relationship with our British socialist party at the time. For my part I knew how hard his task was in getting Spain back on its feet although some acts that were carried out in his name were particularly brutal.

Besides meeting with agents, there were the more tedious aspects of administration to be dealt with, such as personnel, supplies and finally budget! The latter had become a very gloomy prospect for SIS in early peace time as the cold war had not really started and the need for our continued existence was becoming a question of politics as much as military.

Two days before I was due to return home, David Thompson took Pat Dyer and his crowd, Bill Milton and myself out to lunch. Bill Milton, a friend from my previous visit to Madrid, was now processing German, Italian and Japanese assets in Spain on behalf of the Allies. He was working very closely with his American counterpart to try and close down these assets. During the lunch at the Meson we talked about the problems we now faced as Europeans and certainly as British people. Britain made drastic political decisions concerning Spain which had a very serious affect upon our industrial possibilities with Spain. The Meson was an ideal meeting place. The food and wine were invariably good, but more importantly, due to petrol rations the only clients able to frequent a place that far out of town were foreign diplomats, businessmen and Spanish VIPs.

On the drive back to Madrid, David's car skidded on the icy road and crashed into a tree. I remember lying in the back hoping the car would not catch fire as there was no way in hell I could get out due to the pain in my back and leg. As the shock subsided we were relieved to realise none of us were dead. Luckily another patron of the Meson was not far behind. We were rushed to the Madrid General Hospital where we were stitched, plastered, given hot tea and generally taken very good care of. David had hurt a few ribs. Juan, Pat's Basque friend, had split his head and I had fractured my pelvis.

During my examination by the doctors my right leg was allowed to fall off the examination table, and I can still recall the excruciating pain. Later I was transferred to the small British-American hospital in Calle Padilla, where matron Margery Hill OBE, God bless her and her superbly trained Spanish nurses, took care of their then sole inmate.

Thankfully I received visits from my fellow wounded who laughed at my plaster straightjacket.

Three weeks later I was leaning on crutches at Northolt airport in Middlesex while an over-zealous customs officer went through my entire luggage. When I was finally allowed through, Betty, the only person in the lounge laughed and sympathised at my demise.

When the plaster was removed my atrophied right buttock needed to be rebuilt, so I sat in the training tub at London Rowing Club for twelve days and rowed the right portion of my bum back into shape.

After five weeks of absence I returned to the office, limping badly and using my crutches more than necessary; besides winning me more sympathy, my limping act enabled me to receive extra petrol coupons. My G assistant, Paul Boggis Rolfe, who had held the fort in my absence helped maintain my exaggerated limp.

Charles DeSalis, now our section IX man in Paris, and John Bruce Lockhart, head of station on Paris, had expressed a wish to keep a Polish ex-lawyer named Popowski on the payroll. Popowski was a soviet expert having been the state procurator at Vilno, on the Soviet border.

After many trips to the Home Office and much deliberation on their part I was able to eventually secure his naturalization papers. It became necessary for him to change his name, and I suggested he should have a name which would not surprise anyone, like Smith or Jones. We decided on Pope, (after all, he had been known as Pope), a strong English name with a literary connection. He said he would like his Christian name to be George. Papers in order, our Russian expert George Pope went back to Paris where he stayed for three busy and useful years.

Sometime in 1946 I met up with Hans Scherrer. Hans had been a German newspaper correspondent in Spain during the Civil War. When the Second World War broke out the Abwehr had employed him to operate as an agent in Lisbon. By 1943 he had become disillusioned with the Nazis and decided to defect. He supplied our Lisbon station with a lot of information on the Abwehr. At one point he felt he had been detected by the Germans and asked to be evacuated. Hans's apartment was raided. As his German employers broke down the door, he climbed out of the window, shinned down the drainpipe and ran to an MI6 safety house that Gene Risso Gill had told him about.

After a few days Ralph Jarvis gave Hans a British travel document and put him on the train to Seville where Jorge Joseph (Antonio Joseph's brother) picked him up and drove him to Gibraltar. Donald Darling organised safe passage aboard a ship and Hans, one of the first German defectors, arrived in England. For the last part of the war Hans was an adviser on the Germans and how to turn them. He was able to tell who was a Nazi and who was a German.

When I met him in 1946 he asked if I could organise for him to be sent to Spain, where he felt there was more opportunity for him as a journalist, and his mother wanted to buy a house. I agreed to help him and he agreed to pass on any information which could possibly be useful to us. After all, he did have a lot of Falange friends from his Civil War days and would be able to mix with the German colonists arriving in Spain.

The latter part of 1946 consisted of office routine, and many discussions speculating about the new Russian KGB, and the American CIA.

On 2nd October I became the father of my second daughter, Annette; a very happy and strong young lady. Another happy Christmas came and went with all the joys of a big family. The war really was over. Rationing thankfully did not affect us too much as I received special coupons. The cold war was just starting to become a major concern as the Russians proved their intents by building up their arms. Nuclear weapons were becoming a serious threat for both us and the Americans. Industrial espionage was part of the network which monitored its developments.

There are no dates on this particular set of notes, but I can judge they refer to 1947 or thereabouts. My father was invited to join a committee to investigate the activities of a young Czech/Hungarian named Ludvik Hoch. He had fought fiercely with the Czech army and had very strong Jewish feelings having lost many members of his family in Auschwitz. This man was offering to work for Intelligence. Due to his courageous acts during the war, and the contacts he had with the Jews, for some reason it was agreed to give this man money to start in the publishing world.

Robert Maxwell, the publishing king and Mossad spy, was born that day. . Strangely, back in the sixties, my eldest sister got her first job in publishing with Robert Maxwell. I wonder how that came about?

On the death of Maxwell, (his drowning after falling off his yacht), it seems my father was convinced that the Firm dealt with Robert Maxwell, with the agreement of the CIA and possibly Mossad. According to his notes, Maxwell had become involved with some criminal activities at the highest level and knew too much about too many people. How would my father know this? I have no real idea; maybe just suspicions on his behalf.

1n 1946/7 Philby moved to Istanbul and became the head of section over there. Now looking back, this is when he must have been giving considerable information to the KGB concerning agents landing in Russia. How many died or were tortured as a result someone in the archive department must know. Has this been released? No; not yet.

Having agreed the pollution in London was unbearable; in May 1947 we sold the house in Strawberry Hill. Following a dream Betty and I shared of becoming farmers. We bought a small farm in Essex. Betty and I discussed my giving up Government work altogether and putting on a pair of wellingtons to take up farming seriously.

Betty's mother moved in with us to help with the farm and the family, all of whom, at this stage were unaware of my Secret Service status.

The move to the farm was made complicated as in September David Thompson had to resign as head of station in Madrid. One of his agents was found with Spanish War Office papers in their possession. This caused considerable embarrassment for the Foreign Office. Subsequently I was invited to take up the position. This offer meant I had to come to a real decision about the farm; after much deliberation and heart-searching I thought farming would be an ideal family life.

How much heart searching I wonder? Maybe to get away from secrets and secret ghosts.

Betty, saw this as promotion within the Foreign Office and easily persuaded me to accept the role. Her experience in the Land Army had taught her how much capital one needs for farming. We would lie in bed in the mornings, talking over our cups of tea, until eventually I realised how right she was and how much I did enjoy being in the Firm. Besides, living in Madrid would be fun and perhaps I could help relations between England and Spain with my knowledge and basic understanding of the Spanish people. After all Betty's mother and a farm hand named Percy Walsh would help look after the farm. Not that there was much to do in the way of farming as we had not invested in animals. The 75 acres of land was grass and woods with a stretch of river. The house and outbuildings were the only real concern, and Percy would tend those and cut the grass for hay.

The position as head of MI6's Iberian section would allow me to influence many situations.

17   Head of the Iberian Section: Madrid

Before leaving for Madrid I received an invitation from 'C', Major General Sir Stewart Menzies, the chief of MI6. This was the third time I had been in to see him during my career. By us, the younger element in MI6, it was called the August Presence.

He was shy, quiet and displayed an aloofness which served him very well in maintaining a barrier around him. This barrier, whether created purposely or not, kept the crawling members (ass lickers) of the office at bay, and there were quite a few.

I knocked on his door. C invited me in offered me a chair.

'Hello Desmond,' he said in his ramified, somewhat blustery, aristocratic English, 'how are your preparations coming along? I understand you have a farm and family to sort out. From what I have heard, the schools and those sort of things are supposed to be good out there.'

He carried on with his polite social chit-chat for a while, then got to the point.

He pointed out how the business with Thomson's agent had made my initial task difficult.

'We are trying to decide on what cover posting to give you. At the moment we are trying to persuade the Foreign Office to have you as Second Secretary of Chancery.

Whatever position it is, you are going to have to tread carefully at first.'

He turned in his Chesterfield armchair, pressed a button, and asked if I wanted coffee. A secretary brought it in.

Menzies continued.

'We are in a rapidly changing world, politically and economically, since the war ended. Basically it is becoming clear that Germany will slowly become our ally and the Russians our enemy. Spain remains somewhat of an enigma. We do not know how the majority of Spaniards really feel. There is still a strong Communist faction; and there are still a few Nazis running around. Politically Spain is quiet at the moment except for the reports coming in about these political prisons which unfortunately have a fascist ring about them. Which to some of our politicians means there are unsavory aspects to the present regime. You will be monitoring the Soviets as well as the Nazis. Do not forget that although the West is not an enemy of Russia, Russia claims it is, and Spain was the country where the Communists, aided by Russia, lost their first military effort. Stalin is still seething about General Franco. We have it on good authority the Soviets will certainly try to undermine Franco and anyone else in the Iberian sector.'

'Franco, although politically unpopular with our more liberal politicians, has brought a degree of stability to Spain and generally we hope he will remain in power.'

He paused and sipped his coffee. I sat back listening intently, quite surprised at what I was hearing. He continued:

'I have personal admiration for General Martinez-Campo and Vigon, despite their fraternizing with the Germans during the war.'

This really surprised me as both these Generals, certainly Vigon, had very openly fraternized with the Germans. Perhaps Menzies knew something I didn't. Perhaps these Generals had used their friendship with the Germans to keep the Germans out of Spain. Maybe all is on record somewhere. Why Menzies should have any admiration for these men, if not for that reason, I have no idea.

'Anyway, Desmond,' he went on, 'I wish you luck. Give my regards to Alan Hilgarth when you bump into him. Anything you want to talk about directly with me, just do so.'

We stood up and shook hands and I thanked him. As a result of that chat, C took on a completely different hue for me. He had given me very wide latitude, certainly much wider than the one I had formulated in my own mind, about my job in Spain.

Knowing that the farm would be well taken care of, and the flight passages for the children had been booked, Betty and I packed the black Humber supplied by the office and set off to Madrid. We took a slight detour via Paris, where I met up with Charles DeSalis. We discussed how the department in Spain might help keep an eye on KGB activities in southern France, as well as local Communist Party movements. Before leaving Paris I received a telegram from HQ informing me of some problems on the French-Spanish border at Irun, and with the scarcity of petrol, they recommended we delay our journey. After a chat with Charles, whose agents in southern France implied the problems were not bad, I asked him to telegraph HQ to say, "Pressing on regardless of problems!"

At the end of the first day we arrived in Tours and treated ourselves to a gourmet meal. The food in France was very different from in England. The next day we drove across the border without any problems and made our way to San Sebastian. We stayed the night in a little hotel and made arrangements to have lunch with Ernest and Vye Copeland at Doit Ana (Dirty Anas, as Vye called it).

Ernest, the vice consul in San Sebastian, filled me in on the industrial and political situations around the area, which at the time were stable. The local fishing fleets were busy again and many small industries had re-established themselves. He was not too sure what was happening with the Basques, but he was more than happy to keep me updated. What with Ernest and Pat Dyer, the north of Spain was well covered.

After a grueling drive through Northern Spain we arrived in Madrid and settled in to the Hotel Nacional where we stayed for three weeks. There was enough time to look around for a flat, and to look at the international school for the children. Betty was able to find her bearings while I settled in to the office. We looked in the shops and galleries and tried some of the restaurants. The Civil War scars were beginning to heal and affluence was becoming apparent.

C and head office had succeeded in persuading the Foreign Office to give me the title of Second Secretary of Chancery as my cover posting. This meant I had a relativity plush office at the top of the very regal staircase in the Embassy. As head of MI6 I had a chauffeur and other perks unusual for a Second Secretary, which caused me a small problem of explanation. Not for long, however, as in those days it was not uncommon for Embassy people to be privately wealthy; I certainly was not, but perhaps people liked the idea that I was, and this seemed to be how they explained my extra perks.

The Iberian field section consisted of an ex-SOE chap named Kenneth Mills, who was the head of station in Gibraltar; Teddy Dunlop, our lady in Tangiers, a doctor's wife, and Henry Prior, our man in Lisbon, Pat Dyer in Bilbao. Barcelona was vacant as an unfortunate accident had killed our man there just before I arrived; he had been watching his MG being unloaded from a ship when the cable snapped and he was crushed.

Pat was a remarkable agent. He recruited agents in northern Spain from about 1939 until 1944. Many of his 'observers', as he liked to call them, were Basque nationalists and consequently very pro-British. One of his closest collaborators was Flavio Ajuriaguerra, the brother of Juan Ajuriaguerra then head of the Basque nationalist movement. With the help of a Basque dockworker who had many fishermen friends, and a Spaniard who worked for a German typewriter company where all the local German agents were recruited, Pat and the British intelligence network were able to render most of the German operatives in the area useless.

While the watching of the German agents was going on Pat had recruited a group of Basques, then organised the capture of a German merchant ship carrying iron ore. He contacted the navy in Gibraltar and informed them of the estimated time to rendezvous with the ship. He armed and briefed eight Basque volunteers; then with his wife; watched from the wharf while the German boat was captured under the very noses of five or six other Germans vessels. When the pirates had tied up the German crew they set sail in a northerly direction. As soon as they weighed anchor the other German merchant ships, being part of the convoy, followed suit and sailed with them. The pirates waited until dark, when they turned around and set sail for Gibraltar.

With typical English gratitude, when the mission was successfully carried out the Basque pirates were made prisoners of war in England and left to rot. Fortunately Pat heard of their dilemma and created one hell of a stink with Admiral Limpney. The admiral completely agreed with Pat and was able to persuade the government to hand over the money promised. On their release Pat heard that one disappeared and another joined the 8th Army and was killed in North Africa; he is not sure what happened to the other six.

Besides these escapades, Pat ran seventeen independent lines from northern Spain, across the Pyrenees and into France, one of which went as far as Paris. Some of these lines brought intelligence information out of France which was too detailed to be transmitted by wireless. Some of the lines transported wireless sets and money into France, to help keep the Resistance going.

A wireless set was needed in Dax, and Pat was faced with the problem of disguising it. He found an illustrated pamphlet, written in German, advertising portable medical equipment and put it inside a suitcase which contained a transmitter. The medical diagrams were not unlike diagrams of the transmitter. At one stage of the journey it was strapped to the back of a motorcycle. The man riding the bike was stopped by a German control between St Jean Pied de Port and Dax. The control looked at the pamphlet and at the suitcase. After about five minutes, during which time the poor chap almost shit his pants, the officer in charge gave him a friendly tap on the shoulder and sent him on his way.

On a less amusing note, I will add that during some stay-behind preparations Pat organised, in case of a German invasion (very similar to the ones Brian and I prepared in southern Spain), some of his agents were shot by Germanophile Franco troops.

On our second Sunday in Madrid I took Betty for lunch at El Meson, and as we walked in I noticed Bill Milton with his secretary, sitting at a corner table in deep discussion. The place was full, and in Madrid no one knew who was watching who; and with David Thomson's cover being completely blown I was wary of my position.

The people interested in who was head of MI6 in Spain were the Spanish secret police, the members of the Nazi ring who were shipping personnel off to South America, the Dutch, the French, the Russians of course, and the Americans.

My tasks were to monitor the political wrangling's going on in the government, and to help Britain understand Spain's economic movements and requirements. In certain ways this coincided with the task of collecting and assessing information on German-owned assets: businesses, factories, boats, cars, trucks and real estate. This information would help me establish a monitoring system, which would watch the flow of Germans in and out of the country and the number of Germans, especially Nazis, living in Spain.

I needed to find somebody in a position to help me gather this information and update me as time went on; someone in direct contact with German affairs who, would be willing to be a so-called agent for me. It had to be someone already working on and processing this type of information.

I called Bill Milton, whom I had met briefly in Madrid in 1942, and again in January 1946 after my car accident. Bill had visited me in the hospital almost every day, bearing grapes and the occasional bottle of vino. I knew he worked for the Ministry of Economic Warfare (MEW) and had something to do with monitoring German businesses.

'Hello Bill, Desmond here. I have something I need to talk to you about in private; could we meet for lunch at the Argentine restaurant – or perhaps you know somewhere else . . . that only Spaniards go to.'

'I'd be delighted, so long as you are paying. And yes the Argentine is the best place for privacy. Since I know the manager I'll call and make the reservation. See you there at 1.30. Adios amigo.'

In the meantime, while I was putting together a collection of people who could help me gather information, my secretary started some filing systems; Bill Milton being one of the first names.

I left at 1.00 having decided to walk, as walking enabled me to lose anyone who might follow more easily than if I was in my car. I walked out of the Embassy wearing my hat, which I used to enjoy wearing; somehow and rather stupidly I felt as though it was a disguise. Besides if someone was following me I thought I could lose the hat and lose the tail.

I arrived at the restaurant a little early, sat at the bar and ordered a vino tinto. I felt a tap on my shoulder, turned, and saw no one. Then from behind I heard, 'Psssst'. I looked around again. 'Pssst, over here, chum.' There was Bill at a table in the corner, a wide brimmed hat pulled down over his eyes, signaling me by holding out his lapel which had a carnation in the buttonhole. As I arrived at the table he stood up very quickly and put his finger over his lips.

'Sssh, I'm going to check for bugs,' he said. 'Sit down, sit down.'

I laughed as he slunk through the restaurant looking furtively around, whispered in the waiter's ear and went to the bathroom. He obviously ordered wine, as an expensive bottle was placed on the table. I was admiring his choice when he came back laughing.

'Hello, chum, how are you? Ordered a good bottle since the Firm is obviously paying. How's Betty enjoying Madrid? When are the kids coming over from England?'

Bill was always smiling; he liked to have fun, and to make fun of almost everything that was serious. He had tremendous energy, as though he was always in a sort of frenzy. I must add he was always very good at what he did, and very particular.

Before I could get a word in, he continued.

'I've guessed what this is about, I think. You want me to provide information on the German assets and German personnel here in Spain.'

I immediately stopped worrying how I was going to ask him for information and marveled at the speed and accuracy of his guesswork.

'How did you come to that conclusion?' I asked. What his reply was I am not sure. We skirted the subject anyway.

Over a good lunch, Bill agreed to provide me with any information I required about the Germans and their affairs, as and when I needed, and as he came across details. During the course of my German witch hunt, he provided a breakdown of businesses, properties, schools, all their asset information and a who's who of every single German who had been in Spain, was in Spain, and wanted to come to Spain.

I then started thinking about the other people I could contact to help me with the German question and decided to make contact with Hans Scherrer. I picked him up in my car near the fountain of Retiro Park, and for the first few minutes we exchanged the usual pleasantries.

'How's the writing coming along?' I asked.

'Not very well. Germany does not seem very interested in reading about Spain at the moment.'

Hans, on his arrival in Spain in 1946, had started writing articles for a few German publications.

Having established Hans needed money, that he still had contacts with his falange friends and as a journalist he would be able to contact any German, I decided to employ him.

We agreed to meet the following week, when I would drive out to his house at Torrelodones, half an hour north-west of Madrid.

During that week I had a couple more enjoyable and informative meetings with Bill Milton, got my secretary to finish the new filling system, and read through the office records. While sorting through the records I decided to call Tommy Thom in for a meeting. He was Consulate passport control officer. I asked him to liaise with me as much as possible about any Germans or Russians applying for visas, or any other information he might feel relevant. His unwillingness to co-operate bothered me. For a time I wondered if he had been involved with the fiasco before I arrived as Head of Station; then I realised he was upset he had been overlooked. This was ridiculous as he had been a file and passport inspector and had no idea of spying and how it worked. Fortunately there was an old friend of mine from Cambridge within the passport control offices, who had been an MI6 agent for a time. I reported Thom's reluctance to work with me, and sent it back to London. Unfortunately those above showed very little concern. He was not withdrawn from Spain until two years later.

It was early in the morning, frost was on the ground and the car windshield was all white. Having cleaned off the frosty patterns I headed off to Torrelodones. Madrid's very beautiful centre was becoming positively busy again, cafes were full of people eating churros and drinking hot chocolate before they started their daily routine. An increasing number of gasogeno-powered cars were running around, filling the streets with smoke and honking their horns. All this created a very different scene to the Madrid of 1942.

Gasogeno was an alternative fuel to petrol that produced a lot of smoke. Unfortunately, Spain being low on petrol supplies and refusing to buy in quantity, people with the money bought gasogeno-powered cars. The limited amount of petrol was mostly used by government vehicles. All government officials, Spanish or foreign, had to have tokens and a plaque attached to the rear license-plate with the letters PMM (Preferencia Mobil Ministero) which was jokingly referred to as Para Mi Mujer, (for my wife).

The half-hour drive through the very beautiful country north-west of Madrid sped by. I was on my way to ask Hans to become an agent, my mind full of the possible connections he might have and how best to utilize them. At the same time I did not want Hans to jeopardise himself in any way. The Nazis were still a very nasty lot. I decided to codename him Arthur, and have specific places and times to meet, to reduce the amount of telephone contact.

His house was on the outskirts of Torrelodones. He lived with his widowed mother, an avid gardener, who had planted up the front with lots of roses. I remember well; when I knocked on the front door their Alsatian dog barked and jumped up at me, making me step back straight into a pruned and prickly rosebush. As I recovered Hans came out.

'Sorry, Desmond, I should have tied him up. Are you all right?'

'Yes, yes,' I responded making sure no thorn remained embedded in me.

'Please come in and meet my mother, then we'll go for a walk. By the way my mother speaks quite good English; so be . . . you know.'

On our walk, Hans agreed to be my agent, codenamed Arthur. He emphasized how many people he knew in the Falange party, and how many of them were friends with German businessman. Although he had positive details he could give me at that first meeting, he made it clear he was aware of many Spanish-named companies, with Spanish personnel, that were either wholly owned by Germans, or run by Spanish-German partnership. Hans was well liked by the Germans and Spanish Germanophile elements in Madrid; after all, he was one of the few journalists writing articles about the peninsula being read in Germany. He and I made very strict arrangements. We would lunch on Tuesdays at a small restaurant, always full of artists and musicians, as a public place to chat where he could give undetailed information. During lunch he would say whether it was necessary to meet again in more private circumstances, when he would give me dossiers and sometimes photographs of personnel and places. I told Hans about Bill Milton, and suggested we all lunch together the following Tuesday. I drove back to Madrid feeling satisfied.

Hans was to prove a very valuable source of information and enabled me to build up an intricate and detailed file on the movements and businesses of Germans and Spanish Germanophiles. After the first lunch he suggested we meet at Bill's flat that Friday, and from then on we had our private meetings at Bill's. This worked out very well since a lot of Hans's information was useful to Bill. In fact, I can safely say that Hans Scherrer helped MEW close down or confiscate many German assets which, without his help might never have detected.

In early 1948, wanting to appear a little interested in the duties of my cover position as second Secretary, I made a trip with Brian Wallace, the third secretary, to Barcelona. I introduced myself to the consul general and familiarized myself with some of the staff. I seem to remember I made a point of making sure the Spanish knew I went on the trip. Not long after, HQ decided to send my old assistant of G section days, Paul Boggis Rolfe, as our man in Barcelona, why I have no idea; he spoke no Spanish at all. Consequently he was not very useful and his stay was brief. Thankfully the post was taken over by my feluccing friend, Fergie Dempster.

By September 1948 I had settled into a routine of liaison with the various heads of station and agents. Tommy Thom being not yet out of the country but basically out of the way, friction with passport control was over. The monitoring of German and any other foreign economic or political activity was now well oiled and had become routine. Assessing and analyzing Spain and General Franco's policies was also becoming easier. Franco was not following a military policy; he was intent on rebuilding a very broken up country. Even so, while he was encouraging foreign investments he was not prepared to sell out to anybody. Britain's policy towards Spain continued to be one of ostracism. We had withdrawn our ambassador in 1946 and our politicians continued with this policy, the French and the Americans also had no ambassador, but the politicians of these countries did not hold back their larger companies from investing in Spain.

We, the Bristow family, had moved into a beautiful house two miles outside Madrid. The house with its magnificent walled garden had once belonged to the sister of the King of Spain. We moved around May or June, and not long after that I had my first personal experience with bugging devices.

In May, I had a suspicion that the Spanish were bugging the phones in the Embassy. The anti-bug man arrived from England with instructions to test not only the Embassy but also certain houses, including ours. A faulty bug was discovered on the phone line at the Embassy. In our house, he found one little microphone in the bedroom, and one on the phone line. The idea of my family's private life being invaded to that extent was upsetting for me, but more especially for Betty.

In mid-1948 I remember a stepping up of agents reporting on the state of the political prisons and prisoners, whose welfare was increasingly becoming the concern of some leading politicians in Britain. Some trade union activitists were also creating about the prison situation. The Foreign Office was under increasing pressure to look into the fate of some named prisoners and rattle the sabre against the regime. Except in a few cases this was not diplomatically acceptable. Nevertheless Bernard Malley, our locally employed counsellor, often attended trials and visited the infamous prison at O'Cana, sixty kilometers south of Madrid, where most political prisoners were held. I decided that it would be good policy to accompany him on some of his visits, partly for cover, and partly to see for myself what was really going on.

Despite the apparent viciousness of some court sentences, the general atmosphere within the prison walls was very informal. Guards and prisoners had card games going, families were allowed to visit, cigarettes and even the odd Marxist tract, which the guards also appeared to read. It was obvious to me that the leftwing politicians in England were looking for excuses to undermine Franco. No doubt our visits and British interest made life easier for the prisoners, many of whose sentences were extreme, but left-wing politicians used this to try and undermine the delicate stability Spain was experiencing for the first time in years. Maybe because of my Spanish upbringing and my having seen widespread poverty and starvation before Franco arrived, I became frustrated with left-wing tittle-tattle. Did the people really want a revolution in Spain again?

I have been asked many times why the West allowed the Franco regime to continue in power. My answer is that the West was not in a position to initiate any real alternative; as such an undertaking could only have been achieved by military intervention resulting in loss of life. At the same time we were looking at the Soviet machinations with ever-increasing concern. Britain and the US were beginning to face up to the impending cold war, and realising that to wage war we needed as many allies as we could muster.

One afternoon as I was finishing up my analysis of information from Hans, the security porter Hilario, rang me on the intercom to tell me someone was in reception wanting to see me. He was an American, calling himself Ricardo.

I quickly folded my papers and descended the grand Embassy staircase. My visitor came towards me with a big smile-yes, it was indeed Ricardo Sicre.

'Hey, Desmond, you look like the Duke himself standing on that staircase. So this is the British Embassy; regal but threadbare.'

'What the hell are you doing here?' I asked. 'Come on up to my chamber.' I offered him a whisky.

He went on to explain.

'I am working for an American set-up called Ryan. As you know, Betty and I married after we dropped into France. She was an amazing radio operator, you know. Anyway, Cornelius Ryan is a friend of Betty's father and a big business man, who needed a rep in Barcelona, so out I came. I have just made a deal with the Japs and Spanish; Spanish rice for Japanese potash.'

He looked around my big office.

'You look as though you are rather important these days.'

'No, no, they have mistaken me for someone else, but since the whisky is free and I have this big desk and comfy chair, I thought I would wait for them to realise their blunder.'

Ryan Cornelius was a close associate of William Stevenson, better known as A Man Called Intrepid. My guess was Ricardo had been working for the OSS (CIA). He flatly denied it when asked.

He asked if I was able to find out if he was on a wanted list in Spain.

Slightly set back by the directness of his question I replied.

'Yes, I can find out for you; but why on earth would you be on such a list?

He explained that his father had been a doctor near Barcelona, and he, Ricardo, during the first six months of the Civil War had fought for the Republicans. That was until he witnessed the Communists line up some people against a wall and shoot them for no apparent reason. After that he deserted and was on the run. He met up with Robert Graves who assisted him with papers and put him on a boat bound for England. Here he worked as a barber in Great Bardfield, Essex; the shop was called the barber of Seville.

'My God! That is where Betty and I have a farm. What an amazing coincidence.'

We talked about the little village of Great Bardfield; then I asked him where he was living.

He explained how he and his wife Betty Sicre were living in central Barcelona but wanted to move to Madrid.

As he left I called after him,

'By the way, I am going to be in Barcelona next week, visiting my old pal Fergie Dempster.'

We agreed to meet up, and in the meantime I would find out how wanted he was.

I called my contact at Spanish internal security, whose name I am not going to disclose. He told me the only information they had on a Ricardo Sicre was that he was dead.

The following week, Betty and I drove to Barcelona. We had a marvellous dinner and get-together with Fergie and his wife Diana, Ricardo and his wife Betty. We stayed the night with Ricardo and Betty, since Fergie's flat was too small. I was able to tell Ricardo he was not on any Spanish wanted lists, added to which he was dead; for which information he was very grateful.

While in Barcelona, Betty and I went to see the now famous monastery on Montserrat, today the stage of one of the best choirs in the world. Gaudi's work was not advertised as much as today. The Cathedral fascinated my wife and she went on a tour with a mutual friend. In those days Barcelona was a medium sized port town with wonderful Spanish houses. Fish salesmen would push their wheelbarrows along the cobblestones, yelling out the catch of the day.

I went to Fergie's office to talk about MI6 affairs. Fergie had developed a relationship with a senior officer in the Spanish military security department, who was fascinating and very well informed on the subject of the Spanish

Communist Party. The gentleman was a strong Anglophile, and later on in the relationship, and with very little persuasion, gave Fergie a long report, about twenty five pages, on the Spanish Communist Party's structure before the Civil War, and how it had operated during World War Two. Unfortunately it did not contain many names. I translated it into English and sent one copy to the Foreign Office and a copy to head office.

During this trip, I decided my friendship with the FBI man in Spain, Joe Presley, could possibly raise suspicion against me. The Americans were never shy about their CIA or FBI members, consequently everybody who watched Joe would notice if we saw a lot if each other and would realise I was involved with the British Secret Service.

Joe and I met two or three times a week exchanging information about Germans and other causes of concern for both our countries; there was never anything of great importance, but it was an open co-operation between an FBI man and an MI6 man. I had taken it upon myself to cultivate our friendship and therefore our flow of information, as we were on the same side. On our return to Madrid from Barcelona I invited Joe to join our small shooting syndicate which Bill Milton and a Rumanian had organised. We spent many an afternoon in the campo near Naval Casnero, one hour north of Madrid, shooting the odd rabbit or partridge while we exchanged information.

At the end of 1949 a German working with a company based in Bilbao put in an application for a visa to visit the

U.S. Joe Presley (FBI) asked if I had any information on this man. Through Bill Milton and Pat Dyre I was able to inform Joe that Florian Hendricks had some shady dealings during the war and seemed to be an avid Nazi. Joe told his passport control officer to refuse this man entry to the States. On occasions Joe was able to do the same for me.

This makes no sense to me. In my father's notes made sometime in the 1960s he mentions meetings with Skorzeny and most of the time it was on the behalf of the FBI and CIA. Again why did he not want to reveal this when he was alive? Why did he leave notes for me to find? For all his light hearted ways and his apparent public school boy approach to matters there appears to be some possible serious implications here. This is why he did not want this mentioned in our book 'A Game of Moles'; or is it? Perhaps he never intended for me to discover these notes.

The shooting trips were always fun; Betty and the children, Joe's wife Marjorie and their children would usually join us and we would have enormous picnics. Bill always had new stories, jokes about politics and funny things that happened at the MEW. The shoot enabled Bill, Joe and I to have three way conversations enabling us to swap information without constantly looking over our shoulders.

In the middle of 1949, Al Almer arrived from Washington with his family and a few weeks after his arrival Joe and Marjorie held a July 4th celebration party. It was fun attending a celebration of a time of discord between our two countries, during a time when we had only recently become hard and fast allies, (World War Two brought England and America together in a very fundamental way). Unfortunately, in my opinion, England has never fully accepted or appreciated this fact. Our stubborn pride and unwillingness to accept we no longer are the empire we once were has held us back from taking advantage of many opportunities, certainly as far as America is concerned.

At that party I met and became friendly with the very busy American military attaché Charlie Dasher. He was successfully securing military bases for the American air force, (bases used heavily during the recent Gulf War), and the use of Spanish ports for the American navy.

During the party Al Almer teasingly said to Joe,

'One of my boys reported seeing you driving down the Calle de Granada in Desmond's sleuthing car a few days ago.'

'Oh!' exclaimed Joe. 'I'm glad you CIA boys have nothing better to do than watch me.'

'Actually Joe he wasn't, he was watching Desmond's car, wondering what MI6 could be doing outside the Spanish police department when he realised it was you.'

Al was head of the CIA in Madrid and he helped keep me abreast of some of the American economic activities in Spain, while I reported sadly on Britain's economic non-activity there; (I hope of some the members of SIS who happen to be reading this book are turning uncomfortably in their chairs). Although most of the information we exchanged is insignificant, just the fact that I maintained such an open rapport with our American friends was not even known by head office in England, and would certainly not have been appreciated.

This open relationship my father mentions was much more involved than he implies. He writes a great deal about his close line of communication with both the FBI and CIA men in Madrid at that time.

At the end of the war the Spanish government had readily accepted the Safe Haven Report. And for the most part complied with the rules, although obviously given the amount of involvement the Germans had had with Spain before the war, there was some prevarication on the part of certain ministers. Nevertheless, the Allied Commission responsible had completed many of the investigations by 1947. But it was clear that much of the prevarication was to buy time for many Spaniards to hide their German-linked assets, which left many outstanding and important questions to be answered by Bill Milton's, and partly by MI6's investigations.

My discussions with Bill centred on who had been what, and which Spaniards had played any role, sinister or not, on behalf of the Germans during the war. Firms like Bayer, the worldwide chemical company, had several Abwehr agents on their payroll. A very slippery customer named Geronimo Yplano had worked on direct orders from the German naval attaché in Barcelona. Geronimo was responsible for looking after a small fleet of boats (mostly fishing) that were owned by the German navy. The fleet was camouflaged under the name of Jesus Franqueza of Barcelona. The purpose of the fleet was to run supplies out to German submarines operating in that area of the Mediterranean. Many German aircraft such as Heinkels and Messerschmitts had either crashed or force landed or just plain disappeared. Investigations on these went on until 1950. Many ended up in the Spanish air force. As investigations took place we monitored the behavior of the Spanish, even those who readily complied with the so called rules.

Had it not been for Bill Milton's sagacity, experience and knowledge of Spaniards, negotiations on that whole touchy subject would more than likely have been pursued in a very acrimonious manner. Bill's respected toughness and honesty, and his ability to communicate openly with the Spanish, meant that even those who had their German assets frozen or confiscated recognized he always adjudicated fairly. God knows how many lucrative backhanders he might have taken, if he had not been straight as a die.

Bill helped me understand a part of Spain that I had not been at all familiar with. His pre-war experience as an administrator for the iron mines of Whitehall Securities (a city-based mining finance company) around Seron in Almeria, and before that in Vizeu in Portugal, gave him knowledge of business practices in the Iberian Peninsula making him a key figure for MEW both during and after the war.

From our discussions it became clear to me how important a role MEW had played in Spain. For example, the manner in which some essential supplies were obtained from Switzerland via Spain is fascinating. In 1943 the British commercial counselor in Spain, named Lomax, purchased a Swiss design of quick-firing cannon for our Spitfires and Hurricanes. He initially negotiated through a Swiss gentleman named Birkigt who worked in Barcelona. Due to the success of the initial negotiations, Lomax was able to secure financing from MEW and went to Switzerland and finalised the deal. The contract papers were sent to Spain, where they were handed to a visiting MP named Kendall, who flew back to England from Lisbon. Why they trusted an MP with the papers is beyond me. Kendall left the papers on the plane. Fortunately for him, and Britain, they were retrieved. MPs, even today, are apt to leave confidential papers in taxis, or whatever.

Another MEW operation was to obtain a heavy industry lathe manufactured in Switzerland. Shipping was a problem, but MEW created a way around it. They blacklisted the Swiss company and made sure the list fell into the hands of the Germans, thus erasing any suspicion the enemy might have had of the goods being delivered from that company to Spain. The blacklisting enabled the lathe to be transported through occupied France into Spain, and then by boat back to England. A more amusing example of their shipping techniques concerns a special type of ball-bearing needed for Britain's fighter planes, which was manufactured in Sweden and Switzerland. The diplomatic bag from these two countries to Madrid was often used to carry the valuable bearings; once in Madrid they would be transported, usually by train, to Gibraltar and from there shipped back to England. As you can imagine the bag was quite heavy.

The way in which MEW operated, and the depth of their knowledge of German assets in Spain, made my task easier. We knew the Germans had some $100M of assets in Spain in 1945, which in comparison to Britain's or any other country's was an enormous amount. Part of my job was to monitor where these assets went and who had access to them. Many Germans escaped the Nuremberg trials and with this money they could easily influence politicians in need of finance to become leaders; especially in South America.

18   Guy Burgess and Liddell

As 1949 rolled on, the only matter that caused any real concern and needed careful monitoring was the question constantly being raised about Gibraltar. I put together a detailed report on the activities of the Communists in Spain. The centre of this group tended to be in the Northern areas and Cataluna. The south of Spain was divided by so many small mountain ranges and large distances and the means for any strong political group to gather strength were very restricted. The Guardia Civil kept its eye on everything. There were still bandits in the mountains behind the south coast. This left Spain's Communist Party, although vocal, relatively ineffectual, and the Russians certainly had very little influence in Spain. I would send in regular reports on Communist activities. Pat Dyer kept a strong watch on the Basque movements and the workers and Communist interests in Bilbao and Santander. Fergie Dempster would often send messages of some workers' skirmish in one of the newly found factories in the Barcelona area. Nothing of any serious nature was developing which might threaten Britain's interests. As a consequence head office decided to reduce the network of the Iberian section.

At this period my father was involved with watching German activity in Spain, and often on behalf of the FBI.

Spanish politicians usually took hold of the question of Gibraltar only when they needed to create a rise of nationalism, and apart from this almost continuous hot potato, I agreed that we no longer needed more than a few agents in the field in Iberia. Teddy Dunlop, in Tangiers, continued to monitor the small skirmishes which were continually taking place amongst the Arabs, but she had never required large funds for her agents, and the way she ran her field was her own affair. Henry Prior, in Lisbon, monitored the Spanish Royal family living in exile at Estoril. Portugal had the odd Russian wandering around, and like every country in Europe was busy trying to increase its trade; but nothing ever happened to cause real concern.

I did a tour of the peninsula, going to see Pat Dyer in Bilbao, Fergie Dempster in Barcelona and Henry Prior in Lisbon. Teddy Dunlop came to see me. They all agreed with the decision to reduce the number of field agents, and started to decrease their networks. The increase in telephone systems made communication easier.

Of course we maintained our most important and hard-working agents. In November I had a meeting with Hans Scherrer, who, besides giving me information about the Falange and a couple of German newspaper men, said he heard something about the monarchists. Apparently they were making noises with the idea of creating interesting in putting the King back into power; but he felt it was nothing serious. I was leaving for Lisbon in a few days and said I would check up on what the exiled king was up to. He asked if he could come with me, as he had left some documents and personal belongings in his old Lisbon apartment, which he would like to collect.

'I don't see why not,' I replied. 'I'll organise some English papers for you to travel on.'

Lisbon was quiet and instead of posing as a tourist as I had on my last visit, this time I was able to actually be one, taking Betty around the town. The secret police were not interested in spies' there were no spies to be interested in. For Britain now, the only political point of interest was the activity of, and around, the exiled Spanish monarch living in Estoril.

Hans collected his belongings from his old apartment, and then took Betty shopping while I had my rendezvous with Henry Prior. I asked Henry what was going on with the monarchy as I had heard very small rumours in Madrid.

'Well,' he replied, 'Senor Gill Robles has just returned from Madrid where he had talks with various monarchist sympathisers and all seem to be of pretty much the same opinion; that without outside help they are unable to do anything.'

'That's good; the last thing Spain can take at this moment is another revolution. Food is still in short supply for most people.'

We talked for an hour or so, and I told him about the cutbacks in agents, which did not really affect him very much.

I went to join Hans and Betty for lunch at the Palace Hotel. Crossing the road in front of the hotel reminded me of the time I had been arrested with Klop; those weeks in

1944 with Klop, the secret police, the possible German agents and all the hustle and bustle had been two of the most thrilling weeks of my work in the SIS.

After lunch Hans went off to see some old acquaintances and I took Betty to see Estoril. The next morning we headed back to Madrid, via Salamanca. Hans wanted to call in at the Irish College where, during the Civil War, he, Kim Philby and other foreign journalists had taken shelter before moving on to Burgos.

At the college Hans, who knew the building well, led the way to a large door and knocked on it. There was no reply, so knocking again Hans pushed the door open to find the rector, Father McCabe, sitting in his chair and slumped over his large desk, breathing very heavily, a large bottle of brandy in one hand and a pistol in the other. He had obviously consumed over half the bottle and was lying on paperwork which looked like deeds of some kind. Hans went over to him, accidently kicking over an empty brandy bottle. At the sound of the bottle rattling over the stone floor, Father McCabe stirred from his stupor, looked up at Hans though bloodshot eyes, and in a strong Irish accent said,

'Hans, Hans Scherrer, me boy, father in Heaven and Saints preserves us, have ye come to help me fend off those Spanish bastards? They are trying to take me College away from me, lad.'

He kept on and on about his College and how the Spanish bastards were going to take it away.

Betty made him coffee, while Hans and I walked him around outside. It had surprised me how in his condition he had recognized Hans so quickly. But as he slowly recovered he kept repeating,

'I never forget a face ye know. Fancy old Hansy, a god-dammed kraut, being the one to come to me rescue. God does work in mysterious ways, ye know. What was yer name again?'

'Desmond Bristow,' I replied.

He then went into more surprised profanities as he slowly realised I was English and a Protestant. We sobered him up and persuaded him to come with us to Madrid and stay until I was able to organise his return to Ireland. On the journey back he kept on about the mysterious ways in which God worked. Looking up at the roof of the car, he would ask,

'What are Yer trying to do to me? First off he's a Protestant kraut, second off these other two are English Protestants. What are Yer thinking of, sending the likes of them to help me?'

It appeared that Father McCabe had been left in the College alone for years and the Spanish prelates had threatened to take over the College. He had been sitting behind his desk, a bottle in one hand and a pistol in the other, for two days before we arrived; quite prepared to shoot any of the Spanish representatives had they gone near him.

The Irish legation refused to deal with the problem or even take care of Father McCabe, so on Betty's insistence he stayed with us until he was sober and I could organise his return to Ireland. Betty was incredible, and the father was soon dried out, healthy, and good company for the children and for us. After ten days, the Armagh (the Irish Vatican) organised the Father's return.

Father McCabe was replaced by Father Ransome; who in gratitude for our help offered us the use of the College house at Pendueles, in northern Spain, for our summer holidays. Father Ransome would join us for the three week's holiday and would be part of the family. The Bristow heretics enjoyed the Father's company as much as I know he enjoyed ours.

For the second summer at Pendueles, Father Ransome was accompanied by a young Polish priest who had been first interned with the Poles at Dachau, then a captain chaplain in the Polish army. He had initially come to Spain to serve God, but during one of our discussions he turned to Betty and said,

'I am returning to England next week.'

Betty asked, 'Why? I thought you had decided to stay in Spain and were looking for a place to work?'

'Yes, that is true, but I have to come to realise I do not fit in here. I claim to be a good Catholic Christian, but sadly see so very little connection between the Spanish Church and the teachings I have received; so much so that I do not feel I could happily carry on my spiritual work in

Spain…a so called catholic country. Ironically I think I'll be able to work better in England.'

We had many more conversations about religion, politics, wine and food.

The last port of call on my tour around the peninsula was Gibraltar, which was uneventful. Betty and I enjoyed the company of Ken and Patricia Mills; I explained the need to cut back, and that several agents had to paid be off, (in most cases the paying off of agents simply meant them being 'laid off'). There was no British agents' union to argue for just reward! SIS was poor financially as well as in personnel. Ken Mills was the MI5 head based on Gibraltar. He would report to me as I was the Foreign Office representative in the Iberian sector. As I was the head of MI6 as well he would report to me due to the amount of information which was of mutual importance to both MI5 and MI6.

Shortly after my visit to Gibraltar, Ken phoned and asked me if I knew a chap called Guy Burgess?

'Yes, unfortunately I do know the little poof, not well, I might add. The little shit is a friend of Philby's and Tommy Harris's. God knows why they like him. Why do you ask?'

'He's here in Gib, claiming that he's a good friend of Philby, that he knows you and is personal assistant to Sir Hector McNeil, and has asked me to change money for him. When I said I would have to check with you first, he went on to explain that he was on very friendly terms with

315

Guy Liddel, (deputy director of MI5), and did I know Dick White. . . again I told him I would have to check with you. Well, he continued rattling on, then he started asking questions, persistently. What really rocked me was the way he slanged off the Americans, and expressed great admiration for Mao Tse Tung. Tell me, what do I do?'

In a very exasperated tone, I replied,

'Fuck him! On second thoughts no, he'd probably enjoy that. Just chuck him out; even though he is in the FO.'

'Don't exchange any money or do anything? We must not get involved?' asked Ken.

'No bloody fear,' I said. And that was that; or so I thought at the time.

The telephone conversation worried me. Guy Burgess, a friend of Kim Philby's. What was he doing in Gibraltar stirring up trouble? Why did he need to change money?

A week or two later, it must have been January 1950, as we had just had Christmas; the telephone rang. It was Teddy Dunlop calling from Tangier.

'Hello Desmond, I have a problem in the name of Guy Burgess. He's rude, keeps pestering me for money and generally behaving in an appalling fashion.' She sounded very irritated.

'Well, for a start don't give him a penny and keep him out of the office.'

'But Desmond, he knows everyone! How can I just have him kicked out?'

'I don't know. Let me think.'

'Maybe he's an FO agent spying on us,' I added, jokingly.

'Well, if that's the case he should not have gone around broadcasting the name of the Swiss diplomat who allowed the British to use the Swiss diplomatic bag to bring rare pieces of equipment and information out of Switzerland.'

She continued with more horrifying news about Burgess.

'Also he should not have pinched Harry Dean's Arab bum boy. He has created one hell of a scandal and that alone has really fixed him in Tangiers.'

Harry owned a famous bar in Tangier and was a roaring queer, but a very likeable chap, who was well known in the area and had a lot of powerful friends. Burgees had set the gays of Tangier alight, it seemed.

Teddy was concerned. The Tangier community was scandalised by the behavior of this member of the British Foreign Service. I told Teddy to collaborate with Ken and send the report to head office. Ken sent his report to MI5, in which he boldly stated that Burgess should not be in the employ of the Foreign Office let alone be a personal assistant for a minister of the Crown. Teddy sent a report to me and I sent my report to head office (MI6) with a covering report to the Foreign Office. To the three of us, official reaction, as witnessed later, was very strange and illogical. In February 1950 Ken had to go to England on personal business; on arrival he was called to a meeting with Guy Liddell and Bernard Hill, MI5's legal adviser.

Here follows a précis of a tape-recording, which Ken gave me shortly before his sad death, recounting this meeting:

"Guy Liddell cross-questioned me on most of the contents of my report, inferring I possibly had motives for slandering Burgess. I told him not to be so ridiculous. His most reluctant attitude to forwarding my report about Burgess to the Foreign Office astounded me. Here was a member of the Foreign Office behaving in a mad, wild and totally irresponsible manner abroad, throwing names around with complete abandon. Bernard Hill interrupted my report to Guy Liddell and pointed out that if Liddell was to refuse to support a trusted member of his own department in MI5 and refuse to pass on this information to the Foreign Office, the Foreign Office should be advised not to accept any more MI5 reports. Besides, either Liddell trusted his representatives and should have them investigated. When Bernard Hill finished his barrage on Liddell, I added that if Liddell did not accept what I had to say there were plenty of people in the Rock Hotel and in Gibraltar who would more than willingly provide statements pertaining to Burgess's wild, decadent and insidious behavior. Three days later I heard that the Foreign Office had reprimanded Burgess. Burgess had then immediately reported back to Liddell about his reprimand due to my report, and inferred to Liddell that I was running a currency racket. What a terrible individual he was".

When Ken gave me the tape, he and I discussed it; this was after Blunt had been exposed. We were agreed about Blunt; even just after Maclean and Burgess escaped we thought Blunt must have tipped them off.

During our discussion we talked about Roger Hollis, who I might add had become the head of MI5 and been knighted for his services. I felt that someone else must have been involved other than Blunt, during the Burgess Maclean affair, and I thought it was Hollis and I still do. My argument was based on a brief history about Hollis that had come my way, concerning his involvement with Agnes Smedley in 1936 when Hollis was working for British American Tobacco in China. Agnes Smedley was a known KGB agent and Communists supporter. They had casually met at a party in Shanghai. Not long after this meeting he returned to England, owing to tuberculosis. When he had recovered he became obsessive about joining the Secret Service and succeeded by socializing with the right people at a tennis club.

Later in 1945, he was chosen by Philby to interrogate Igor Gouzenko, the Russian cipher expert who defected to Canada. Why did Philby suggest Hollis, and why did the conversation Hollis had with Gouzenko take only about 20 minutes? Cyril Mills should have been the person to have gone, since he had well-established connections within the Canadian police. Moreover, besides the fact that the interview Hollis had with Gouzenko should have lasted a lot longer, he dismissed the information he did receive as worthless. The Canadians and the Americans who acted upon the information they obtained from Gouzenko successfully arrested a number of Soviet spies.

Despite my fairly strong evidence, Ken never agreed with me about Hollis.

My own unanswered questions remain: what were the motives? What could Guy Liddell have been thinking? Blunt had been in Liddell's department earlier on; and now here was Liddell supporting Burgess, and basically trying to cover up his behavior in Gibraltar and Tangier. Curiouser and curiouser!

In March 1950 I returned to England to attend a course, housed in an old turreted mansion in Hampshire. We carried out night landings in rubber boats, learned how to use explosives, and the destructive power of two gallons of petrol. We were receiving lessons on wartime special operations. Our instructor was a tough man, about the same age as I was, of Spanish decent, named Fernandez. He was expert, meticulous and a very able and amiable teacher. He had been a member of the diving group which successfully breached the underwater barbed-wire entanglements laid by the Germans around the Normandy beaches, (I last saw him in 1987-88 when he was vice consul in Algeciras).

Why were these heads of Secret Service departments attending courses on Wartime Special operations in 1950?

I then went to London to talk with the heads of department who were receiving reports from my section. My last call was on David Footman; the receiver of some of my reports from Madrid. He was an old hand in SIS and the expert on the Balkan states. I arrived at his office in a mood of irritated curiosity; his assistant had told me that he had not forwarded my report on Spanish Communism to the Foreign Office.

'Hello, David, how are you getting along?'

'I am glad you have come, Desmond. I was just preparing a note asking you to explain why Pat Dyer should be kept on; he seems very pro-Franco to me.'

I laughed.

'My God! David, out of all of us in my section, who less so?'

'I don't think he should be kept on,' said Footman.

I disagreed entirely, and gave my reasons. I then asked,

'I was wondering if you knew why Section IX has not responded to my report on Spanish Communism?'

He coughed and shuffled uncomfortably in his chair.

'I did not feel it worthwhile or relevant; consequently I didn't send it to the Foreign Office.'

'How funny, you should not find it relevant. You clearly do not realise I am attached to the Foreign Office via Chancery, and therefore sent my report directly to them. As a result I have received several pointed follow-up questions which leads me to believe they found it very interesting.'

Footman's face dropped. Then in an attempt to sidestep the issue he said,

'Oh by the way, I do not think you or your colleagues should write reports about other colleagues.'

'What are you talking about, David?'

Suddenly I realised he meant the Burgess affair, which made me really cross.

'Listen Footman; one, Burgess is no colleague of mine or of any of us in SIS for that matter and therefore should be no colleague of yours; two, I think I shall go straight up to C and have him read my report, then we can discuss the subject again.'

'C is not here today,' replied Footman.

'How very fortunate for you, Footman.'

He continued,

'All I am trying to say is that we must not act as if we are Gestapo!'

I was dumbfounded by his comment. Feeling very angry, I got up, walked out and slammed the door.

Why was Footman defending Burgess's behavior? What was it about the man that made so many people in responsible positions defend him, even like him? Perhaps it was his theatrical gaiety, supported by his blue blood, which possibly made him amusing and interestingly eccentric. I don't know if it was any more sinister than that. When all hell broke loose over Maclean's and Burgess's escape to Russia, Footman's remarks echoed in my head. They echoed again, when Philby defected in 1963. As for Guy Liddell and his involvement, he certainly allowed Blunt into the Service. He knew Burgess and Philby very well. This may have been nothing more than homosexual friendship.

On my flight back to Madrid I mulled over Footman's outrageous remarks about Pat Dyer. Pat had done wonders during the war for MEW, MI9, SIS and Section V. He was producing good, clear reports on the Basques and their aspirations, a subject the Foreign Office and SIS were very interested in. The Bilbao consul had recently reported how extremely helpful Pat was. For someone like Footman to be raising doubts about Pat was inconceivable; was it just economy?

One week after my return to Madrid, I called the general meeting of Ken, Teddy, Pat and Fergie Dempster, who could not attend. I reported on the Burgess affair, and Footman's comments. We debated the situation – not in terms of moles or double agents, we were still blissfully naïve on that topic (!), but as truly concerned members of the British Secret Service; and for my part as a member of the Foreign Service. At the end of the meeting we decided to 'press on regardless'. We were not in a position to take or recommend further action. We agreed to ignore Footman's remarks and recommendations. We decided that in the unlikely event of any other employee of His Majesty's Government behaving in our territory in a comparably bad way, we would behave like the Gestapo again and file a report directly to C.

According to some details in his notes my father pointed out the need to watch for any German individuals in the area. The reports from Joe Presley and Al Almer, (FBI and CIA), of Germans escaping to South America was a secret my father seemed to have kept to himself. Why? He certainly asked his heads of the various stations to watch and monitor German individuals. Did he tell them he received information from our American allies or not? Perhaps he felt people like Footman or Liddell should not know.

The arrival of Otto Skorzeny in Madrid in 1950 was of major concern as he had escaped from the Nuremburg trials and Germany in 1948. Herr Skorzeny had been the commander of the German Commandoes. Under his leadership the German Commando force carried out the escape of Mussolini from Monte Casino. In 1944 his unit dressed as American soldiers, penetrated behind American lines and carried out several acts of sabotage and cold blooded killings. Again in 1948 while in transit to Nuremberg for a hearing, the transport unit dressed as Americans disappeared along with Skorzeny. The post war German government has listed him as missing. In light of him turning up in Madrid, and apparently with quite a lot of money, he raised many questions. In fact Otto Skorzeny seemed to be quite a gentleman, and avoided association with Nazis in Madrid. Joe Prestley (FBI) met him a few times, when he would forward information about fellow Germans who were undesirable characters quite readily. He also gave Joe information about hidden German assets which Joe passed on to me.

"I met Otto Skorzeny after his trip to Egypt. Bill Milton was monitoring his engineering company, which had bought interests in the States and Paraguay. Joe Presley informed me of the FBI investigations into Skorzeny's connections with some CIA agents in the States and an oilman named Bush. I was a little apprehensive of this meeting as Skorzeny was a tough and ruthless individual. Having said that, I enjoyed my meetings with him as he stretched my mind and espionage work beyond pen pushing; it became clear after learning more, by 1952 he was potentially very dangerous. How involved were Al Almer or Joe involved? I asked casual questions about his trips and suggested we meet up in the States sometime. He responded very positively. We talked of art. He mentioned some works of art of which I was quite ignorant, and he even knew of Tommy Harris.

I discovered he was soon to leave for a round trip to the States and Paraguay. The rest of the conversations were fictional for me as I had never been to the States but I could talk about Washington to some degree. We parted and agreed to be in touch on his return in 6 months' time. It was clear to me he was helping Germans get out of Europe, it also seemed that the Americans were quite tolerant of this ex-Nazi as he gained entry visas with no problems. When I informed Joe (FBI) he asked me not to mention any of this to Al (CIA). Two weeks later we all went shooting and Joe raised the subject. Al Almer seemed very surprised and rather angry with both Joe and I for not keeping him informed. Joe explained his reasons, which were to do with an investigation being carried out by the FBI under Hoover's supervision.

Al admitted they were watching Skorzeny as it seemed he was supporting a Nazi group in the States and moving money and ex-Nazis to South America. The best way for them to watch this trail was to quietly help Skorzeny. This is what I imagine Hoover was investigating. Hans was able to gather some information from some journalist friends of his in Germany, nothing of any real value, other than his case had been closed. Hans refused to meet up with Skorzeny. This surprised me as I would have thought this would have made a great story for him. Especially after Otto Skorzeny had published his book in France which had had quite serious consequences for the French Publisher; I wonder why they did publish. Hans was just too scared, and would often comment on how Skorzeny had been by Hitler's side until the very end. He was a cold blooded killer without a doubt."

After reading these notes I was quite shocked.

Is the man named Bush mentioned here the grandfather of George? Or some other relative. He has got to be connected, as there are not too many Bushes who have been in the Oil game and close to the CIA.

It seems after Menzies retired my father felt far less inclined to deal with MI6 head office in London.I suspect mostly due to Footman and Hollis He must have reported this to the Foreign Office though. If my father had reported this to the foreign office; at least the information would not have gone to Philby. Besides Philby was now in Washington and on the verge of being investigated. .I am sure had Philby seen the information he would have passed this onto his KGB masters. I am almost sure my father passed very little information pertaining to Skorzeny back to London. Why not? Sinclair was not like Menzies; the Cold War was becoming more threatening, and men like Skorzeny might be needed in that arena? I really have no idea. Perhaps he was doing this for his friends in the FBI and CIA?

This makes no sense to me.

In my father's notes made sometime in the 1960s, he mentions meetings with Skorzeny and most of the time it was on the behalf of the FBI and CIA. Again why did he not want to reveal this when he was alive? Why did he leave notes for me to find? For all his light hearted ways and his apparent public school boy approach to matters there appears to be some possible serious implications here. This is why he did not want this mentioned in our book 'A Game of Moles'; or is it? Perhaps he never intended for me to discover these notes?

Al Almer had impressed upon my father the CIA's suspicions of a mole either within their service or SIS. His notes refer to conversations with Joe Presley of the FBI about Hoover and the agreement between some factions of the British Secret Service and the FBI to work together.

Considering how closely he worked with Al Almer and Joe did my father know more about this?

Quite clearly the other main concern, besides Skorzeny and his taking up residence in Madrid, was the cold war and double agents; and Franco's government. As for Skorzeny, Many notes refer to meetings in tapas bars and cafes with him. Again my father has not mentioned any of this to me in person. My only rationalization of this is due to his working so closely with the Americans. He quite clearly did not report very much of this back to London. He was acting on his own; as he had done with the French.

Otto Skorzeny was a very important man to the Nazi movement. He was Hitler's right hand man during the last three months of the war. His links within the Nazi movement were at the highest levels. It is clear to me any information he gave to my father or Joe Presley or Al Almer, (MI6, FBI, or CIA), concerning Germans and their activities was probably because he thought they would be imprisoned and removed from his chain of contacts.

He was building up the line which became known as ODESSA. Whatever, his willingness to give information gave the impression he was collaborating. (ODESSA was the escape line which Skorzeny ran aiding Nazi leaders to escape to the States and to South America). He helped them change their identities, and transported many treasure for them. He became very rich from this endeavor, and saved many war criminals as a result.

It is claimed he worked for the CIA and that they had a deal with him that enabled them to watch the movement of these retired Nazis. Skorzeny provided funds for Nazi groups in the States which were also watched by the CIA. How much of this is true or not I do not know. I know my father helped the CIA gather information on Skorzeny and some of his activities.

Bill Milton helped with some of the monitoring of Otto Skorzeny, by providing information on any companies the Germans had interests in. Over the period from 1950 to 1954, my father would meet Herr Skorzeny as a British member of trade. He would talk about his business interests in America. He mentioned his contact in Venezuela, Juan Pujol.

This next section shows how my father was involved with industrial relations between Spain and Britain.

After the war British and Spanish representatives met twice a year to discuss their trade dealings. There was an ongoing wrangle between the two countries. Britain was invariably represented by a member of the Treasury, someone from the Board of Trade, our minister and of course the resident commercial counselor of the Embassy. Spain was purchasing little from England and each year the balance grew in Spain's favor. We continually tried to persuade them to buy British cars, a difficult deal for them to accept, with petrol being rationed and their need for more essential items. But besides the question of cars, Spain was not playing the game.

I was asked to find out what their attitude was likely to be at the second meeting of 1949. On my asking a few pertinent questions, 'a friend' in the Ministry of Economics assured me that at long last they wanted spares and castings for their newly electrified train, their pride and joy, the famous articulated 'Talgo'.

'What about buying more quality coal, such as anthracite?' I asked.

'I don't know about that; our mines in Asturias are producing large quantities of lower grade coal; I will have to check up about anthracite and the cleaner burning types,' he replied.

Our recently appointed commercial counselor, Pelham (known as Pompous Pelham) was determined to make a name for himself. At a meeting a few days before the trade mission arrived, Pelham stated in the event of Spain prevaricating, he would pick up the phone in the middle of the meeting, call the Board of Trade and request them to stop all anthracite supplies to Spain. The threat hung on the fact of anthracite being quite rare, and essential for firing sensitive chemical and engineering plants. All present, except me, agreed this would be a good tactic. I tried pointing out it seemed rather a purile move, besides which the idea was to increase purchases of British goods, not lessen them. The meeting was broken up with Pelham sticking to his plan of action.

The day before the meeting a Spanish friend from Galicia, known as Jock Ochoa, (real name Jesus Ochoa) educated at Fettes School in Scotland, came down to Madrid. He was in the coaling business and therefore interested in the forthcoming Anglo-Spanish agreement. He spoke perfect Spanish and English with a Scottish accent. We met at one of my favorite little tapas bars around the corner from the Embassy.

'Jock, Pelham is going to perform at tomorrow's meeting.'

'Perform! What do you mean, do monkey tricks?'

I told him of Pelham's plan.

'Desmond! For God's sake don't let him try to pull that schoolboy trick. I cannot believe someone in his position is capable of such stupid behaviour. It would be better for him if he did some monkey tricks, or swung on a trapeze.'

'Oh, he's quite capable of it. I don't think he will take any notice of me,' I said, knowing Pelham did not approve of me. Besides he resented my close friendships with so many Spanish business people due to my ability to speak perfect Spanish.

'Well, he is going to look a total idiot. We have already imported 200,000 tons more anthracite than our quota, and we have more on its way before the year is through; and believe me it will arrive. We have been trading with the mines in Cardiff for over eighty years, and the Welsh don't like being told what to do by the British Board of Trade.'

I called Pelham and explained how the quota had been exceeded already; but he took no notice, implying I was making it up and he knew it was not true. The meeting went ahead, Pelham pulled his trick. That afternoon I received a phone call from my friend Antonio Martin in the Spanish ministry.

'Desmond, I'm curious as to who this Pelham chap is, and why the British have chosen such an idiot to be in his position? He must be very unaware of life. If we had not restrained ourselves the meeting would have become a total farce. You know we like the British, but this man...well, anyway, we are not thinking of selling our surplus coal to Poland, but don't tell Pelham.'

No more was said, and the coal and anthracite trade continued. Pelham later became HMG's ambassador in Tel Aviv.

When I read this, added to the extra notes I have found, I am appalled by individuals within the British Government with their arrogance, and consequently their lack of understanding of how destructive their attitudes are towards other countries and Britain's foreign relationships.

19   Garbo: A Question of Resurrection

Tommy Harris was a frequent visitor to Madrid, and by 1950 was living most of the time in Camp de Mar, Majorca. He would come to Madrid to sell or exhibit his paintings, coloured glass, ceramics and etchings. He was a prolific artist as well as dealing in others' works. I had been corresponding with Juan Pujol (Garbo) who was living in Caracas, Venezuela. I had suggested he join the only Venezuelan Eastern bloc society (the Czech Society) with the idea of gaining their trust. Obviously the idea was to find out about their interests in South America, but more importantly, once he was trusted by them I planned to have him transferred to Paris where he would try to infiltrate the Soviet subversive 'Juggernaut' operating in France.

I discussed my plan with Tommy, who was able to give me more insight into Pujol's character and abilities. At first Tommy thought it a very good idea, and offered his help. I wrote a letter with my ideas to Pujol. When I heard back from Pujol, who expressed his willingness and wholehearted co-operation, I started negotiating with head office. Two or three weeks went by and Tommy, who in the meantime had been to Majorca, returned to Madrid. On the visit he was much less supportive, having discussed the whole idea with Philby. He did say that he had arranged for Pujol to visit him in Majorca to discuss some other business, and would send him on to Madrid to see me.

Pujol visited and we talked the idea over for a few days. He flew back to Caracas, leaving me with the impression that he was keen to go ahead; then head office sent me a message, with very little explanation, telling me to drop the plan. I telegraphed Pujol informing him the plan was aborted.

I can only assume the head office dropped this idea as suspicion was growing around Philby, and by the fact Tommy had included Philby in the idea the KGB would have been fully aware of the scheme. My father would not have realized this.

Some very strange things happened around Pujol, and he certainly was a most capable liar with very few morals. According to him, his wife Aracelli Gonzalez, who had supported them all through the Civil War and had been by his side while he was playing Garbo, had deserted him and was living somewhere in Madrid. In 1980 Betty and I met up with Aracelli and after so many years we became good friends. She told us a very different story. In 1948, Pujol sent her and their two sons and daughter back to Madrid. After a year she realised that Pujol had deserted her and, by then completely broke, she managed to rent a house from an old friend, paying the rent and for food by taking in paying guests. I was even more shocked when she went on to tell us that she had called on passport control for help, and been refused. Why this matter was not referred to me at the time, I do not know. According to her, the person who refused to help her answered a description of David Thomson. Very curious.

How very insidious of Pujol to lie to me.

Anyway, I was disappointed about Garbo not being resurrected; it rather took the wind out of my sails. Not long after, in about June of that year, I was in my office one evening trying to continue to think outwardly and sustain my counter-espionage instinct somehow, when the telephone rang. The duty lady on the Embassy switchboard said there was a gentleman on the phone wanting to speak to the military attaché's assistant urgently. I asked her to tell him he was out. In fact I was the only one in the Embassy at the time; why, I cannot recall.

Upon the gentleman's insistence I accepted the call, and an excited young man told me he was on the run from the police and had important information to report. I asked if he had been to the United States Embassy.

No, was his somewhat angry reply. I prefer this Embassy.

I told him to call back the next morning as I had no charter to listen to him. He became very agitated and insistent, so I eventually agreed to meet him the next morning. He gave his name as Jose Ponce de Leon.

The following day, posing as the military attaché's assistant (there wasn't one in our Embassy), I interviewed Jose. He was shaggy, dirty and unshaven, and gave me a long and reasonably authentic sounding story, which concerned a possible coup against Franco. I emphasized that the possible coup was of course of interest but our interests had better not be misconstrued. I started to suspect he was a plant by the Spanish security service who were trying to discover who was head of MI6 in Madrid.

I sent him over to passport control, where he was given a little money and sent to a well-known safe house which the Spanish secret police would have under surveillance. He spent one night there and disappeared the next morning.

1950 passed slowly. My work with Bill Milton was drawing to an end; of course we stayed close friends, shooting and going to guitar recitals by Segovia. Betty and I were doing quite a lot of diplomatic entertainment at home, some of which was fun, but too expensive, considering how little we received from the Foreign Office. In those days it was assumed that all diplomats had large private incomes, part of which could be spent on behalf of the country, maintaining liaison and social contact if nothing else.

Towards the end of the year rumors started to filter through about the appointment of an ambassador. It was time; the Spanish were starting to resent Britain's continued ostracism, and we in the Embassy were starting to resent the extra workload.

The Ambassador, Sir John Balfour, and his wife arrived early in 1951 and as is the custom a ceremony was held where the ambassador was received by, and presented himself to the head of the state, in this case General Franco. The ceremony was very grand. Franco wanted to show off some of the splendor of Spain. The streets of Madrid echoed with the sound of horses' hooves and carriage wheels; the pavements were filled with flag-waving, confetti-throwing people; chauffeur-driven cars bearing flags followed in procession; army uniforms and polished buttons, shining shoes and twinkling medals. I arrived at the royal palace, having chosen not to wear my medals. I wanted to draw as little attention to myself as possible. I suppose I felt my true line of work would be questioned if I pinned them on.

We were ushered to our places. We shuffled around and bowed our heads, and then there I was shaking hands with the Generalissimo, the man who had been the military leader who had won Spain's Civil War. Now under whose leadership Spain was recovering fast. His character had been smeared and attacked at every possible opportunity by liberals and socialists. Yes, it was Franco who was blamed for the Civil War, yet no one man can start a war. I knew what Spain had been suffering before: constant political upheaval, starvation, disease, and due to the lack of roads and communications. isolation for many villages from the rest of the country, Spain had suffered from a total lack of central organization; in short; economic and political chaos. Besides, in my opinion, if Franco had not joined the Civil war, Spain would not have survived much longer without some sort of revolution; and it was a virtual certainty that had the Republic continued, Germany would have walked into Spain after the fall of France.

So there I was, shaking hands with the so-called butcher of Guernica.

The arrival of the Ambassador certainly warmed things up socially, with highbrow parties and social events. Economically, our relationship did not change at all; Britain continued to maintain a critical and aloof attitude of superiority. France and Italy were winning out. The Renault car factory installation, and the marriage of Fiat to a Spanish company which produced Seat, resulted in an increasing number of cars being made in Spain which started to fill up the roads. The number of American bases and naval vessels docked was evidence of a military relationships co-relating to the cold war. The Americans were trying desperately to woo Franco with economic aid and always failing. In his words: 'Spain is not for sale to anyone.'

Because I knew the Spanish were fond of us Brits, and wanted to work with us more than with most others, I became frustrated as I watched so many opportunities for Britain fall into the hands of other countries purely because of our off-hand arrogance.

As for MI6, we continued to monitor the political and economic jockeying, but for me and my colleagues, our enthusiasm was faltering. I would occasionally go over to passport control in Calle Montesquinza on the pretext that I needed to check up on information pertaining to some minor historical fact about relations between England and Spain. In reality I was liaising with my friend from Cambridge, the archivist who was working with a great many MI6 operations and was still one of the most successful agent operators in Madrid. We were able to converse in French if necessary, since she was trilingual like me. (Her usual line of communication to me was via the small diplomatic bag that went from passport control over to the Embassy.)

My training for deception and undercover work had most definitely included routine; but I was never subjected to routine for any length of time, and unfortunately when I was, I became bored.

Not long after the arrival of the Ambassador, head office instructed me to meet a Mr. Dowding and his colleague at the airport, explaining that he was the head of HM's customs investigation branch. I duly met the bright and friendly Mr. Dowding, who explained how his department wished to arrive at a modus vivendi with the Spanish head of customs. A subsequent meeting between the two opened the door to a continuing relationship of free-flowing information. This apparently insignificant arrangement was to benefit not only me but MI6 in the future.

At the end of May 1951, my life as a Secret Service man fell prey to doubt and misconceptions. The news of Burgess's and Maclean's flight especially disturbed me when I heard about the inefficiency of Dick White (MI5's director of counter-espionage) from internal sources. As soon as he heard about the flight of Burgess and Maclean, White had gone to Newhaven to follow their trail. On presenting his passport to immigration he was informed it was six months out of date; and they did not care who he was, he could not leave the country with an out-of-date passport. I was beginning to wonder about SIS.

My friend Kim Philby was then withdrawn from Washington due to demands from the CIA. Kim was suspected of informing Burgess and Maclean about the up-and-coming investigation of Maclean. I was stunned and shaken by what I was hearing through the service grapevine, and by what I was reading in the newspapers. Kim was politely forced to resign by Sir Stewart Menzies.

Trying to avoid thinking about Kim's possible treachery was virtually impossible. Joe Presley (FBI), Al Almer (CIA), Bill Milton, Tommy Harris and all of us could not help speculating. In the autumn Kim was cross-questioned and found not guilty, despite the amount of circumstantial evidence provided. Where was the flower without the petals; not to ask about being loved or not, but was he? Or wasn't he?

I wrote privately to head office saying the uncertainty was intolerable, and suggested "Why not lock him up in a flat with two bottles of whisky and see if he confesses?" Needless to say I had no response. But I did receive a visit from a member of the London office, Margery Bray; this was the first official visit in three years by a head office representative.

At first Margery Bray was very guarded and asked a lot of questions. I remember being irritated by the officialness of her visit, in light of the fact that head office had hitherto left us alone in the Iberian section.

Perhaps I was under suspicion as well.

After she left I met with Al Almer who informed me that the CIA had been trying to warn Britain about a 'mole'. Al could not believe we had blundered so badly over Burgess and Maclean.

This statement made by my father is quite a cover up. As his private notes reveal.

Date 1965. Notes Desmond Bristow:

"Al Almer and I had so many discussions during the late 40s and early 50s. Al had made it quite clear to me of the suspicion held by the CIA that SIS had Russian informants within its staff members. I always argued how this could not be. Joe Presley would back up Al's information. I sent a message to Stewart Menzies in 1950 informing him of the CIA reports I was receiving in Madrid. I could only assume the CIA in London was passing on their fears to him also."

'Do you mean to say they escaped, or were allowed to escape?' Al asked.

'When you tell me that Dick White arrived with an out-of-date passport I have to think it was deliberate.'

'I don't know, but it would seem that way to me." I replied rather despondently.

'Do you mean to say that it is possible for your lot, having orchestrated the D Day deception, to suddenly turn into an outfit not worthy of the Keystone Cops? Oh no! There must be more in it than that! And what about your friend who is being interrogated, or has just been interrogated, Philby? Is he in it too?'

'I hope not. Kim is someone I consider quite a close friend. . . I just don't know. I find it very hard to think about, let alone believe. Burgess, well, the couple of times I have run across him I have, I can honestly say, despised him. He must have got to know that Maclean was a Soviet spy. Perhaps he saw some communication in Philby's office. After all he was living with Philby in Washington, much to poor Aileen Philby's horror.'

Accepting the drink Al offered, I continued.

'Listen, Al! Here I am in Madrid; all I can do is surmise what happened or why. All I can say is that no one seems to be saying anything definitive to anyone. I have been on the best of terms with Philby, and the office well know that, but that does not mean to say I would be kept informed of any developments. In fact with him being interrogated and now thrown out I would say the opposite. It is all very confusing and I just do not know what to think. I simply hope head office knows what's going on and what it is doing.'

We talked back and forth for a long time. Fortunately, Joe Presley did not press me on the subject and just left Al to quiz me.

I did trust head office to sort the mess out, so that things would settle down. Unfortunately this was not to be. The internal bush telegraph, the press and others continued to ask the same questions. It tuned into a perennial cloud of doubt hanging over the present, the past and the future. I lived up to my Gemini birth sign. I did not want to believe that Philby was the Third Man, as MP Marcus Lipton had called him; yet I could not clear my head of nagging doubts, not least of which was his friendship with Burgess, which I never understood.

In early 1953 I received a message from head office advising me "Philby is due to arrive in Madrid on a contract for the Observer, and has been briefed not to have anything to do with you! We strongly advise you not to have any contact with him."

I did not know whether to laugh or cry. Philby and I were good friends; we had worked together during the war. He had been my boss and in many ways my teacher in the ways of espionage. For him to come to Madrid and for me to pretend that I did not want to see him would have been ridiculous and could possibly have raised his suspicion. I telegraphed London saying that I was well aware of the circumstances, but if the situation arose I would see Philby.

It was a Tuesday at 2.30 pm; a tremendous thunderstorm was raging when the phone rang.

'Desmond.' I immediately recognized the voice.

'Hello, Kim. Where are you?'

'I'm at the Iberian bus t-t-terminal in the m-m-middle of M-Madrid and I'm stuck. I was wondering if you might know of a small hotel.'

My father clearly did not want Kim to feel as though he had any suspicions of him being a KGB agent. My father informed both Joe and Al of Kim's arrival in Madrid. I think my father thought he would be able to get some indication of Kim's loyalties.

'Oh, don't worry, I'll come and fetch you and we'll see what we can sort out.'

Confronted by him directly like that I could not bring myself to think of him as a Soviet agent.

I telephoned Bill Milton who lived near the city centre and organised to meet him after I had picked up Kim. In the event, Bill offered to put Kim up for that night, taking him next day to a small hotel in Calle Miguel Angel.

I warned Joe Presley and Al Wallace of Kim Philby's presence. We agreed to play the game with him as though nothing had happened. He might make a false move, suggested Al.

Well, Kim was looking for journalists so I introduced him to Sam Brewer of United Press and Bobby Papworth of Reuters. Through them Kim was able to meet all the Anglo-American journalists in Madrid, and become a member of the journalist's club.

Kim's friend, Lady Frances Lindsay-Hogg, arrived during his stay. They joined us on of our picnics. Kim and I spoke very little about the Burgess and Maclean affair. He once reminded me of how I had never liked Burgess.

'How on earth do you remember that?' I asked.

'Oh, just one of those things.' Somehow we never discussed politics, or the weight of suspicion he was carrying on his shoulders.

He seemed to enjoy his months in Spain, and being a journalist.

We gave a party for him when he left.

I think my father was too hurt or felt too stupid to really want to find out the truth for himself. My father was a great conversationalist and a political beast. For him to have apparently not spoken about Burgess and Maclean makes me think he did not want to know or he already knew. He did not want anyone else to know; which can be perceived as being party to the Double agent network. It is easy for me to sit here and judge. But if one of my close friends had done something very serious which would warrant the death penalty, and the collapse of everything I believed in; what would I have done?

The big question mark remained. Despite him being cleared by the Prime Minister, Harold Macmillan, I could not make up my mind. Why should the firm have found him a job in Spain? Was it to string him along? Was it to see who he made contact with? What was at the back of it all? By this time the damage caused by Burgess and Maclean was starting to take effect; and was Kim guilty? Or was he our double agent? Head office must know something which those of us in the field did not. This period of uncertainty had a most demoralizing effect on many of us; it certainly did on me.

Added to this Sir Stewart Menzies retired in mid-1952; a man who I believed could have cleared up this problem. I had always had a good relationship with him and had a great deal of respect for him. Yet he seemed to be running away in the middle of this dilemma. Stewart Menzies was replaced by Sir John Sinclair. Sinclair was not the same caliber of a man as Menzies. As was shown when he had to retire in 1956 over the Crab affair. The Service was changing I was under suspicion and I felt very betrayed by the whole set up."

Surely Kim must have been working for us, and reported on Burgess and Maclean, so he now posed as a journalist and come to Spain as a safe haven; but then, why the letter from head office? My imagination ran wild with questions. Had I been instructed not to see him to save me from being blown? Or to save him from arousing the Spanish seguridad's suspicion? Here was a journalist, in good standing with the Spanish authorities due to his correspondent work during the Civil War, in touch with a member of HM's Embassy; why? But then all foreign journalists were frequently in the company of diplomats.

His visit caused Bill, Joe, Al and I to talk about him more than ever, and made my mind more of a muddle than ever.

At times I felt like talking about him with anyone around who might have an opinion, but of course I did not. However there was no bridle or bit, on the mad galloping of my imagination. If Philby was a Soviet agent then all those who knew him at St Albans would fall under a cloud of doubt. Doubt was starting to plague me, though I was certain I personally had no real reason to worry. But the wrong fish can often get caught in a net. I realised that, of the Iberian Section, I was closer to Kim than anyone. His only other close friend in that part of the world was Tommy Harris. I remember reminiscing with Tommy about the war days and wondering if it was possible that Kim, whom we had got drunk with, who had ridden so often on the back of my motorcycle, who had introduced the two of us, was really a Soviet spy.

That summer was our last holiday in northern Spain.

Speculation about Philby subsided.

From notes it is clear my father fell into quite a depression. He expresses his confusion and anger. His notes refer to the incredible lack of serious interest from the main body of MI6 and even the Government. What must it have been like to have one of your best friends and your ex-boss within the British Secret Service to suddenly be suspected of being a traitor? Kim Philby, if found guilty, would have been hung; as would Burgess and Maclean had they not escaped.

In January 1953 head office started intimating that my days in Madrid were numbered, and I was soon to return to England. I was told so often I was leaving, and then not leaving, that Betty and I must have attended six or seven farewell parties. Eventually head office was sure it had found my replacement and on 1st April we left Madrid.

Rosanne, our eldest daughter, flew back to England with Tommy and Hilda Harris, making room in the car for Pepe, a friend's young servant who had decided he wanted to come to England with us. We packed as much as we could into our Austin; the rest of our belongings went by freight. John and Annette went in the back with Pepe Betty and Dardo, the English setter, sat in the passenger seat and I drove. For the first hour Berry and I discussed whether she had left anything behind, while John, Annette and Pepe played the irritating game of 'I-Spy'. The family disputes and Dardo getting car sick must have made Pepe wonder why he had decided to come to England with us; or even why we had decided to go to England at all. I know it annoyed the hell out of me.

Our first stop was San Sebastian, where we had lobster, mussels, fresh sardines and a marvellous bottle of wine (or two) at a restaurant overlooking the moonlit Bay of Biscay. We stayed in a new high-rise hotel. In the morning we were awakened by Pepe, in a panic.

'Senor, Senor,' he yelled, pounding on our door.

Sleepily, Betty and I got out of bed, as Pepe rushed in explaining that Annette and John were climbing from their balcony onto the next in a daring attempt to surprise us. This would have been good fun, had our rooms not been a hundred feet above the road. I peered around the corner of the window just in time to see Annette land safely on the balcony next to ours. Betty yelled for them to stay where they were. I rushed out of the room and knocked on the door of our sleepy neighbor.

'Excuse me senor.' I said in Spanish. 'Our children are on your balcony and I would like to retrieve them before they attempt to climb onto ours.'

With a look of horror he invited me in and opened the window fastenings as fast as he could. I grabbed Annette, who smiled broadly and said in Spanish,

'Good morning, Papa, how are you today? We were going to surprise you by climbing in your bedroom window while you were asleep.'

When she realised how upset we were, she kept explaining why they had attempted their death-defying act. Betty and I knew full well that John had persuaded Annette it would be a good idea, and the more she reasoned with us on their behalf the less upset Betty and I became. Of course her brother kept his mouth firmly shut, and looked as though he was about to burst into tears. After about half an hour we all calmed down, had breakfast and set off to Le Touquet. By the time we arrived, we were all laughing about the children's climbing exploits.

Le Tourquet retained some of the grandeur of the days when it had been as important to tennis tournaments as Wimbledon. Because of the dog we had decided to fly him by the short route from Le Touquet to Lydd in Kent. A dog box was prepared, Dardo was immunized and we said goodbye to him, not to see his muddy paws in our home for six months, when he would emerge from rabies quarantine.

After five and a half years in Madrid it was somewhat of a culture shock to be back at Hawkins Harvest, our small farm near Great Bardfield in Essex. Betty and I could see a thousand and one alternations and repairs that needed to be done; our budget would cover about half of them. I had two weeks' leave in which to help Betty unpack, do some minor plumbing, electrical repairs and carpentry and purchase an old jeep that had been in North Africa about the same time as I was. As we settled in the change in environment and the physical labour helped me to brainwash myself about Spain.

When my leave was up, I drove to Chelmsford station early on Monday morning and caught the train to Liverpool Street. It was time for me to report to head office and find out what they had in store for me.

I was invited to become the head of a newly formed section of MI6 which dealt with the very complicated problem of strategic trade. This obscure title referred to about one hundred items which the United States and Britain had decided must be prevented from reaching the Warsaw Pact countries.

Priority goods on the list were copper in any shape or form, aluminium, diamonds and a host of accessories not available behind the Iron Curtain, especially electrical goods and embryonic electronic parts. This represented a great challenge and I felt very enthusiastic about my new position.

That first journey home went very quickly as my mind was occupied with details of my new responsibilities in the office and at home; ships full of copper during the weekdays, horses, cattle, chickens and pigs during the evenings and weekends. The clickety-clack of the train wheels put my mind in a condition for daydreaming. The rich Essex countryside slipped past as condensation on the window clouded my vision; very green grass, full oak and chestnut trees, crops covering the gently undulating fields.

My daydreaming was about farming. Farmyards stood beside the railway line, and I imagined our little farm; Betty collecting the eggs, the milking of the cows, the tractor driving and gymkhanas at the weekends.

I could not help wondering if Betty and I were not trying to do too much, as the new job was more exciting and responsible than I had expected. Getting out at Chelmsford with all the other commuters and walking to the car felt like fun on that first evening. The drive to Hawkins Harvest was beautiful. The narrow lanes around our house were lined with high banks and thick hedgerows, apple orchards, woods and little country cottages; in most places only one car could pass along them. In those days we were one of the few families that had a car; most others who had lived in the area for years used bicycles or old tractors. It was very romantic and a lot of hard work. Thank goodness Pepe had come with us; he was a great help to Betty in the garden, with the outbuildings and animals.

20   Diamonds Are a Girl's Best Friend

I had a meeting with Sir John Sinclair who struck me as a rather arrogant and slack individual. He informed me of changes taking place, but never mentioned Philby, Burgess or Maclean. This struck me as odd. At the time I asked about this when his secretary came in with an urgent message from the Home Secretary. I was excused and went on my way.

For the next week Jack Sharp, my assistant, showed me how the office worked. He explained who gave what information and to whom in the offices down the hallway; the system for monitoring the strategically listed exports, and who were our representatives abroad, providing much of the information. I was now involved in the cold war.

The Bill of Landing had become ineffective as a means of monitoring the passage of goods, as ships often changed their route and destination while on the high seas. Before I headed this new department the Allies had established a shipping intervention programme using receivers. Each country was consigned a particular number of receiving companies, which would receive incoming goods that were on the strategic trade list. But without constant vigilance this method was full of holes, and goods continued to go behind the Iron Curtain, the office and the CIA set up agents in jobs that would enable us to monitor sea traffic as closely as possible. Once goods arrived in the country, customs officers would carry out random investigations on the receiving companies.

I will use Chile as an example since it produced copper, which was in very high demand behind the Iron Curtain. In Chile both the consul and the commercial counselor worked for us and had a network of agents who passed on information about shipping. These agents usually worked in the import and export department, or in the shipping telegraph station. When the consul or commercial counselor heard about a particular ship, carrying copper, which had been leaving for Oslo and then received instructions to redirect to Gdansk, they would send me details, often very explicit, perhaps even including the captain's name. I would then inform the naval intelligence department. The navy would follow the passage of the copper-carrying ship, and at a strategic point intercept it and redirect it to an English or French port. The cargo would usually be confiscated and put on the market, and the receiving company in Oslo would be investigated and blacklisted. We worked very closely with the CIA in our endeavours to monitor shipping and the developments of strategic trade.

During my second week, Jack and I needed the help of U.K.'s customs investigation branch. I called the head of the department, to discover I was speaking to Mr. Dowding, whom I had introduced to the Spanish customs authorities.

Jack came into my office with a telegram from the consul in Chile about a shipment of copper due to arrive in England. The copper had been bought by a well-known English trading house which in itself would be good enough for most people. The consul's agent in the telegraph office picked up a message requesting the ship to change its final destination. Instead of Liverpool, the ship was ordered to go to Newcastle. This was strange; Liverpool, being on the Atlantic side of England, was the natural port for industrial goods arriving from the Americas. Also most copper processing plants were in Manchester or Preston, both of which are within easier access of Liverpool than Newcastle.

I called Mr. Dowding and explained the situation. Two or three weeks later Dowding called me back.

'Mr. Bristow, the copper carrying ship has apparently finished unloading its cargo, but the quantity in the warehouse is one quarter of the quantity you told me the ship was carrying. The receiving company's receipt, made out by the trading company, seems to be in order. They apparently were only expecting one quarter of the load. The captain had departure papers dated for tomorrow.'

'Has the ship taken on any cargo since its arrival?' I asked.

'Besides normal food rations and medical supplies for the crew, no it has not, and the captain's papers are all in order, with export approved instructions issued by the trading company for him to deliver the remaining copper to Stockholm, so I'm unable to hold him or the ship.'

This seemed rather curious so I thought about how to dig a little deeper.

Jack called up his friend in the navy to find out if they had a ship in the northern part of the Channel, near Holland or

Denmark. I called naval intelligence and informed them of the situation. While I was giving the details to naval intelligence, Jack was on the other phone taking details of naval vessels on maneuvers near Denmark. Jack always took details of naval vessels in these situations as sometimes the officer at the other end of the phone was slow to react, or made a fuss. When that happened Jack and I would give the details of ships' positions and tell the liaison officer at the other end of the phone to get on with it. It was quite amazing how some people reacted in these situations. I'm sure they were fed up with war, and basically we were fighting a strategic goods war.

Back to the ship leaving Newcastle. Four days later it was stopped by the navy as it sailed passed Stockholm, quite obviously on its way to Gdansk. The ship was forced to return to England where it was impounded by customs. As a result of this the English trading company was blacklisted by us and carefully watched. During my time as head of strategic trade, Jack, and I managed to stop four or five more shipments, organised by the same trader, reaching the Eastern bloc.

While this copper escapade was going on, of course a lot of other trading movements were taking place. One involved the CIA, the American navy, and some classified electronic components being shipped to England. They were to do with fighter planes. I don't remember all the details. As a result of the liaison and between me and the CIA man in London we became friends. He shall remain anonymous, and during the next few paragraphs I refer to him as John X.

I cannot find notes relating to this episode directly. One point is he was quite aware of was the CIA following him and he surmised this was due to his friendship with Philby. Al Almer had clearly introduced my father to the CIA in London. Although Al Almer had cleared his name as far as working with Philby was concerned, there was always suspicion. My father was quite obviously fascinated by the CIA and their ability to act fast. He often refers to the slow deliberations of the internal workings of the U.K. government and how this slowness was used to cover so much corruption within the upper factions of English society. He was clearly unaware of the much more mercenary attitude of the CIA towards politicians and people in general. For me, the British Secret Service was and hopefully still is far more human in their approach to their position and work.

It happened around the time Tommy Harris had one of his parties, a big bash. Kim Philby was there, and Blunt, and a host of others; a very social gathering. Tommy wanted Kim to write a book about his being withdrawn from Washington and ousted from the Service, due to his knowing Burgess and Maclean. Up to that point, as far as we all knew, Kim had been very a good head of several departments and to all appearances a very successful operator, quite possibly due for the position of C.

The following Monday Kim and I had lunch. Kim, broke and at a loose end, told me that he did not think he would be able to write his book, and the more pressure Tommy put on him the less inclined he felt to put pen to paper. I felt sorry for him at the time and encouraged him to write the book. I thought it was a good idea. He changed the subject and asked after the family, and vaguely asked about the firm. I walked back to the office feeling some doubt once again about everything to do with the Service.

Back in the office, I was pulled out of my gloomy mood. Jack told me that John X wanted to see me and it sounded rather urgent. I called John X and agreed to go to his office in the American Embassy in Grosvenor Square.

I hailed a cab, felling curious, because John X, normally a rather cool character, had sounded very concerned. At the Embassy, I showed my pass to the guard, and was escorted by another guard along the passage to the elevators and up to John X's floor. The floor number was marked with some cover name and I remember thinking how crazy for them to bother. Everybody knew the CIA was there.

John X offered me coffee, and gestured to one of his comfortable chairs. The CIA had large offices which looked and smelled wealthy and efficient compared to ours. His room was very comfortable, with Chesterfield chairs and couch. His bookshelves were full of American and English law books. Next to the picture of the President was a photograph of John at Harvard receiving his graduation papers. The secretary brought in the coffee.

'So what's all this about?' I asked.

'Diamonds, Desmond; you know, a girl's best friend. Except these are industrial diamonds.' He went on to explain, in his mild American accent,

'I have received a message form Washington saying that they believe diamonds are reaching Poland and East Germany, obviously for their wire-making and metal-finishing factories.'

'So, how does that affect us?'

'My colleagues at home seem to have information which points the finger towards the Diamond Trading Company; you know part of the De Beers set-up.'

I knew very well the company he was referring to. I also knew the Diamond Trading Company (DTC), and the trade of diamonds was then (as now) a very important contributor to Britain's balance of payments. It was essential that this highly regarded international business should not have its reputation tarnished. If it was indeed involved with marketing diamonds to the Eastern bloc, America would, as John X said, blacklist the company and stop importing.

'We are talking big bucks here, Desmond.'

Speaking my thoughts out loud I said,

'I cannot believe the Diamonds Trading Company is involved, or even aware of any of its diamonds reaching behind the Iron Curtain. If they are indeed getting to Poland or East Germany, it must be through one of the Belgium buyers, in Antwerp.'

We discussed various possibilities for the remainder of the afternoon.

On the train going home that evening I looked at the faces around me; I wondered if any of these men worked at DTC and if so, whether they knew of any Russian trade. No; they would be blissfully ignorant, I thought. I shuddered at the idea of the international scandal it would cause if indeed De Beers were trading with the Eastern bloc. The financial blow to the City as a whole if the Americans stopped buying industrial diamonds would be terrible.

The next morning I called Peter Bowie, our liaison officer with the international operating companies, who I knew had contact with one of the directors of DTC (The Diamond Trading Company). I asked Peter to get the up-to-date list of all the European diamond buyers. In the meantime Jack and I started checking through intercepts and telegrams to and from DTC and the buying companies in Belgium. We even looked into the possibility of getting the Belgian security services to tap certain Belgian buyers' phones, but it became too complicated and political.

Working in strategic trade was refreshing; it seemed as though it was one of the very few departments that was able to pull in the co-operation of all other departments without the normal back stabbing and silly games. I suppose that's what comes of being in the department dealing with the physical elements of the Cold War.

After a month of reading through thousands of intercepts, and thoroughly investigating all the international trading companies and analyzing information from many commercial counselors and consuls, we found no evidence that any European company was involved in diamond smuggling to the Eastern bloc. What we did discover was an ancient diamond trading trail going from West Africa via the Lebanon. A lot of the diamonds that went to India, and certainly Russia before the revolution were bought and sold by Lebanese traders. We concluded that the diamonds reaching the Iron Curtain countries emanated from what we thought of as the illicit diamond trade centred mostly in Liberia and other West African countries, and still run by Lebanese traders.

Peter Bowie, Jack and I went for a celebration drink at the club. The three of us wondered where the CIA had received its information implicating DTC.

'You, know. The CIA has a lot of chaps in West Africa and Lebanon.' Peter said thoughtfully. 'I wonder why they are not aware of the diamonds circulating in those areas, which are nothing to do with De Beers?'

'God only knows! I would imagine they are too busy worrying about oil. Besides, aren't they under the illusion that DTC is a world monopoly, and that all diamonds go through their hands?'

'Yes, Desmond, and that has made business difficult for DTC in America. But even so it surprises me that our American friends seem so ignorant. When you go to see John X, ask him about it.'

'I will. I'm seeing him tomorrow.'

Jack offered his cigarettes around. 'You know, what puzzles me is where the Americans got their information from.'

After a few more drinks, and conversations that went around and around the same subject, we came to the conclusion that the KGB had possibly fed a CIA agent with the rumour in order to tarnish the name of De Beers, thus reducing American trade with the company, which would indirectly have a very damaging effect on Britain.

The next day I convinced John X of DTC's innocence, and that none of the European buyers were in any way involved. I told him and showed evidence, some of it historical, about the diamond business run by the Lebanese in West Africa.

It was true; the CIA had no idea, or at least John X told me they had no idea, of the Lebanese traders. Quite surprising really, since historically the Lebanese had been trading in diamonds long before the DTC and so many of the CIA chaps were history buffs.

He was as glad to hear the news as I was in giving it to him. I broached the next subject with caution as it could have been a bit touchy.

'John,' I said clearing my throat, 'Peter, Jack and myself believe the KGB fed misinformation to one of your agents, perhaps in Poland. The idea would obviously be to tarnish De Beers with your country, thus undermining the company's trade with the US which would potentially have the devastating effect on Britain we have already discussed.' Lighting a cigarette I continued, 'It means they know the identity of your agent.'

'Yes, Desmond, you could be right.' He thought for a moment, and exclaimed, 'My God! This could be very tricky. I'll have someone look into this idea of yours; you just never know.'

Whether his agent was exposed to the KGB I never found out, but I'm sure if there was a problem John sorted it out. This was the last exciting assignment I was involved in.

Although working in strategic trade was fascinating, there was no way in which this prophylactic exercise achieved more than fifty per cent success. It did, however, slow down the development of the war machine in Russia. Unfortunately this had no effect on Soviet espionage, subversion, disinformation or any other undermining tactics in which Russia and some of its reluctant allies were engaged.

Radio Moscow broadcast the Communist Party rules, and repeatedly slanged Imperialism, a practice at which Russia had become ruthlessly expert. Hypocritically, it remained the masthead of their anti-democratic propaganda. Every time the subject was raised, or I read a newspaper article about the Communist Party or a Communist-organised strike, Burgess and Maclean would come to mind , and then, invariably, the uncertainty around Kim Philby.

We were witnessing Soviet Russia practicing one of its basic commandments: The Communist Parties in the Imperialist countries must render systematic aid to the colonial revolutionary liberation movement of oppressed nationalities generally. The duty of rendering active support to the movements rests primarily upon the workers in the countries upon which the oppressed nations are economically, financially or politically dependent. The Communist Parties must openly recognize the right of colonies from the Imperialist state. They must recognize their right of armed defence against Imperialism and give active support to this defence by all means in their power. This policy must be adopted by the Communist Party in regard to all oppressed nations.

This avalanche of directed subversion was what we in the West were up against. The cloud of political fall-out was as effective as the atomic bomb. It permeated the minds of a great percentage of academics, journalists and the so-called intelligentsia of Western Europe. It certainly affected our workforce, causing strikes and a strong rise in the political strength of left-wing unions.

America was also under verbal attack, and the fear this generated led to the McCarthy period of Reds under the bed.

The slowing down of technical aid and supplies was initiated to put off the day when Soviet words of abuse might be turned into active weapons of war.

My section, because it was actively achieving visible results, became the object of curiosity from other incumbents of 54 Broadway. Fortunately our two officers were at the end of a tortuous corridor at the back of the first floor which kept the less zealous away. One afternoon

I returned to my office to find a chap dressed in naval uniform, khaki anorak and tilted naval cap standing in the doorway talking to Jack.

'Excuse me, but what are you doing here? And what is your name?'

'I just thought I would come and have a look at the department that seems to be faring well against our Russian friends.'

He edged into the office. I moved in front of him.

'I have just returned from Germany and heard several reports about your work.'

'Oh, really . . . What was your name again?'

'Blake, George Blake.'

'Well, George, unless you are here officially you can f--- off, since we are very busy and don't really appreciate snoopers.'

He turned on his heel.

'Not very friendly, are you?'

'No, we are not, now get out of here,' I retorted angrily.

George Blake was arrested as a Soviet spy some years later, and like the others managed to escape from prison so he could reside in Russia, (lucky fellow).

It is clear from his secret notes how badly my father was being affected by the internal workings of the SIS. Sinclair was worse than useless. He apparently had very little time for the Americans, who had been involved in the Korean War and consequently had a great deal of direct hostility towards communism. The tortuous way bureaucracy had of dealing with situations made immediate solutions unacceptable.

"There was a very damaging war taking place within the political arena, and the slowness of our government and industry to change made it very easy for the workers to gain strength and cause immeasurable economic damage. Had the leading industrial groups and politicians woken up to the need of a fairer society then the idea of Communism would not have gained so much strength. There was a great deal that needed to be done, and these leaders opened the gates of revolt by not changing."

My good friend Ken Mills was back in London working for MI5 and we lunched together regularly when we would discuss work, Philby, Burgess, and the extraordinary behavior of Liddell; but usually have a good laugh. We were both still shaken by the Burgess-Mclean affair. In early 1954 I met up with Ken at his club for lunch. He wanted my opinion. There was snow on the ground and London was at a standstill.

I have been offered a job outside the Service and don't know what to do. He explained that Sir Percy Sillitoe, his old boss in MI5, had been invited to take up a post with De Beers. Percy wants me to join him. The company is going to set up a security organization in South Africa to cover its diamonds and gold mining interests.

Hearing the excitement in Ken's voice, and knowing how disillusioned he was with MI5, I told him to go for it, and he did.

I envied Ken a little, and again thought of leaving the Service. By April 1954 the strategic trade work had become more or less routine and the list of goods and companies we were watching had been whittled down to ten or twenty. The main concern was in the atomic field and in electronic components, mostly manufactured by America. There was neither the workload nor the room left for both Jack and me; and Jack seemed to enjoy the routine, which I did not.

Head office got to hear of my dissatisfaction and, in an attempt to keep me on, asked if I would be interested in going to Buenos Aires as head of MI6 in South America. My cover position would have been passport control officer. I was dumbfounded; so far as we were concerned, passport control was all very well, but every country's security service was well aware that this was British Secret Service cover. Besides, I did not want another upheaval for the family, or to leave the farm. I refused their offer of Buenos Aires and informed them I was going to start looking around for other work.

In May, at one of our weekly lunches, I told Ken of my desire to leave. Two weeks later he invited me to have a chat with Percy Sillitoe at their office at St Andrew's House, High Holborn.

Percy and Ken told me about the diamond smuggling in Liberia and other parts of West Africa, and the problems it was creating for De Beers. They needed another person to join them and wondered if I was interested. Little did either of them realise how close the diamond smuggling game in West Africa had come to causing the possible collapse of the mighty financial empire of De Beers. At that time, neither Ken nor Percy knew that I had been dealing with diamonds and so-called smuggling.

I thought about their offer and talked about it with Betty over the next few days. She reminded me of how unhappy I had been since Philby's retirement. Besides I felt the climate in the Service was getting worse, not better. Everybody was suspicious of everybody else.

I accepted Sir Percy's offer. I said goodbye to Jack and a couple of the secretaries; all my pals had left the Service long before. I went up to Sinclair, and shook his hand.

I received a cheque for two thousand pounds as my payoff.

In the late summer of 1954 I was still commuting on the train up and down to London. We were still farming; we had pigs, cows, and an old Fordson tractor and horses. Pepe had married and moved to Chelmsford. The children were fit and well; Rosanne had been to a couple of schools; she just could not settle down. That was rather how I felt, I suppose, but I was now employed by De Beers and chasing diamonds smugglers around and I could feel myself settling down slowly into a much more normal life without the need of deception or secretiveness with family or friends.

21   Questioned by Peter Wright

For the next eighteen months Ken and I thoroughly investigated the illicit diamond trade in West Africa. This included the countries of Sierra Leone, Liberia and the Gold Coast. Sir Percy Sillitoe spent most of his time asleep, dreaming of the sweetshop in Eastbourne which he had purchased on his retirement as chief of MI5.

At the end of October 1955 Christopher Robert William Tomas (Bill) was born. It was rather traumatic as Rosanne resented his birth and in some ways was perhaps rather disgusted by him since he was so much younger. His birth seemed to cause some domestic friction except for Annette who became Bill's best friend.

As I have already mentioned, the so-called illicit diamond trade was a well-established business, with many of the West African governments in the pockets of the Lebanese traders (smugglers). We had meetings with a few government representatives and tried pointing out that this business was paying no taxes to the government, but they were not interested. We were trying to break into a trade that had been established for at least three hundred years. As far as the governments were concerned, the smugglers may not have been paying taxes, but indirectly they were bringing money into the area; as indeed they were.

'After all,' said one Sierra Leone representative in his Eton-cum-Oxford accent, 'the diggers, as you call them, the people picking up or digging up the diamonds are paid with foreign money and then they spend it in our shops or put it in our banks.'

The good looking, well educated, very black African was right. What's more, policing frontiers against smuggling would be very costly, and virtually impossible due to the wide-open nature of the bush land and semi-desert. Consequently we gave up trying to convince the governments to illegalize the smuggling.

However, we did suggest that De Beers set up a buying company with outpost buying houses to purchase diamonds directly from the diggers. We also suggested that the company should start buying from some of the larger smuggling organizations which would make it possible to infiltrate their influence over some of the government officials involved. When they asked how they would persuade smugglers to sell them their goods, we pointed out that selling to De Beers in Africa would save the Lebanese carriers the long, expensive and dangerous journey back home. De Beers took up our suggestion and shortly afterwards had a very successful business going in West Africa, with small buying houses spread around the diamond producing areas.

Ken, Percy and I were now out of a job. Ken returned to MI5, Percy retired to his sweetshop in Eastbourne, and I accepted Sir Philip Oppenheimer's offer to stay on with De Beers and head up a security and property department.

Later in 1956 I received a surprise phone call from Ken; a surprise because I had lost touch with him since our lives had taken different directions.

'Hey Des, how are you, old chap?' asked his familiar, well-educated, throaty voice.

I was looking at the plans of a new building which DTC were constructing.

'Very well, old boy, busy as a beaver; and you? How is the old Firm treating you?' I asked, realizing how little I missed the SIS.

'I was wondering if you would like to meet for lunch at my club; you do remember it's the Garrick?' he added sarcastically, rubbing in the fact that we had not met for a long time.

'By the way, hope you don't mind, old chum, but I'm bringing along a friend who wants to meet you, what with you knowing Philby and all that sort of thing. He is one of our new boffins, come here from Marconi, got all sorts of new devices for listening in on people. Anyway he is fascinated by Philby and has implied on several occasions that he would like to meet you.'

'Sounds good. I'll see you there,' I replied. 'By the way, what's his name?'

'Peter, Peter Wright. You'll like him. Cheerio.'

The Garrick was always a lively club, full of distinguished academics, artists, actors, some famous lawyers and not too many businessmen. Ken and I ordered Campari and soda.

Peter said, 'I could do with a large gin and tonic, if that's OK.'

I still remember his slightly odd pronunciation of 'tonic'.

After the initial social niceties, Ken told Peter about Guy Burgess's antics in Gibraltar and Tangier, and referred to Liddell's comments at the time. The conversation, quite naturally, centred around Burgess and Maclean; this was still a topic of interest and concern, drawing attention as it did to the crass inefficiency of MI5.

Peter asked me a lot of questions about Philby, and wondered if I had any insight into Philby's loyalties.

'I imagine you are concerned about Philby's relationship with that arch-bugger Burgess. I had lunch with Kim not long ago; he is still broke, starting to look scruffy. Drinking a lot and looking for a job. I just don't know how he ever tolerated Burgess. Certainly Burgess had put him in the shit. But who in hell tipped off Burgess, and who called off the watchers at Maclean's house over the weekend they disappeared? That is what I would like to know!'

'Well, from what I know now of office procedure, I just don't know who it might have been. It could have been Liddell himself,' Peter conjectured.

'Do you think Philby had anything to do with Burgess being tipped off about Maclean?' I suggested, hoping for a definite answer one way or the other.

Peter chuckled.

'As you know, Burgess lived with Philby for some time in Washington. It seems obvious the leak was via Philby, and surely it might have been done wittingly, but whether it was any more than a friend telling his friends they were about to get into a lot of trouble, no one knows. Your old Firm, Desmond, seems convinced of his innocence; at least that is the official line.'

'Yes I know, but if they genuinely believe in his innocence, why virtually sack him? And if there is any doubt, why not investigate him more thoroughly? Kim had no difficulty in answering the questions from Milmo. Kim is far too bright for the likes of Milmo. In a situation like that he would just put on his stutter. Peter, I have had many long chats with Kim when he never stuttered; other times, when it suited him, he stuttered so badly I had to stop listening.'

We talked about my new work while the waiter served us, then I continued.

'I was about to say about Philby, and indeed Burgess and Maclean, but for me more Kim, because I consider him a friend. . . quite a close friend; the whole affair has completely demoralized me as far as ever working for MI6 again is concerned. Let's face it, the Russians must know an awful lot about our whole set-up thanks to Burgess, and just having to wonder whether Kim Philby is or isn't, is paralyzing. The whole thing is a joke and I am sure Moscow is laughing at us all.'

I was on my high horse and letting out some of my frustration.

Peter put in, 'We in 5 do not believe Philby is innocent, and we are still trying to build a case. Our problem is not being able to find any real proof.'

'What is real proof, Peter?' I asked, bewildered. 'How can any of us who have anything to do with espionage expect real proof by British law standards? Our whole existence is due to the fact that we operate (or operated) outside the law.'

'Yes of course; but when it comes to trying to prove a person's guilt we have to have hard evidence,' said Ken, pointing out that I might well be under suspicion also.

'You have known Kim a long time, Des. You are great friends with Tommy Harris, and he was great friends with Burgess, still is with Kim. According to you Blunt and Liddell are often at Harris's parties; and if there is one bugger I don't trust in all of this, it is Blunt.'

Peter looked at me out of the corner of his eye. We decided to change the subject as Ken and I were becoming a bit rattled, and as people filtered out of the club our voices carried further. Peter told me about his work for Marconi before he joined MI5. We discovered we lived close to each other in Essex and decided that if we should meet on the train we would go out for a drink.

'Perhaps at the Queen Anne's Castle, the old pub near Great Leighs,' suggested Peter.

Back in the office, I felt very glad to be working for a company that cared for its members and was operating in a relatively sane area of the business world, instead of walking along mind- twisting hallways infested with the suspicious thinking of espionage and counter-espionage.

About two months later Peter and I did meet on the train, and went for a drink in the Queen Anne's Castle, where the low oak beams made it necessary for me to duck; the smoky, noisy atmosphere and the smell of keg beer were intoxicating and we could talk without fear of being overheard since the noise level was good and loud.

'Peter, I heard a few days ago from my Spanish tutor at Cambridge; he told me that someone, he thinks from the Service; had been asking him a lot of questions about my political views during the Civil War and if I had been a member of any of the Communist groups at Cambridge.'

'Well, were you?' he asked.

'No most certainly not.'

I went on to explain my views. We then talked about his investigations, how things were with the Americans and Mr. Hoover, the Suez Canal crisis, and how Mr. Hollis, the director General, was coping.

Peter did not have much to say about Hollis.

'As for Hoover, Desmond, he is not a nice a man in the least. He is paranoid about Communism, cannot and will not get over Maclean, thinks Philby should be in jail; but he is at least talking to us again.'

Peter and I met a few more times, when he would invariably ask more questions about Philby, and what I knew of Tommy Harris, and kept on about Philby's proposed book. I saw him not long after Philby had gone to Beirut. Tommy had reimbursed Andre Deutsch Ltd, the publishing company, the sum of 3000 pounds; the advance Kim had received from them to write the book. When I told Peter this he remarked, with a twinkle in his eye,

'You do know them well, don't you, Desmond?'

I didn't see him again for some time.

By Christmas 1958 I had completely settled into my work in the normal world. Life at De Beers was both interesting and straightforward and I was enjoying being who I was supposed to be, instead of always pretending. Santa Claus was my only secret identity, the Diamond Trading Company was growing by leaps and bounds; the buying office in West Africa was very successful, the new building was finished. Apart from my odd meetings with Ken and Peter my connection with old Firm grew fainter and fainter.

The farm in Essex was coming along slowly. I had four stockings to fill that Christmas. Bill's presence was becoming less of a problem especially as Rosanne was away at school. His godfathers were Tommy Harris and Ken Mills. (Perhaps it is because he had two MI5 chaps as godparents, and me as his father, that he is writing this book with me now; an inherited interest.)

Actually I wanted to find out who my father was. As I mentioned for a time I wondered if he had been a traitor. I could never understand why he had such a close relationship with the French and why De Gaulle had bestowed such high commendations upon him. My father was a very jovial man and yet would have bouts of depression, and terrible bouts of anger. His years of deception never left him; that is quite clear as even now I have discovered some very important aspects of his life which I would have loved to have discussed with him.

It has often been said to me, once a member of the Secret Service, always a member. One day in late January 1958 the telephone rang. It was Margery Bray, the London representative who had come out to Madrid. Since our return to England, her family and ours had become friends, and I was expecting her to ask us to an after-Christmas party or something. Instead she asked if I would be prepared to undertake a mission for the old Firm which would last about a week, and would involve my going to Tangiers.

Rather taken aback, I said, it depends what it is. Then, realizing my duties lay elsewhere, I added, and whether the managing director here will give me clearance.

The managing director, knowing about my previous occupation, readily agreed. The next day I telephoned

Margery and suggested we meet somewhere away from the old Firm's offices as I did not want to be seen anywhere near them. I don't know why I even entertained the idea of working for them again. Looking back I'm not sure if it was not due to nostalgia as much as anything.

We met at a Chinese restaurant in Soho. She was early, as usual, and had already ordered for both of us by the time I arrived. The slow ting-tang chimes of Chinese music and the dull light of the Chinese lanterns created a very appropriate atmosphere.

Margery was very businesslike, and got straight to the point. She asked if I remembered a Moroccan sergeant who I had harboured, and MI6 had taken on, while I was in Algiers. I certainly did. He had been recommended to me by Doudot for his initiative, savoir-faire and general reliability, along with his hatred of the Germans. I had last seen him when he had just volunteered for active service and was about to be parachuted into Italy behind German lines.

'So what is this to do with me now?' I asked.

'Well, he is now the head of the newly formed Moroccan security service and he has contacted our agent in Tangiers (David Y) a newspaper correspondent; you know Teddy Dunlop resigned not long after you left Madrid? Anyway, our friend has spoken to David about you and has stated quite firmly that before establishing any kind of liaison with MI6 he wants to discuss the details with you.'

'How very flattering,'

377

I must admit it was a bit of a thrill to be asked back in, especially knowing it was only going to last for a week. A quick in and out, as it were. She gave me a few more details, and I thought for a while.

'OK, providing you let me make my own travel arrangements and the company reimburses my expenses through an exterior account of theirs, I'll go.'

I smiled.

'But this will be the one and only time.'

Maybe my condition about travel arrangements was paranoia on my part, but as I told her, all Firm travel outfits are blown. That is certainly what I thought then, and whether they were or not, she agreed to my conditions.

The restaurant had filled up with tourists and when an American couple sat at the table next to us Margery reduced her voice to almost a whisper.

'You will meet David Furgueson, our head man in Rabat, at the bar of the Hotel Minza in Tangiers, where he will organise a room for you to stay.'

I interrupted, and wagged my finger at her. 'No! I would rather organise my own Hotel thank you."

'OK. You will meet him at the Hotel Minza bar where he will brief you. I don't have the details with me, for obvious reasons.'

On the appointed day in March I found myself on the BOAC flight from Heathrow. I must confess it was exciting to be back in the world of secrets; it was like going on an exciting adventure, and maybe I overplayed the importance of it, but it was fun.

I arrived in the early evening; the sunset was creating a wonderful red glow in the rapidly disappearing heat haze coming off the desert sands. I was reminded of how very quickly the evenings became cold in that part of the world.

The last time I had been in North Africa was in the middle of the war, and things had changed a little. Tangiers airport had been modernized and seemed very busy, with hundreds of Arab families arriving and leaving. There were still one or two jeeps, now operating as taxis. I jumped in one and asked for my hotel. The streets were full of people wrapped up in bundles of clothes, walking around and shopping. Chickens, goats, cheese, fruit, vegetables, carpets, lamps, camels, all sorts of things were on the market considering how late in the day it was. And the air was thick; amazingly, the smell of the animals was completely overpowered by the strong scents of herbs and spices- vanilla, cinnamon, cumin, cillentro, mint, pepper; it was almost intoxicating.

I checked in at the little hotel I had chosen and decided to walk to the Minza. Besides thinking it would be quicker in such traffic, I thought it would give me a chance to feel part of the hustle and bustle, and get used to moving amongst the Arabs. Straight from London as I was, I could not help being conspicuous, and at every other corner a young man would come up and offer hash; men with trays gold and silver trinkets tried everything to entice money out of my pocket, and carpet traders grabbed my sleeves. By the time I arrived at the Minza, I had learnt to spot the more aggressive traders, and had developed a sidestepping technique.

Why my father lies here I have no idea. The whole trip was organised by Margery Bray and he stayed at the Hotel Minza. I found this out when I went to Morocco and he suggested I stay there as he had such a good memory of it. He could not help but deceive even with this small episode. What goes on in the head of a SPY?

I walked through the beautifully tiled lobby of the Hotel Minza, with its arched windows and doorways, into the lounge bar with its sumptuous Persian carpets. Our man in Rabat, David Furgueson, was easy to recognize. He looked very much the English charmer, and was reading The Times. He obviously recognized me, as he got up when I entered and asked if I wanted a drink.

'Very much so,' I answered feeling a little worn out by my walk. 'What the hell is going on here? It's not Ramadan is it?'

'Well, Desmond, as a matter of fact it is.'

'Oh God! I thought so. Even the airport was packed and the Arabs don't like to fly all that much; unless it's on a carpet of course,' I added somewhat sarcastically.

The French bartender, wearing a fez, nodded a greeting of recognition to David. I guessed he must have been one of his agents.

David was younger that myself, well-tanned and tough-looking, and very charming. I had made a point of reading up on his background on the plane trip over. I can't say I liked him at that moment; I was annoyed that neither he nor anyone else in the Firm's office had thought about Ramadan.

This is the period in the Islamic calendar when Muslims are required to fast during the day; they then eat, and eat, and eat at night. It is a very family orientated period, when an Arab meeting a European in a public place would be very noticeable, and it would be impossible to meet at his house. It would only be possible to meet at some unearthly hour of the night.

I put this over to David, letting him know I was none too pleased. He then informed me he had not been able to fix a time with the head of security, and hoped our Moroccan friend would be able to see me later that evening.

I had a short meeting with my old acquaintance, who was very glad to see me, as I was him. We talked about his appointment as head of security and what he wanted from me. When he explained his requirements I realised it would take more than a week to sort out all the details, especially liaising with London. I explained I only had a week; he explained apologetically that after that evening he would not be able to do anything for the month of

Ramadan. I persuaded him to liaise with the head of station in Tangiers when the month was over.

The next morning I called David and asked him to organise my trip home. Three days later I landed at Heathrow feeling furious. What a waste of taxpayers' money. Could the Firm not get anything right? Fancy them not checking on the dates of Ramadan, and David Furgueson for not having established that I was available for only a limited time. I realised how glad I was not to be surrounded by their crass inefficiency any longer. It reminded me of how often agents had been sent into the field wearing English clothes with the labels still attached, and the agent in Algiers whom they were sending to Italy with an ID photograph showing him wearing a specifically English shirt. No wonder the Americans lost faith; so had I.

Poor Betty; when I got home I verbalized my outrage about the Firm to her; and I was angry. The next day I wrote a stinking letter informing head office of my opinion, and that under no circumstances would I ever do anything for them ever again. Whether they built up a successful relationship with the Moroccan security department or not, I don't know; I didn't care then and I still don't.

The fact is he did care and right up until his death. He could not stop on about how much opportunity Britain had had and yet let it go to waste due to its arrogance and stuffy attitudes to so many aspects of itself. His anger and frustration expressed here shows me how depressed and unhappy he was. Sadly for all of us at home this anger would explode upon us and mother.

In September 1962 Peter Wright called me in my office, asking to meet me at Liverpool Street Station one evening. I suggested that same evening by the shoe-repair shop next to platform 9. I arrived a little early and watched one or two of the remaining steam trains puff out of the station, and the commuters coming from the underground in their droves. The evening standard paper man yelled out the latest headlines: read all about it. I wondered what Peter Wright could want; he would not have called me after all this time just to have a chat for old times' sake; we did not know each other well enough.

It had not been a good year. I was fed up with commuting such a distance; the farm had become much harder work with very little financial reward; John, my eldest son, wanted to emigrate to Canada and become a Mountie, or sail to Australia. What the hell did someone from MI5 want with me now? I made up my mind before Peter arrived that I was not going to accept a job of any sort.

I saw him walking slowly over. He was easy to pick out as everyone around him was in a hurry. He looked older and worried.

'Hello, Desmond,' he sounded tired.

'Hello, Peter, you look as though you need a drink.'

'Yes, I do. Do you mind if we wait for the buffet train?'

'Fine by me.'

I checked the time on the departure board. We had fifteen minutes.

'Let's have a quick snifter in the pub,' I suggested.

We chatted casually. Peter had moved to Thorpe Le Soken, near Frinton. We were looking for a house near Witham as the drive from the farm to Chelmsford station was too tiring, and the farm was too much work.

We were the first on the buffet train. Peter walked straight to the bar and bought a gin and tonic and a whisky and soda. We sat down. Peter took a gulp of his gin, looked me straight in the face and said,

'Desmond, I need a full written report on everything you can remember about Philby, from the day you met him.'

I looked at Peter and thought about what he was asking me to do.

'You must have found something new on him, or are your masters just creating a fuss again?'

'No they are not. I am though, and I have some information which confirms our worst suspicions; and it seems as though he is going to confess.'

'So what do you need a written report from me for?'

Peter did not answer straight away. I felt my bubble of delusion about Philby burst completely. Well, at least all my questioning about him was over. Somehow I was not as angry about his deception as I might have been. I still vaguely wondered if he might be a double agent (romantic folly). When Peter said what he said, I felt a tightening in my stomach.

'Well it seems as though you are one of his close friends who was on the right side, and I am collecting every piece of information on him possible.'

I remember thinking how convenient for the present day office to have its old members to spy on. It annoyed me.

'Why the hell are you bothering with all this? The Secret Service is about as secret as the Eamonn Andrews Show, the office treats us all so badly. Why the hell did they re-employ Kim; just to get him to admit to being a bad boy so you can bring him home, smack his hand and make him stand in the corner with a dunce's hat on? Besides, I don't suppose you will bring him home. If those idiots Burgess and Maclean got away, I can't imagine 5 outsmarting Kim at this stage of the game.'

I realised it must have been Peter who had sent someone to question my old tutor at Cambridge about my political views. I wondered if he was still delving, even still suspicious that I might be involved with Philby, or if his investigations had made it clear I was not.

However, I agreed to write a report on Philby. Here it is, as close to the original as I can remember.

September 1962

Dear Peter,

The day I met Kim Philby was at my initial interview with Felix Cowgirl in 1941. Kim, a gentle-looking man with smiling eyes and an air of confidence, was wearing an old jacket with leather elbows. He sat behind Felix making notes, and only interrupted a few times to ask me to repeat myself. My first impression was of a man with quiet, inquisitive, intellectual charm.

My second meeting with Kim Philby took place when he drove me up to St Albans. During this drive I realised he was in charge of organizing the Iberian section of Section V of MI6. I immediately liked him and knew working with him was going to be fun and interesting. He had a spiritual tranquility about him. He was very unassuming and modest.

From before I arrived and for a little time afterwards, Section V increased in numbers, as Philby gathered together a team of intellectual adventurers all of us speaking at least two languages fluently. During my nine and a half months at St Albans we had many discussions and even arguments, but never any rows. Philby was an able 'chef d'orchestre'. I never witnessed him lose his temper. He and I would often go to the pub together, either on my motorcycle, in his car or on foot. My conversations with Kim were often about hypothetical political situations, consisting of a lot of ifs and buts. Our families would always enter as a point of interest of health and well-being, and he would always encourage me to have them near me, certainly while I was at St Albans. He and his wife, Aileen, my wife and I would often have meals together. The evening sessions in the Snake pit were usually called by Philby and terminated by him, unless members of other departments appeared. He was invariably the centre of the group, and even those from other departments found themselves drawn to his magnetic personality.

He had great admiration for Hugh Trevor-Roper, but the association was purely business. Hugh did not fall for his charm and remained aloof.

For the game of espionage and counter-espionage we could not have had a better teacher and leader; he guided the department with careful, disciplined and good humoured warmth. We worked hard, long hours, enjoying every minute as our imaginations were allowed to flow and be expressed. I certainly feel the success of our department was largely due to Philby. He was very thorough and he himself worked harder than anyone.

As far as friends go, he was certainly one of my best friends at that time. We had some common ground: Cambridge, the fact that we were raised as expatriates, that our parents had lived abroad and sent us to England for our education. We both liked art; we both liked drinking and conversation, whether idle or constructive.

I can say without any doubts his best friend was and is Tommy Harris, whom Kim introduced me to at Christmas 1941, the same time I met Kim's mother. He spent a lot of time talking with Herbert Hart (MI5's ISOS specialist) and appeared to have a close relationship with him. A person Kim expressed admiration for was Tar Robertson.

I remember Kim having a certain conflict with Felix Cowgill. He wanted ISOS Ultra information to be shared with more departments, whereas Felix wanted to retain control. On the one hand, Felix was almost too possessive; but on the other hand, Kim often appeared to be quite prepared to pass on information freely and risk knowledge of ISOS reaching the Germans.

The Garbo situation. As far as our department was concerned, Philby made all the major decisions, as Cowgill would not make a move without him. Kim remained calm, slightly aloof and very much in control of every move.

From 1942-44 I was abroad as the Section V man in Gibraltar and then Algiers. From those two stations Philby seemed to be running the English end very well.

After the war Philby and I moved into different departments and only saw each other socially, usually at Tommy and Hilda Harris's rather decadent parties. Always a heavy drinker, he appeared to have started drinking excessively.

1947 I was stationed in Madrid and from then on my only contact with Kim was the occasional phone call and letter. Visits to Tommy and Hilda's house in Majorca, or their visits to Madrid, would often include a conversation or two about Kim.

After the flight of Burgess and Maclean he was posted to Madrid by the Observer. During his stay we saw a certain amount of each other despite my being warned not to by the office. We did not talk about their defection, or about Kim being asked to leave the Service; he always sidestepped the issue. I assumed at the time that he was very upset about the whole affair. I would say he was preoccupied. He was joined by Lady Frances Lindsay-Hogg, about whom he told me very little, other than that she was a friend from the Civil War days. With most of my friends, and with Philby in the past, we would have talked about Frances, about who she was, etc. He even avoided talking about Tommy and Hilda. He maintained a barrier I did not want to transgress.

On my return to London, again I met up with Kim at Tommy and Hilda's parties. When I left the Service he and I would have lunch together. It was during this period I noticed a decline in his outward appearance, especially after his acquittal by Macmillan in 1955. To round off, Peter, I regard Kim Philby as a friend who has partially died, as far as I'm concerned. The suspicion about his loyalties has created so much doubt in my mind about him as a friend, but more doubt about the abilities of my past employers, that I find it hard and somewhat painful to think about him in a clear, positive fashion. Whether your present investigations prove he is a Soviet agent or not, the fact that he has shaken the very foundation of the Secret Service in the way he has is partly his doing and partly the doing of the Services themselves.

Yours sincerely

Now, with the privilege of hindsight, it is easy for me to see suspicious acts and searching words in conversations, but to say I was truly suspicious of Kim at the time would be a lie.

Perhaps I should have been angry with him for coming to see me in Madrid after he had been let off the hook, and was still under suspicion, but it was, and still is, very difficult to contemplate one's good friend being a traitor whether for a worthy cause (in his eyes) or not.

At Christmas 1962-63 Betty and I received a card from Beirut. The picture on the front was of three Bedouins heading east. The message read simply,

'Have a Happy Christmas and a Happy New Year. May not see you for a while. Love Kim.'

It was his way of telling me he was the third man. I wrote my report. Philby defected. We sold up the farm as it was proving too much work and the commute to London was long. We moved house to Rivenhall, near Witham; much nearer to London. Peter and I became regular train-travelling companions. On the train, and in the pub near the station in Witham, Peter started to confide in me much of the contents of his book. I remember he was scared and felt very lonely.

One evening we were at our usual table in the buffet carriage. A cricket match was in progress on the playing fields of Brentwood School, and I commented that it must have been a good game to have lasted so late into the evening. We were talking about Harold Wilson and the unions, when Peter sat forward in his chair and indicated that he wanted to say something quietly in my ear.

'Desmond, I am at the point where I cannot talk to anybody in the office and I only trust a couple of my colleagues. It is quite awful. But I am convinced there is still a mole in MI5 and I do not know what to do about it.'

Not quite sure what to say or why Peter was suddenly using me as his father confessor, I replied,

'Peter, when I left MI6 I thought the whole outfit was full of moles and as it turned out I was not far wrong.'

Of course I was joking, trying to make light of what he had said. There were many loyal people still working for MI6 when I left, but I did not really want to talk about them or the Service very much. Do you not think one gets to the stage when one starts to suffer from mole mania?

I do not want to repeat the contents of Spycatcher, but over the next year or so Peter confided in me about many of the suspicions he disclosed in the book. He convinced me that Sir Roger Hollis was definitely a Russian mole, and I convinced him that Liddell, if not actively a Russian mole, had certainly helped the cause by defending Burgess and Blunt, and that it was Liddell who had brought Blunt out of retirement from the Service to check all of Burgess's personal belongings.

Despite my father feeling safe within the walls of De Beers, his work with MI6 was to continually haunt him and his personal life. Sometime in the 1970s De Beers signed a deal with the British and Russian Government, which would allow the sale of Russian Diamonds through the Diamond Trading Office in London. There was a large celebratory diner attended by Sir Phillip Oppenheimer, Harry Oppenheimer, other senior directors of De Beers, my father being one of them. My mother who accompanied him, sat next to one of the Russian directors. He was supposedly the senior member of the Russian party. My mother noticed how he would constantly refer to the Russian woman on the opposite side of the table. She was the boss not the gentleman next to my mother. She was a KGB senior officer, as were the others. After the diner my father got in touch with the Old Firm, and gave a description of the woman and the men. He was informed by MI6 who she was and they were well aware of her presence. This was quite discomforting for my father and mother. By this stage Kim Philby would have informed his masters of every single member of MI6, especially men such as my father. This made my mother very nervous. Would my father be under any threat at this stage? I do not think so. He did not either, at the time. But he had to calm my mother's fears down.

In 1976 my father retired from De Beers, sold up in the U.K. and moved to a village near Nerja in Andalucia, Spain. The old mill in Frigiliana needed to be rebuilt, it was, and my parents turned it into a wonderful home. During his time there, my father had visits from various members of MI6 and even MI5. He has never explained *why or what the visits were about. My mother by this time had her suspicions that it was to do with his friendship with Philby, etc. After all, Philby's funeral received a lot of attention during this era. He also received Nigel West sometime in the 1980s who was looking for Pujol. My father knew that MI5 had moved Pujol to Angola and faked his death. He also knew he had at one time lived in Venezuela. Not being sure if he had not since died, my father suggested Nigel follow up all those named Pujol, suggesting he start in Barcelona. This put Nigel on the track of Juan Pujol (Garbo). In 1984 my father accompanied Juan Pujol to the Normandy Beaches to be part of the 40th anniversary of the D-Day landings.*

Back to the Peter Wright case....

Cyril Mills has accused Peter Wright of being a traitor and a liar; perhaps that means that Mills himself had something to hide, or perhaps he was ashamed of having been duped by the Russian moles, or of having lied about his own accomplishment connected with Garbo. Whatever Mills's motive, there is no conceivable way in which Peter has ever betrayed his country. My feeling is that the security service or the politicians betrayed him, as they betrayed many loyal employees through sheer lack of compassion or understanding. Perhaps the politicians were so ashamed of the way in which the government has ignored information and advice from people such as Peter Wright that they tried to create a block, and paid dearly for it.

My last meeting with Peter was in 1988 when Betty and I were visiting our eldest son and his family in Australia. I called from my son's house just outside Melbourne and arranged to visit Peter. He seemed very hesitant at first. Undaunted by his reserve, Betty, John and I, after a wonderful drive through Tasmania, arrived in Cygnet, where I telephoned Peter again.

He still seemed hesitant, but agreed to see us. I don't know if he thought I had come to check up on him, or whether he was embarrassed by his living conditions. We arrived at a shack which consisted of three rooms covered with tin sheet roofing, sheltered by gum trees. The surrounding fields were very waterlogged, which was marvelous for the mosquitoes, not for the Wrights. The floors were filthy dirty, the kitchen was in chaos and quite obviously every penny went into the horses. Once over his initial surprise at seeing me and Betty again, Peter relaxed and showed us the stables.

'The Horses have been our savior from financial ruin, would you believe?'

He explained how the area was infested with deadly poisonous tiger snakes, and how when walking outside one always had to wear wellington boots to avoid being bitten.

The case against him still seems very strange to me. I cannot see why Spycatcher was so disturbing to Maggie Thatcher and the government. OK, Hollis was knighted, but so was Blunt, and that is their fault, not Wright's. Peter on his retirement, received a pension of 2000 pounds per annum.

As we were saying goodbye I remembered the time Peter had come to me with tears in his eyes.

'Desmond, I simply cannot afford the Welsh farm; the office have cheated me on my pension,' he had told me. I had been slightly incredulous.

'Yes. Like a fool I took their word for it, and did not insist on a contract and they have cheated me, and I cannot live on 2000 pounds a year.'

When we left Peter's shack we decided to spend another day exploring Tasmania, and we learnt about the terrible massacre of the Aboriginals on the island. The following day we took off from the little airport, and as I looked down on the sumptuous green of Tasmania, my last conversation with Peter ran through my mind; I thought about some of the amazing achievements of England, and Englishmen, and how far the Empire had once stretched, and some of the atrocities committed to further it.

Peter had had no part in such dishonorable deeds. Yet he would have been better off betraying his country, confessing and being granted immunity like Sir Anthony Blunt; or defecting and running to Russia. Instead he had worked conscientiously, and applied himself wholeheartedly to the security of the country, to end up living in a shack surrounded by snakes because the government had reneged on his pension. What a terrible and sad truth about my country. Peter Wright is not the only person who has been treated like a disposable piece of human rubbish by the security services.

I went over in my mind once again the whole affair which led to Peter Wright's investigations of the Service as head of the Fluency committee, starting with the defection of Maclean and Burgess. Why were the people watching Maclean taken off duty, allowing the two of them to escape to Russia? Why did Dick White arrive at their port of departure with an out-of-date passport? My conclusion is that the government did not want to deal with two traitors publicly; it might have led to a hanging and have caused a great deal of friction with the Soviet Union. I feel sure the same applies to the inadequate cross-examinations and investigations of Kim Philby, which came to the public conclusion of unsubstantial evidence. The government just hoped he would run for the skirts of mother Russia sooner than he did.

Now onto my Godfather Tommy Harris; who I really did not know.

22   Tommy Harris, My Godfather

Anyone who has read anything about Tommy Harris before will realise there are many questions about him which are and will probably remain unanswered. It is true to say that I knew Tommy Harris well; on the other hand there is part of him I perhaps knew then, and know now, but did not and do not want to believe.

He was a romantic figure, often referred to as Jesus Christ because he looked like the paintings. He was an explorer with his mind and with art. These days, living in Spain, I will often smell the smoke of black tobacco cigarettes, which reminds me of him. With the number of his pictures hanging on our walls, and the pieces of furniture he gave us scattered through our house, few days go by when he does not enter our thoughts and conversations. Yes, I am saying he has a permanent presence in our house. He was perhaps one of the most complete human beings I have ever known; he was capable of tremendous displays of generosity, giving friends wonderful gifts yet at times he could be very intolerant, especially towards his wife Hilda. He had a penetrating imagination and a far-reaching intellect. His soft, soulful eyes would suddenly take on a wild look when he had a bright idea, and would retain a certain wild, glazed look when he was painting or sculpting.

Some of the following details were written by Anthony Blunt in the foreword to the catalogue of the Lefevre Gallery when they held an exhibition of Tommy's work in

1954. The foreword is long and perhaps over-detailed, but gives an in-depth account of his background.

"Tomas Harris was born in 1908, in London; whither his English father Lionel and his Spanish mother Enriqueta had returned after many years in Spain. During their life in Spain Lionel and Enriqueta had accumulated a great deal of knowledge and artifacts of Spanish furniture, ceramics, tapestries, jewelry, lace and paintings. On returning to London the Harris's opened a gallery in the rich and fashionable Conduit Street, Mayfair, enabling the public and connoisseurs to admire and buy Spanish works of art, ranging from the fifteen up to the nineteenth century, never seen before in England. Royalty and dignitaries became regular visitors to the Spanish Art Gallery. Tommy, growing up in this world of art and beautiful things, showed his artistic talent at a very early age. He was fourteen and a half when he won a Trevelyan-Goodall Scholarship to the Slade School of Art (at that time the most important art school in England). When he had completed his course at the Slade he spent a year at the British Academy in Rome, where he developed an interest in Goya and El Greco. In 1930 his career as an artist was interrupted by his decision to enter his father's firm, but while working there he continued to paint, and used his opportunities to enlarge and deepen his knowledge of the great artists of the past, particularly Goya and El Greco. In the business, he very quickly showed an uncanny talent for dealing in antique furniture and paintings.

During the Civil War Tommy made numerous trips to northern Spain where he purchased many paintings and pieces of antique furniture and jewelry from Spanish refugees. He liaised from time to time with a Russian art dealer supposedly practicing the same trade. On one such trip he apparently met Philby, I believe in Burgos, and I have heard tales of Tommy acting as a courier for Kim, taking Times correspondence to France.

In 1937, Tommy and his father decided to hold an exhibition of their own large Goya collection, to raise money for the Spanish Red Cross who were helping victims of the Civil War. The exhibition was opened by Tommy's friend, the art historian Anthony Blunt. The exhibition, a resounding success, instantly aroused great interest in Goya, up till then generally ignored in England."

At the outbreak of World War Two Tommy and Hilda were recruited by Burgess as cook and housekeeper for Section D of MI5, which was later disbanded and made into SOE.

When section D was disbanded Tommy was kept on and moved to B Section of MI5; a surprising jump, except that Blunt was Liddell's assistant at the time. Tommy was more than capable of the work intellectually, but had Blunt not introduced him to Liddell (who was a sucker for artists and art connoisseurs), Liddell would have been unaware of Tommy's potential. By 1941 Tommy was in a position to recommend Philby as head of the Iberian section of Section V.

Tommy, well established in B section, in the bowels of MI5, later became case officer to Juan Pujol (otherwise known as Garbo). The success with which Garbo was built up over the years prior to D Day is certainly due in part to Juan Pujol (Garbo), but it owes much more to the penetrating imagination of Tomas Harris.

I had witnessed the way in which Tommy started his initial correspondence with the Germans. After the war was over, Tommy would sometimes talk about the fun he and Garbo had had creating fictitious characters dotted around various parts of the world. He explained that the real problem had been convincing the Germans that their imaginary characters existed; once the Germans showed their belief, the fun was in the making up of stories to send to Abwehr, rather like writing a play for an already captive audience. Cyril Mills has been heard to claim that he was responsible for bringing Garbo into England, and acted as his case officer. Cowgill and Philby were responsible for bringing Garbo into England. I interviewed Garbo under the administrative eye of Mills, but as the latter could speak no language except English he was sent to Canada as a liaison officer with the Mounties and from time to time acted as an agent for Garbo.

Anyone who has read about the exploits of Garbo will be well aware of Tommy's contribution. I remember him receiving the OBE, and after the ceremony telling me about his interview with General Eisenhower.

'At the end of our talk, Desmond, the General leant across his very large and very ugly desk and congratulated me on my work with Pujol.'

Again.

Many people have suggested Tommy was a Russian agent; and from the point of view of a Soviet spy set-up he was in ideal situation. There was Blunt as Liddell's personal secretary, Philby as head of Iberian Section V – and Tommy as head of the Iberian section of MI5, and then as a case officer of the world's most successful wartime deception agent.

During and after the war, the Harris parties were the congregating ground for Blunt, Burgess, Philby and, to a lesser extent, Maclean.

After the war Tommy wrote a report containing a very detailed account of his work with Garbo. He showed me his copy just before handing it over to Liddell. According to someone who was searching through the files for a copy of this report, it is now missing; or maybe MI5 are reluctant to reveal its contents for some strange reason; or Liddell misplaced it; perhaps he sent it to the Russians. Or perhaps Tommy never submitted it to Liddell.

This report has since shown up and is now a book.

I have been told that Tommy managed to persuade Blunt to authenticate fake paintings, which would relate to something Aracelli (Juan Pujol's wife) told Betty and me during a conversation in 1986. She said that shortly after the war Juan and Tommy started up a fake painting business in Caracas. They had sold several fakes when their business was cut short by a Venezuelan art expert, who discovered one or two of the forgeries in a famous collection. So it would seem Blunt was indeed persuaded by Tommy to authenticate the fakes. My question is whether it was for money, or perhaps as a favor to a Soviet agent colleague?

Another nagging question, and I have many about Tommy, which concern Aracelli, goes back to 1947 when I became head of station in Madrid. Aracelli returned to Madrid and was expecting Juan Pujol to follow her but after six months she realised she had been abandoned. According to Aracelli, Tommy would sometimes see her and help her out financially; when he stopped helping her, she rented a house from friends and in turn rented out rooms to support herself. Juan Pujol had sold all her jewelry and belongings to finance himself. Why did Tommy never tell me about this situation, I ask myself. He would have known that I would have helped Aracelli; he would also have known I would have contacted Pujol about her. There was definitely a conspiratory aspect to the post-war Pujol-Harris relationship.

I was blissfully unaware of this during my time as the MI6 man in the Iberian Peninsula, and Betty and I spent some wonderful weekends at Tommy and Hilda's retreat house at Camp de Mar, near Palma in Majorca. Back in England we went to most of the parties at their wonderful house at 1 Logan Place. Of course Blunt and Philby were at several of these, and it was at one of these parties that Tommy had publicly suggested Kim should write a book about his achievements and work for the Services, and about his withdrawal from Washington and early retirement because of his relationship with Guy Burgess. It was Tommy who secured the contract to publish with Andre Deutsch Ltd on Kim's behalf, and Tommy who, after a year of trying to persuade Kim to write the book, reimbursed the 3000 pounds advance. Why, I wonder? Perhaps it was Russian money.

In 1955 Betty and I invited Tommy to be our fourth child's godfather.

In the late autumn of 1958, on a Sunday evening after one of their big Saturday night parties, Hilda, Betty, Tommy and I were about to sit down to scrambled eggs. Tommy had gone to the kitchen for a serving spoon when the door buzzer buzzed; they had a security system with a camera at the door and an intercom. Tommy pressed the enter button and walked into the dining room. As soon as Tommy sat down there was a knock on the kitchen door, which Tommy had left open, and a voice said, 'Hello, I'm back for Christmas.'

Much to our surprise Kim Philby walked into the dining room. We had not seen Kim for some time. His wife Aileen had recently died under strange circumstances; it had even been suggested that he might have murdered her, or had her killed. He was rather taken aback to see Betty and myself, and started backing out of the room, apologising that he could not stay as he was catching a train to Oxford. It was very obvious that he had needed to talk to Tommy. Later that evening, after we had all retired to bed, the telephone rang and Tommy had a very long conversation. The next morning Betty asked Hilda who the late call was from.

'Oh, Kim.'

She sounded irritated.

'He often calls but I never know what about.'

Not long after the New Year we went to a party with
Tommy and Hilda. We drove back with them to Logan
Place, and had just got out of the car when they started to
argue. By the time we had reached the house they were
yelling and screaming at each other. Hilda walked into the
kitchen and poured herself a drink. Tommy followed, only
to have a plate thrown at him. Tommy started to yell in
such a fashion that Betty and I began to feel nervous for
their safety. Hilda began crying hysterically and came
rushing out of the kitchen and into the living room. Betty
followed and tried to comfort her. I went in and asked
Tommy if he was all right. There were a couple of broken
plates on the kitchen floor. Tommy was sitting on a stool,
running his hands through his hair.

'Oh, Christ, Desmond, I am sorry about this.'

Betty convinced me that, if we could possibly persuade
them to, they should come with us to Essex instead of
staying in London for the weekend. Tommy accepted. He
walked over and put his hand on my shoulder.

'Can Betty take Hilly to the car, and I'll collect a few
belongings. Could you pour me a scotch?'

I asked no questions and on the drive I think Betty and I
talked about the cows.

The next morning Betty asked Hilda why they had suddenly started to argue. Hilda explained that it happened a lot, and if the argument wasn't about the book on Goya that Tommy was working on, then it was often about Philby.

Tommy and Hilda started to spend much more time in Majorca, only coming over to London occasionally to shop, or when Tommy wanted to sell some paintings. Consequently we saw very little of them between then and the fateful day in 1964 when Tommy crashed his car and died.

The day after the accident Betty answered the telephone to a very distraught Hilda.

'Betty, Tommy is dead; he killed himself in a car accident yesterday.'

Betty, in a state of semi-shock, asked if he had been alone, and Hilda explained how she had been in the car with him and felt it was her fault, and so on, and so on. Poor Hilda. I agreed to fly out and help her however I could. On my arrival I retrieved the smashed up car from Spanish customs. Hilda was very upset at the sight of the car and that evening she told me the whole story.

'Oh, Desmond! What have I done?' She said. I poured her a large brandy and asked,

'What do you mean? For God's sake tell me what happened, Hilly.'

'Tommy and I went to Palma; he had a meeting with his antique dealer, Senor Acosta. After the meeting Tommy wanted to take some of his latest ceramics to the ceramist to be fired. I went off to do some shopping while he went to see Acosta. We agreed to meet down by the little port. I finished shopping so I went and sat down outside the port restaurant to wait for him. When Tommy arrived he seemed in a tetchy mood. We had a couple of drinks and then an argument ensued; don't ask me what about, I haven't a clue; most probably I was angry with him for being late.'

Her hands were shaking so much she split some brandy on the floor. She took a deep breath and continued.

'Well, we set off, and Tommy drove like hell, and the more I asked him to be careful the faster he went, until we crossed a small humpback bridge, the car left the ground, he lost control, we skidded into a tree and I was thrown out. When I came to he was still in the car, not moving or breathing or anything. I can't believe it.'

She took another large sip of brandy, and wiped the tears off her face. She rocked back and forth in her chair.

'Why, Desmond. Why?'

I did not know what to say. I am not very good in that sort of situation; besides, it was a bit of a shock for me. Sniffing hard she continued,

'He was killed instantly. As you can see, I received a few bumps and bruises on my face and arm.'

She burst into tears. Unable to restrain my own emotions I walked over, took her in my arms and joined her.

The next day I checked with the police report and everything tallied. Tommy's untimely death at the age of 55 deprived the world of perhaps the foremost post-war Goya specialist, and a very talented artist. I quote from an article written by Enrique Lafuente Ferrari (the director of Museum of Modern Art in Madrid) in 1957.

"Expressionism seems to be the most exact definition of his work, but there is nothing about his draughtsmanship to suggest his Spanish blood. The penetrating precision of his lines suggests something of intellectual torment which certainly is very little Spanish. Some affinity with Grunewald, Van Gogh and Munch seems to proclaim itself in the analytical, bold annotations which Harris uses to give his forms perspective. There was already something of this quality in his Malaga landscapes. Since then his style has deepened its own qualities, gaining in sureness and fire- *a frigid intellectual fire*."

I don't know if Tomas Harris worked for the Russians or not; all I can say is, I find it hard to believe that a man with his talents, his intellect and his imagination would not have known of Philby's, Blunt's and Burgess's activities. For myself I also find it hard to believe he actively participated; knowing Tommy he was more than likely just amused to know he had friends working for the opposite side. My wife Betty, on the other hand, feels very strongly that he did work for the Russians; she also admits it was more than likely for the amusement value. Perhaps I was too personally involved with him, and I admit I was very fond of him, to see or want to see the evidence. Even now, with the evidence in front of me, I want there to be an explanation of his innocence.

Could this be how we all felt at the time of the defections, besides feeling like complete fools? Now, as I finish writing this book, I realise why writing it has been a long process for me; for at the end one very important friend was a traitor and another very important friend may also have been a traitor.

As I sit here with my son Bill reflecting happily for the most part, but sadly as far as the behaviour of those in authority is concerned, I realise that the investigations of Philby, which went on for ten years, and the prolonged investigations of most of the others, and the whole case against Peter Wright served the politicians not the country.

Of course Philby was allowed to escape. Perhaps he was even encouraged. To have brought him back to England and convicted him as a traitor would have been even more embarrassing; and when they convicted him, could they really have hanged him? The press would have had a field day.

I have never seriously thought of life as a Secret Service man as anything but normal, but as Bill points out it is by no means what most people do or even think of doing. In writing this book and having had very lengthy discussions about the politics we played in the Services as opposed to the politics diplomats or politicians played, I realise he is right. As head of the Iberian section, on many occasions I witnessed some terrible diplomatic blunders. Following these blunders, one of my Spanish friends in Government would contact me to talk about the situation. They wanted me to try and rectify when all I could do was pacify and help keep relationships friendly. The work has frustrated me greatly when I think of how much talent Britain truly had, and still has, and how many countries used to respect us. It was soul destroying during the years following the war, witnessing one stupid mistake made after another.

On my retirement from MI6 in 1954 I had regrets about leaving. I rapidly had to 'brainwash' myself of the job, the environment and most of the people. Fortunately, being at home with a young family, a small farm and the animals to attend to, this was not difficult; and Madrid, Gibraltar, Algiers and the 54 Broadway buildings were cast into the oblivion of my subconscious mind. The various jobs and countries I had served in had given me wide experience and some wonderful adventures. Most colleagues and some bosses were amiable, and co-operative. As in any other business, there were those who were objectionable, but for the latter part of my career I was able to pick out those with whom to associate, whether for social or professional reasons. Some stayed friends after I left.

Joining the great big world outside was intimidating, but the transit was helped by working with my old friend Ken Mills, the friendliness and sense of humor of the Diamond Trading directors and the clear welcome I received from almost all in that enterprise.

It was not long before I realised how happy I was to be out of the undercover world espionage and counter espionage work in peacetime. The sheer façade to be constantly maintained; not being able to chat about my day's work with my wife and family or friends had been highly frustrating. Chinks in my self-discipline might have manifested themselves at awkward moments, with consequences which might have jeopardised one situation or another; especially after all the doubts surrounding Kim at that time. If I had remained in the Service and therefore been a part of it when he finally ran to Moscow, God knows what effect it might have had on me.

Looking back and remembering Peter Wright's remark:

'Desmond, you do know them all!' I wonder whether the moles, in an indirect way, helped break down the fear which Soviet Russia had of the West and the West had of the Soviets. Could some of their activities and a few drops of their revelations have led to Glasnost, and the wall coming down?

In 1979 my father retired from De Beers.

All this considered, and despite my own 'brainwashing devices' being involved in that, work has kept my mind very active. Frequently, discussions in our household are about world political behavior. Of course during the Peter Wright case the conversation was heated, and I was very upset by the pathetic behavior of the Government from beginning to end. Brian Morrison after returning to England from Gibraltar at the end of 1943 spent time training at HQ and St Albans in preparation for the invasion of Europe. Up to this point he had been a civilian and it was deemed necessary for him to become an officer in the Army. The selection committee known as the Warrant Officers Selection Board (WOSB) interviewed him. The first question asked by a rather typical small-minded pen-pushing individual was 'What's a mouse when it spins?' Well this was too much for Brian to tolerate. Brian made some rude comment, 'What the hell has that got to do with anything?' got up and walked out. Brian was failed and spent the rest of the war as a Corporal in an SCI unit. After the war he was not offered a position with the Secret Service, despite the conflict with the Russians and Chinese, and discarded. He died tragically, an alcoholic, in Granada in 1983.

As for Donald Darling, after the war he spent time visiting and helping European members of the Allied Escape lines. In 1949 he was posted to San Paulo in Brazil to be locally engaged as the Press Officer, a rather lowly position for somebody of his caliber. On his return to England he was offered nothing and discarded. Donald died in 1980, alone in a small room of a public house near Trafalgar Square, having been befriended by the publican.

What is a mouse when it spins? It's a weaving shuttle. Excuse this digression, but it does make me angry when I think how badly many worthy people have been treated by the powers that be, especially in the case of Britain.

When discussions are not about politics, they are about the garden or a new terrace or wall for the house, or some new business venture I am involved in; and very often about art and wine.

Now the book is over and finished I will talk less about politics. As for the years of government investigations and the soul-destroying moments, here is a little Churchillian-type quote which I think sums it up:

"Never was so much time wasted by so many people keeping non-secrets secret from their own people - Tapwater."

My father's notes on Kim Philby. Dated 1968.

Kim Philby was a rebel like his father. Kim Philby's father St John Philby had lived with the Arabs. Converted to Islam, he had helped the Americans form a union with the Saudi Family back in the 1930s. His arguments with the British authorities and with Lawrence of Arabia made him a very rebellious character; this had clearly influenced Kim. Kim, a very bright and deep individual had an ego which centred on his secret worship of his own ideology of social reform. In my opinion he genuinely believed that Communism was the solution to the social imbalance of society. A good belief from someone of our background: colonial, public school, Cambridge, the arts.

I can never forgive him for his ruthless acts which resulted in agents being killed. He caused these deaths when he was getting close to being discovered and could be seen as acts of desperation. His deception towards me personally has not angered me as his belief was like a deep religion for him. And whatever ones beliefs are, it is up to the individual as to whether they want to share them or not. The acts that one carries out in following those beliefs; in Kim's case nothing less than murder and social destruction, cannot be forgiven or ignored. What I find so very hard to cope with is how the Government allowed him to get away with it. These agents died on foreign lands without any mention in newspapers or any sort of recognition for their work for the United Kingdom. As I once said to some friends, if Kim had turned up at my house I would have offered him a large whisky, had a chat about life in Russia and then I would have shot him.

He hurt me, he hurt MI5 and MI6, and he seriously damaged Britain's relationship with our best ally (America). As for men and women such as me that he created he had a very damaging affect upon our feelings about our country and its unfair behaviour towards him and Burgess and Maclean. How many others feel as I do; who knows. My belief in our Government has never repaired itself.

I wonder what life has been like for Kim Philby's children. One of whom incidentally shares Tommy Harris with me as his Godfather. How does John Philby feel about his Dad?

For me as the son of Desmond Bristow, I feel sad I did not know his world of intrigue and espionage as I think it must have been exciting; to have been so far on the inside of the establishment and yet on the outside of normal life. His work certainly had an effect on the family, and this was not positive. His long absences and his aloofness must have been tough on my elder sisters and brother while living in Spain. Most people will know their father. They may not like their father but they will know him. I am never sure that I knew him. There will always be some doubt as to who he was and what he did. The fact that since writing my first book with him did not reveal much about his work was a surprise in one way and yet not so in another. Whatever you the reader may think, I loved my father very much. He was a very free thinking and intelligent man, who had a temper at times, as we all do. But he was fun, willing to discuss almost everything in a very open fashion, which for his generation was very unusual. He would talk about how Tommy would smoke joints and that he had witnessed the use of cocaine at one or two parties. I miss him and would love to really know the truth.

Perhaps I know more about my father than most children as there are secrets about his personal affairs which I am privy to. I do not find this upsetting as he was in his 20s, away from home for a long time and was quite important. When he transferred to Algiers, his appointment as a Major in the British Intelligence Unit made him one of the youngest officers in the army; he was in charge of his section of MI6; he was a spy. He loved the French he worked with. What could be better?

My father never stopped talking about politics. This is why I never believe the headlines. I always look for the real reason something is acted out by the Government. Did MI6 Kill Lady Diana? They certainly had cause to and anybody who thinks they are not capable of such acts just does not understand the needs of a nation as a whole. The Towers and Bush; to say that it is impossible for the Americans to have done this, those people do not understand how things can work.

But I have to say going through part of my young life wondering if my father was a traitor, or not was not a good feeling. Now feeling that he was involved in an assassination, albeit for the good of the war and certainly De Gaulle, makes me wonder about so many things. The world is never as we think it is. Sadly for me all these spies are now dead and I cannot talk to them about any of my feelings. I certainly had great conversations with my father about the world. I read Marx and Engels when I was 16. My father insisted upon it. I chose not to go to Cambridge or any other university. By the time I was 16 public school, and many of the things it represents, did not feel right to me. I am sure this is due to my father's rather negative feeling towards establishment and how it can work.

I had many arguments with him about Franco; now with the mess the world is getting itself into with our so called freedom I often wonder if he was not right. Yours and my children will pay for our freedom with massive debt and energy crisis after crisis. Would this have happened had society been kept on a tighter leash? Who knows? For all of his open minded thinking, there was a very troubled man underneath his jovial exterior. His troubled mind was not about the everyday troubles, it was the failure of this great Country of ours to recognize how great we could be and should be.

Obituary

Desmond Bristow

12:00am BST 16th September 2000

Wartime MI6 officer who, with Kim Philby, helped recruit Garbo; one of the Allies' most successful double agents.

DESMOND BRISTOW, who has died in Spain aged 83, was a former head of MI6's operations in the Iberian Peninsula. Between 1942 and 1945 he took part in many strategic deceptions in the Mediterranean theatre, and with his friend Kim Philby was closely involved in the running of Garbo, perhaps the most successful double agent of the war.

Bristow was recruited to the Secret Intelligence Service in 1941 because he spoke good, idiomatic Spanish, and was assigned to Section V(d), which organised counter-intelligence measures in Spain and Portugal. The section was based in St Albans and for nine months Bristow and his boss, the personable Philby, monitored intercepted messages from Abwehr, (the German intelligence service).

One of the section's first coups was to decide correctly that reports being sent to Abwehr by an agent code-named Arabel were fictitious, and when a Catalan named Juan Pujol Garcia approached the British Embassy in Lisbon volunteering to work for the Allies; it was Bristow who guessed he was Arabel.

Philby and Bristow were instrumental in persuading their superiors to accept his offer, and when Pujol arrived in

London in 1942, Bristow interviewed him for a week to establish his *bona fides*. Pujol was run by MI5 under the Double Cross System, which was supervised by the highly secret Twenty (XX) Committee. Bristow, as MI6's liaison officer for Pujol, attended its meetings and advised on how Garbo, (as he had been designated), could best pass convincing falsehoods to the Germans.

Garbo's work subsequently helped to deceive the Germans as to the location and timing of the Normandy landings and later persuaded them to shorten the range of V2 rockets, so that many fell south of London. In May 1942, Bristow went to Gibraltar to supervise the section's work there. This involved aiding SOE agents, stopping German saboteurs and keeping an eye on enemy spies among the 16,000 people who each day came from Spain to work on the Rock.

On one occasion, Bristow learnt that Admiral Canaris, head of the Abwehr, would be visiting Spain. Although a suggestion that he be assassinated was vetoed, Bristow still contrived to have tea in the same hotel as Canaris, who nodded politely to him as he left the room.

Later in the war, Bristow (under the codename Tapwater) ran joint deception operations with the French from Algiers, where he employed a professional safebreaker to steal cyphers from the Spanish consulate. He also worked in Paris and in Lisbon, where he looked after the agent Klop Ustinov, (father of Peter).

After the war, Bristow became head of station for Spain and Portugal, but in 1954 he left MI6, disenchanted by its treatment of some who had served it well and by the climate of suspicion. He thought the defection of Burgess and Maclean had been strangely handled by the secret services, and came to share the belief of his friend Peter Wright that Sir Roger Hollis, head of MI5, was a Soviet agent.

This claim, and those about other MI6 officers, was aired by Bristow in his memoir, A Game of Moles (1993), one of the first by an MI6 agent. Although it dwelt on events of half a century before, MI6 made several attempts to dissuade him from writing the book, and he was warned that he could be sent to prison.

In the event, Bristow published it first in Spanish and, having invoked the protection of the European courts, was not prosecuted.

It was a last success for someone who prized loyalty to friends he had made in the trade above that to any organisation. Although Philby's treachery came as a shock, he had harboured faint suspicions for some time. None the less, in 1962 it was Bristow who gave Philby his last lunch in Britain before the Third Man travelled to Beirut, (and thence to Moscow).
A little later, Bristow received a card depicting three kings heading east. It read: "Happy Christmas. May not see you for a while. Love Kim."

Desmond Arthur Bristow was born in Birmingham on June 1 1917 and grew up near Huelva, southern Spain, where his father, an engineer, oversaw a copper mine. He went to Dulwich College and on to Magdalene Cambridge, where he read French and Spanish. He captained the college at rowing and, to raise money for Poppy Day, once set fire to himself with petrol before jumping into the Cam.

When war came, he joined the Ox and Bucks Light

Infantry before being recruited from the Intelligence Corps to MI6 in 1941. His last post in the service, from 1953-4, was as head of the Strategic Trade section. There he ran Operation Scrum-Half, a joint venture with the Americans to prevent Warsaw Pact countries from receiving materiel such as aluminium, diamonds and electronic goods.

Bristow left MI6 to join De Beers where, working under Sir Percy Sillitoe, a former director-general of MI5, he investigated the illicit trade in smuggled diamonds in West Africa. He later became the company's head of security.

He and his wife retired to Spain, where they made their home in an old sugar cane mill near Malaga. He enjoyed swimming and had recently helped set up a sailing club. He was also a fine carpenter. Desmond Bristow had tremendous curiosity about people and about events in the news. He could be subversive and sometimes curmudgeonly, but was always good company.

He was awarded the Legion d'Honneur and the Croix de Guerre avec Palme in 1947.

49183412R00234

Made in the USA
Middletown, DE
19 June 2019